Praise for *The Four Voices of Preaching*

"In this provocative book, creative and respected scholar of preaching Robert Reid identifies four voices through which preachers tend to speak—the teaching voice, the encouraging voice, the sage voice, and the testifying voice. In engaging prose, the author describes each approach, helps preachers think about when each voice is appropriate, and offers sample sermons. Readers will come away from this book better able to identify their own primary voice while being able to speak in other voices when needed. Few books on preaching combine so deftly important theoretical ideas with practical implications. This book will be a welcome companion in the classroom and would be an excellent resource for clergy colleague groups and for a preacher's own reading."

Ronald J. Allen, Christian Theological Seminary

"Reid is a masterful thinker who has honed his craft to perfection in this volume. *The Four Voices of Preaching* is more than a service to seasoned preachers—it is the *first* book for all reading in homiletics and the *map* to an *authentic* voice."

David Fleer, Rochester College

"Robert Reid has assembled 'a matrix of contemporary Christian voices' while handily employing the rhetorical tradition, social theory, communications studies, diverse theological perspectives, modern and contemporary hermeneutics, and recent homiletic method. *The Four Voices of Preaching* offers the preacher a means for mapping contemporary homiletics and for locating herself or himself within this twenty-first-century matrix. Moreover, the author provides those of us called to preach with specific criteria that constitute authenticity within our dominant preaching voice. Most commendably, Robert Reid treats each of the four voices with a hermeneutics of hospitality, offering helpful insight and criticism while encouraging excellence within each domain. *The Four Voices of Preaching* is an important contribution to contemporary homiletics."

Richard Eslinger, author of *The Web of Preaching: New Options in Homiletic Method*

The Four Voices of Preaching

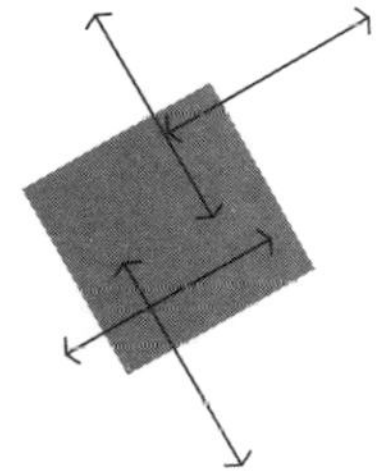

Robert Stephen Reid

BrazosPress
Grand Rapids, Michigan

Published by Brazos Press
a division of Baker Publishing Group
P.O. Box 6287, Grand Rapids, MI 49516-6287
www.brazospress.com

Printed in the United States of America

Library of Congress Cataloging-in-Publication Data

Reid, Robert Stephen.
The four voices of preaching / Robert Stephen Reid.
p. cm.
Includes bibliographical references and index.
ISBN 10: 1-58743-132-7 (pbk.)
ISBN 978-1-58743-132-6 (pbk.)
1. Preaching. I. Title.
BV4211.3.R45 2006
251—dc22 2005031156

The proof of a map is in how well you can get around when you use it.

Charles Taylor
Philosophical Papers, 1985

Contents

Preface

The pastor standing at the practical theology bookshelf is often bewildered by the choices. The student in the seminary homiletics class looking at the variety of books at the library reserve shelf can be equally puzzled. There are more resources than they know what to do with, more issues than they can begin to make sense of, more possibilities than can be practically implemented. This should be a wonderful problem. So why, with such a wealth of resources, do they stand bewildered? For most seminarians, the library reserve shelf seems more like a smorgasbord of homiletical perspectives with no clear compass providing a way through the maze. For pastors standing in a store or browsing the internet bookshops, they see an array of how-to manuals with no clear sense of which approach will best serve their preaching ministry.

I stood near a pastor in a bookstore recently who looked across a choice of about fifteen different homiletics books and said, "I need a map." Often, more than a "Where are these books coming from theologically?" guide, preachers actually need assistance in understanding how to distinguish which of these resources will help them strengthen the authenticity of the voice they already employ in proclaiming the gospel. What preachers and teachers of homiletics courses are looking for are the resources that can support a ministry of faithfulness in preaching the gospel. They need a map.

A wonderfully stylized reproduction of the Henricus Hondius map of the world dated 1630 hangs on my office wall. Most of the continents are depicted, but their proportions are far from how they would be rendered today. The map tells us more about Monsieur Hondius's understanding of the world in 1630 than the world's actual relationship between land and water. The farther one moves away from its depiction of the European continent the less meaningful the map becomes as an accurate guide for negotiating a trip. Maps are always products of their time and their place. This is equally true with the map provided by this book.

In *The Four Voices of Preaching* I offer a map—in this case "map" as an external representation that arrays knowledge of a field of study—with all the strengths and weaknesses of this kind of guide. The good thing about maps is they help us to figure out how to get where we want to go and how to keep from going on unplanned side trips. The problem with maps is that they are always wrong in one way or another. Distortion is impossible to avoid when trying to represent complex terrain. In this case, the complex terrain is the language of the discipline of homiletics and the implied cultural assumptions a preacher takes up in order to be able to answer the question, "What do I want to have happen as a result of people listening to this sermon?"

As a map, *The Four Voices of Preaching* reveals as much the journey of my own social, cultural, and theological location as it reveals the "reality" of the terrain of contemporary homiletic practice. However, before I make this map sound too idiosyncratic, like Monsieur Hondius, I can take comfort that when it comes to the discipline of mapmaking I have been able to depend on several significant guides who already mapped this terrain for other disciplines in the social sciences.[1] So, for now it is enough to say that *The Four Voices of Preaching* provides a map of various sensibilities by which preachers frame their understanding of life and world as cultural commitments to what

1. I refer to these studies in chapter one.

counts as truth and what counts as the "social mooring" of their faith commitment.

I approach my cartography from the perspective of communication theory and practice as well as homiletics and assume a rhetorical perspective in discussing the shape of the voices explored in this book.[2] I am particularly interested in how voice is a function of a way of looking at the world. Kenneth Burke once referred to this way of seeing as the "terministic screen" humans employ in viewing the world. Burke argued that all people intuitively employ a specific set of language symbols and cultural assumptions that provide a "grid of intelligibility" as their basic guide in sense-making. This screen represents the individual's negotiation of language and that person's implicit ideology as it affects how the individual selects ideas, deflects ideas, and reflects on the result that makes up what counts as his or her "reality."[3] Each of the four voices examined in this book represents a different "terministic screen" that I refer to as a "cultural consciousness" shaping the way preachers tend to look at and understand the world.

My map is stylized. It treats some features of homiletics as more salient while ignoring others. Mapmakers do this—even mapmakers who try to reproduce the maps of others. For example, the map in my office is a commercial reproduction that has turned all the original color of Hondius's map into shades of green and gold leaf better designed to match modern décor. Of course, one can deplore the reduction of great art into mere décor, but we could also ask what role color played in the effort to represent reality in Hondius's original map.[4] Colorfulness is simply another dimension of how realities are stylized. In deciding

2. *The Four Voices of Preaching* is intended to serve as a contribution to the effort to employ rhetoric as a resource in theological education. For a recent contribution to the effort to redress the crumbling foundations of modernist assumptions in theological education, see the essays in *To Teach, To Delight, and To Move: Theological Education in a Post-Christian World*, David S. Cunningham, ed. (Eugene, OR: Wipf and Stock, 2004).

3. Kenneth D. Burke, *Language as Symbolic Action: Essays on Life, Literature, and Method* (Berkeley: University of California Press, 1966), 45.

4. This map may be viewed at http://www.raremaps.com/cgi-bin/map-builder.cgi?World+World+8078.

what is salient, I am selecting, deflecting, and then reflecting on the array of current issues and theories in homiletics in the hope that my effort will prove useful to people who would like a map. To any homiletician who finds my description of the terrain of his or her theory too flattened, I can only plead the necessity of utility—the making of a useful map. To teachers of homiletics who array the terrain differently, I can only plead the argument of a perspective shaped by my dependence on the worldviews of the cartographers who have preceded me.

The map that is *The Four Voices of Preaching* is rendered as a Matrix of Contemporary Christian Voices rather than merely a matrix of preaching voices, because my intention is to propose a theory of Christian discourse that locates the distinctions of cultural consciousnesses for any religious communicator writing and speaking today. The study is both descriptive of existing practice and prescriptive in making recommendations to achieve more congruence of voice. I have already employed the matrix as a means to conduct a brief cultural account of the discourse of denominational schism among Southern Baptists at the outset of the twenty-first century.[5] My purpose here is to provide the map as a first step in the development of an anthropology of preaching that also serves as an anthropology of Christian discourse. Such pretensions to develop this project further will only be cordially received if you, the reader, find this map useful in negotiating the terrain of the bookstore, the reading list, the desire to bring more authenticity to your witness to God in preaching, or your ability to experience how listening to a ministry of preaching affects the shape of your own faith.

A formative version of the argument of this book can be found in chapter six of *Connecting with the Congregation*, a book I cowrote with Lucy Lind Hogan. The first version of the argument that considers theories of contemporary preaching as expressions of a cultural consciousness was published as an essay in *Preaching the Eighth Century Prophets*. Readers who wish to see the four voices used to explore sermons based on a text from Amos are

5. Robert Stephen Reid, "Being Baptist," *Rhetoric and Public Affairs* 7, 4 (2004): 587–602.

directed to that essay. My use of Fowler's concept of faith stages in chapter six was developed in an essay published in the *Journal of Communication and Religion.* I have adapted portions of the text from the latter two in this book.[6]

The Four Voices of Preaching was written in the nooks and crannies of time otherwise spent on a full load of teaching, directing a graduate program of communication, and sustaining a marriage with my life partner, Professor Barbara Reid. Two academics in one household is either a dire circumstance or a true encouragement. While I was writing this book Barbara was pursuing a Doctor of Worship Studies degree. The intersection of these two projects provided a context for wonderful conversations in my effort to understand the role of preaching as part of the fabric of worship in a community of faith. Since I am proposing a typology for the worldviews of contemporary Christian discourse, I have come to believe that the book can be as readily applied to interpreting theological and cultural commitments of worship as to preaching.[7] Barbara listened to drafts read aloud and served as an able critic. Where the text is still either too dense or too obscure it is not for lack of her suggestions. Nor is this problem due to any lack of suggestions for clarity and concision from Rodney Clapp of Brazos Press.

I extend my appreciation to Craig L. Blomberg, the Distinguished Professor of New Testament at Denver Theological Seminary, and Barbara Brown Taylor, the Harry R. Butman Chair of Religion and Philosophy at Piedmont College, who both graciously permitted me to use one of their previously published sermons as an exemplar in this volume. I also wish to thank Ronald J. Allen, the Nettie Sweeny and Hugh Th. Miller Profes-

6. See Lucy Lind Hogan and Robert Reid, *Connecting with the Congregation: Rhetoric and the Art of Preaching* (Nashville: Abingdon Press, 1999); Robert Stephen Reid, "Exploring Preaching's Voices from *Ex Cathedra* to Exilic," in *The Cry of the Eighth Century Prophets,* David Fleer and Dave Bland, eds. (Abilene, TX: ACU Press, 2004), 135–64; and Robert Stephen Reid, "Faithful Preaching: Faith Stages, Preaching Strategies, and Rhetorical Practice," *Journal of Communication and Religion* 21, 2 (1998): 164–99.

7. It provides a somewhat different set of cultural indicators by which to array orientations to worship than the continuum of orientations offered in M. Rex Miller, *The Millennium Matrix: Reclaiming the Past, Reframing the Future of the Church* (San Francisco: Jossey-Bass, 2003).

sor of Preaching and New Testament at Christian Theological Seminary, and Professor John M. Rottman, Professor of Preaching at Calvin Theological Seminary, for their willingness to provide a sermon for this volume. Each sermon is offered as an exemplar of excellence in the voice indicated. The identification of each sermon as an expression of a specific voice is mine.

I also wish to express my appreciation to members of the Academy of Homiletics whose conversations have also enriched my understanding of this terrain, especially to Ron Allen as well as Lucy Hogan, John McClure, Paul Wilson, Dale Andrews, David Randolph, Bob Howard, Dick Eslinger, David Fleer, and Dave Bland. I also wish to thank members of the Rhetoric and Preaching Working Group of the Academy of Homiletics who in numerous sessions during the past few years have been patient with my efforts to determine the parameters of voices as a dimension of preaching. John Hatch and John Stewart, members of the communication department at the University of Dubuque, have offered important critiques of this argument along the way. Les Longden of University of Dubuque Theological Seminary read a first draft of this manuscript and offered helpful comments on its readability and its applicability in the field of evangelism. Ann Hoch of UDTS field-tested an early version of chapter one in a D.Min. seminar in Chicago.

To my readers, be they preachers, listeners of sermons, or people interested in understanding the cultural consciousnesses of religious discourse, it is my hope that you are able to find here insight into what makes for the coherence of voice that is authentic in its effort to name God and name grace in ways that sustain and enrich faith.

1

The Four Voices of Preaching

As Walter Wangerin Jr. shares the memory in *Miz Lil and the Chronicles of Grace*, the matriarch of the congregation was before him in the Sunday morning greeting line when he got up the nerve to ask the question. What had she meant with her distinctions between the Sundays "you say I teach" and the Sundays "you say I preach."

> Now Miz Lillian was holding my hand in hers, which was work hardened, her little finger fixed forever straight, unable to bend. "When you teach," she said, instructing me, "I learn something for the day. I can take it home and, God willing, I can do it. But when you preach—" She lowered her voice and probed me the deeper with her eyes. "God is here. And sometimes he's smiling," she said, "and sometimes he's frowning surely."[1]

Miz Lillian was keenly aware, probably even more than the pastor, of the different *voices* he assumed from one Sunday to the next.

1. Walter Wangerin Jr., *Miz Lil and the Chronicles of Grace* (San Francisco: Harper and Row, 1988), 37.

Pastor Wangerin thought he just preached sermons. Miz Lillian informed him something more significant was occurring. On some days his sermons provided answers and insights helping her to learn. On other days his sermons literally facilitated her encounter with God.

It often comes as a surprise to preachers new to the ministry that their voice is taken so seriously by congregants. In their enthusiasm to share the faith they often assume that voice is mostly about conveying a sense of authority or about their style and delivery. It comes as a surprise, therefore, to discover that the most enduring effect of sermons may have far more to do with the preacher's *voice* than the content of any particular message. For long after the content of a particular sermon has slipped from memory, its implied assumptions about what counts as truth and how listeners should live into this sermonic truth shape the cultural consciousness of what counts as faith for listeners. These implied assumptions—what I refer to as *voice* in this book—are a sermon's most enduring effect.

For example, some preachers assume that listeners should practice faith as a set of clearly articulated answers to concerns about practical Christian living. Other preachers assume that listeners should acknowledge that life and faith are God-shaped mysteries that can empower the possibilities of change. Some preachers invite listeners to see faith as a way of embracing a connectedness with a confessional tradition, with sacred space, and with the wisdom of ordered Christian practices. Other preachers invite listeners to see faith as a journey of self-discovery that can lead to personal transformation. Though, as we shall see, there is overlap in these assumptions, no preacher can simultaneously give voice to all of these perspectives, nor would they want to. Yet over the months and years of a ministry of preaching, the residue of what is retained is often more an artifact of the preacher's voice in such matters than the particular theological content of specific sermons.

This is not news to preachers several years into a parish ministry. At an intuitive level experienced preachers know that what counts as authenticity for listeners has as much to do with the expression of their pastoral persona as with what they say. Most parishioners come to see their pastor's passions, convictions, interests, questions, sensibilities, and affirmations as familiar perspectives that reflect the pastor's identity as a person of faith. Over time what gets communicated in the best preaching is the preacher's authenticity—the parishioners' perception of the preacher's personal integrity and his or her willingness to be "real" in matters of faith. Even for those preachers who avoid telling first-person stories in the pulpit, authenticity is revealed in their honest wrestling with matters of faith in ways that model the way for listeners.[2] This is why the preacher's voice becomes the medium of his or her authenticity and a trusted resource for the listener's own faith formation.

Of course, this is no accident. In summarizing the essential resources of human communication, Aristotle argued that the speaker's character—the personal identity that the speaker communicates to his or her listeners—is persuasion's most powerful resource.[3] Yes, preachers clearly desire to be faithful interpreters of the gospel message, but as pastors they also desire to be viewed as the faith community's *phronimos*—Aristotle's word for an individual perceived to be a wise and prudent person capable of sensible judgment and goodwill, who is both just and one who speaks the truth.[4] Congregants come to trust wise counsel (*logos*) from the preacher who seems to possess good character (*ethos*), who becomes appropriately passionate (*pathos*) about matters that the community views as central to their cor-

2. Ronald J. Allen, *Hearing the Sermon: Relationship/Content/Feeling* (St. Louis: Chalice Press, 2004), 24–26.

3. Aristotle found that persuasion effected by the speaker's character as understood out of the speech, rather than from a previous opinion of the speaker, may well be "the controlling factor in persuasion" (1.2.4). *Aristotle on Rhetoric: A Theory of Civic Discourse: Newly Translated, with Introduction, Notes, and Appendices*, George Kennedy, trans. and ed. (New York: Oxford University Press, 1991), 38.

4. In discussing the role of character affected in a speech, Aristotle maintained that "There are three reasons why speakers themselves are persuasive; for there are three things we trust other than logical demonstrations. These are practical wisdom [*phronēsis*] and virtue [*aretē*] and good will [*eunoia*]; for speakers make mistakes . . . [[if they fail] to exhibit] either all or one of these" (2.1.5). *Aristotle on Rhetoric*, 120–21. On *phronēsis* see Aristotle, *Nichomachean Ethics* 6.9.30.

porate, shared identity.[5] Yet, of these three resources by which preachers implicitly communicate their identity—*ethos*, *pathos*, and *logos*—the resource that translates most directly into what counts as authenticity for the listeners is the *ethos* revealed in the interpersonal, social, and cultural convictions of the preacher's judgment about what is central in matters of faith.[6]

Anyone who preaches the gospel communicates an implied personal identity as one who has convictions about this message. Hence the *character* of this identity is revealed by the personal assumptions the preacher brings to the pulpit. Many social constraints of contemporary culture also shape this identity. For example, Ronald Osborn argues that ministry faces a crisis of identity because of the contemporary disarray of *social* roles pastors are expected to embody. Historically, congregations variously expect a pastor to be a saint, a priest, a master, an awakener, a pulpiteer, a revivalist, a builder, a missionary, a manager, a counselor, an impresario, and a teacher. Since there is no common agreement concerning appropriate role identity for the ministry, Osborn describes this as "the problem of great expectation joined to hopeless confusion over basic definition."[7]

To this set of social *roles* Avery Dulles adds six additional social *identities* a pastor professionally negotiates as a mediator of the congregation's theological identity: the church as institution, as mystical communion, as sacrament, as herald, as servant, and

5. Lucy Lind Hogan and Robert Reid, *Connecting with the Congregation: Rhetoric and the Art of Preaching* (Nashville: Abingdon Press, 1999), 48–49. See also André Resner Jr., *The Preacher and Cross: Person and Message in Theology and Rhetoric* (Grand Rapids: Eerdmans, 1999); and Allen, *Hearing the Sermon.*

6. On this threefold division of identities when communicating, see John Stewart, "Communicating and Interpersonal Communicating," in *Bridges Not Walls: A Book about Interpersonal Communication,* 8th ed., John Stewart, ed. (Boston: McGraw Hill, 2002), 34–36.

7. Ronald Osborn, *Creative Disarray: Models of Ministry in a Changing America* (St. Louis: Chalice Press, 1991), 5. William Willimon proposes that pastoral ministry can be conceived in twelve diverse roles for ordained professional church leaders. They include clergy as priest, pastor, Scripture interpreter, preacher, counselor, teacher, evangelist, prophet, leader, person of character, and disciplined follower of Christ. See William H. Willimon, *Pastor: The Theology and Practice of Ordained Ministry* (Nashville: Abingdon Press, 2002). Ron Allen treats the relationship between preaching and pastoral identity in five roles—preacher as teacher, pastor, administrator, missionary, and spiritual leader. See Ronald J. Allen, *Preaching and Practical Ministry* (St. Louis: Chalice Press, 2001).

as community of disciples.[8] Dulles is more sanguine about the ability of congregations to negotiate the overlap of these theological identities than Osborn is about the ability of an individual pastor to be all roles to all people. Clergy constantly negotiate some mixture of these social role identities in their ministry of preaching. In preaching, these roles are often indirectly addressed by way of the preacher's personal or convictional understanding. In this sense, pastoral social identities are recognized and regularly addressed in theological training and in pastoral practice. In addition the preacher's own confessional perspective on the pastor's social roles is quickly recognized and internalized by a congregation.

Of the three dimensions of identity (interpersonal, social, and cultural) the way preachers communicate their cultural identity is the least understood. Of course, parishioners readily identify such cultural markers as race, gender, ethnicity, class, regional colloquialisms, and other indicators of difference.[9] Less clearly understood by either preacher or parishioner is the identity expressed in the preacher's *cultural assumptions* about the nature of authority and *cultural assumptions* about the nature of language. These assumptions, perhaps more than any other structures of identity, form the affective quality through which a preacher enacts the sermonic role of a sacred *phronimos*. Social identity and personal identity influence this perception, but it is the depth structures of cultural identity that shape the assumptions for what counts as the resource of practical wisdom in different faith communities in North American Christianity.

Exploring the way these assumptions are taken up in the culturally diverse *voices* preachers adopt is the subject of this book. Typically, these assumptions can be found in the definition or understanding of preaching's purpose that either explicitly or implicitly structures the preaching intention for a sermon. They reveal assumptions about the nature of language and the nature of authority that both constrain the nature of the sermon's wisdom

8. Avery Dulles, *Models of the Church*, exp. ed. (New York: Doubleday, 1987).

9. These dimensions are developed with sensitivity in James R. Nieman and Thomas G. Rogers, *Preaching to Every Pew: Cross-Cultural Strategies* (Minneapolis: Fortress Press, 2001).

and liberate a preacher to powerfully speak the Word of God to a community.

Preaching's Purpose

What is preaching's purpose? A preacher's response to that question affects both questions of craft and questions of theology. The most famous definition of preaching within an American context was offered by Phillips Brooks in his *Yale Lectures on Preaching* in 1877. He proposed, "Preaching is the communication of truth by man to men. It has two essential elements, truth and personality. . . . Preaching is the bringing of truth through personality."[10] With these three words—"truth through personality"—Brooks succinctly balanced preaching's essential truth claim with its human medium of communication. According to Brooks, if either of these dimensions is sacrificed, then it is not preaching. Without a faithful witness to revelation of the Divine Other there would be no truth. Unless the message is mediated through the unique witness of the speaker's experience, its testimony lacks authenticity. In 1877 this definition represented a version of Horace Bushnell's theory of Christian experience as the authorizing agency for truth set alongside a call to faithfulness to the gospel preaching, the latter offered as alternative to the revivalist's willingness to manipulate "truth" to produce results.[11] Brooks's definition has remained durable long after the context that gave birth to it, in part because it captures the tension so eloquently identified by Miz Lil: preaching is a marvelous mixture of the divine and the human.

I raise Brooks's classic definition because most books would offer a definition of the subject at this point. But definitions,

10. Phillips Brooks, *Lectures on Preaching* (New York: E. P. Dutton, 1877), 5. Willimon notes that when coediting *The Concise Encyclopedia of Preaching* he realized that this was the definition most cited by the various contributors. He writes that it is not surprising, because the "definition strikes experienced preachers as essentially right" (Willimon, *Pastor*, 157–58).

11. Richard Lischer, ed., *The Company of Preachers: Wisdom on Preaching: Augustine to the Present* (Grand Rapids: Eerdmans, 2002), 15.

though they seem straightforward, are far from neutral. They represent an effort to offer what should count as a normative understanding of the subject at hand. Definitions place some qualities of an idea in high relief and deflect other qualities by either negating them or leaving them unnamed. In this sense all definitions have contexts and reflect assumptions about the questions at play in a discipline. One need only take an old textbook off the shelf and compare the definition of its subject offered in the first chapter with a current text on the same subject. More than likely the definition will have evolved to account for new dimensions of inquiry in the field.

Definitions also reflect the cultural assumptions of the one offering the definition. Thus, when reading across contemporary definitions of preaching one quickly discovers several areas of difference. These differences will become obvious in subsequent chapters of this book, where I demonstrate how existing definitions of preaching's purpose often reflect a tendency to favor the cultural assumptions of one of four voices of preaching in contemporary North American homiletic practice. Some writers offer definitions; others prefer to speak of understandings. The former tend to operate with more of an objectivist orientation to the nature of language, while the latter tend to assume a subjectivist orientation.[12]

Core to most definitions or understandings of preaching's purpose is the assumption that preaching is the holy calling to name God and to name grace for others. Naming God involves bringing theological reflection to the interpretation of our world and the preacher's convictions about God's purpose as testimony about God.[13] Naming grace involves bringing that same theo-

12. On definitions as a kind of Socratic lust for certitude, see Bernard Lonergan, *Method in Theology* (New York: Seabury Press, 1972), 81–84. Note Schneiders' proposal of an "ideal intention" as a way of permitting more subjectivist ambiguity as an alternative to objectivist certainty; see Sandra M. Schneiders, *The Revelatory Text: Interpreting the New Testament as Sacred Scripture*, 2d ed. (Collegeville, MN: Liturgical Press, 1999), xxx–xxxiv.

13. On "naming God" as the task of preaching see Paul Ricoeur, "The Hermeneutics of Testimony," in *Essays on Biblical Interpretation* (Philadelphia: Fortress Press, 1980), 119–54; and Ricoeur, "Naming God," in *Figuring the Sacred: Religion, Narrative and Imagination*, M. Wallace, ed., D. Pellauer, trans. (Minneapolis: Fortress Press, 1995), 217–35.

logical reflection to identifying the holy in personal religious experience.[14] This is an intentionally succinct understanding of preaching meant to identify that which is common to excellence in all of the culturally diverse *voices* in my proposal of a matrix identifying differences in preaching purposes.

A Matrix of Contemporary Christian Voices

In proposing a Matrix of Contemporary Christian Voices, I suggest that a particular cultural consciousness is the default presence that functions as the determining power in shaping the preacher's voice. This cultural consciousness serves as a paradigmatic orientation to what counts as reality and what counts as a person's personal center of gravity in matters of truth. There are four archetypical voices, and in each case, they reveal implicit assumptions about the nature of language appeals and the nature of authority appeals whenever someone preaches. For example, many preachers and parishioners are still most at home with either a facts-in-dispute view of the sermon as argument or a call-to-action view of the sermon as a reasoned invitation to take the "gospel medicine." Both of these approaches to preaching assume a persuasively determinate/objectivist voice and generally operate with an implicit correspondence theory of the relationship between language and reality. They can be contrasted with approaches to preaching that tend to assume an interpretivist view of the nature of truth and make appeals in a persuasively indeterminate/interpretivist voice. The latter approaches are more collaborative than affirmative, inviting listeners to join with a speaker in the process of arriving at understanding rather than explaining meaning.

If this objectivist-subjectivist tension is viewed as one axis dividing contemporary approaches to preaching, a second axis equally relevant for preachers and parishioners is the tension between order and transformation. Preachers concerned with sacred

14. On "naming grace" see Mary Catherine Hilkert, *Naming Grace: Preaching and the Sacramental Imagination* (New York: Continuum, 2000).

order and solidarity tend to make their appeals with reference to corporate truth, drawing on systems of doctrinal agreement or on traditions of confessional identity. Preachers concerned with change and spiritual transformation tend to make their appeals by way of reflective analysis and perceptive insight that invite an appropriation of personal truth. The Matrix of Contemporary Christian Voices in Figure 1.1 arrays the basis of persuasive appeals of a Christian rhetoric as a negotiation of these tensions between the Nature of Language and the Nature of Authority.[15]

My use of the term *voice* in this matrix implies an identity—who is speaking—as well as the identity of the group that this notion of voice constructs as its implied listeners—who is responding. In this sense voice is identified by the response its intention calls forth. A preacher whose intention is to *explain* meaning adopts a Teaching Voice to argue for a position. A preacher whose intention is to *facilitate an encounter* with the holy adopts an Encouraging Voice advocating solutions

15. This matrix presumes the theoretical findings of several important research typologies. The most significant is that of Gibson Burrell and Gareth Morgan, *Sociological Paradigms and Organizational Analysis: Elements of the Sociology of Corporate Life* (Burlington, VT: Ashgate Publishing, 1979), 22. Burrell and Morgan argue that the various sociological approaches to understanding organizations are reducible to four paradigms. Their paradigms are presented in a matrix that juxtaposes objectivist and subjectivist orientations as one tension with a second tension of theories of regulation (order) versus theories of radical change (transformation). It can also be compared to Aubrey Fisher's perspectives on the study of human communication (1. Mechanistic Views; 2. Psychological Views; 3. Interpretive-Symbolic Views; and 4. Systems-Interaction Views); see B. Aubrey Fisher, *Perspectives on Human Communication* (New York: Macmillan, 1978). The Matrix of Contemporary Christian Voices has its closest parallel with this study. Other studies of significance include the array of five significant tensions of intercultural communication (hierarchy, identity, gender, truth, and virtue) by Hofstede and Hofstede. They create multiple matrices by juxtaposing the data from these tensional concerns. The two axes that are most relevant is their juxtaposition of *identity* (individualist versus collectivist) and *truth* (high uncertainty avoidance versus willingness to embrace ambiguity). See Geert Hofstede and Gert Jan Hofstede, *Cultures and Organizations: Software of the Mind*, rev. and exp. 2d ed. (New York: McGraw-Hill, 2005), 91. For two studies with related matrices of religious communication see the Conceptions of Authority matrix in Jackson W. Carroll, *As One with Authority: Reflective Leadership in Ministry* (Louisville: Westminster/John Knox Press, 1991), 57; and the various ontological-epistemological matrices of Thor Hall in Thor Hall, *The Future Shape of Preaching* (Philadelphia: Fortress Press, 1971), 56. Hall's various matrices juxtaposed a similar objectivist/subjectivist axis as an epistemological plane, but set this in opposition to an ontological plane that assumed an ideational/empirical axis. The result was boldly provocative but proved too abstract to account for the practical expressions of homiletic practice in the subsequent quarter century.

directed toward listeners' felt needs. A preacher whose intention is to create an event of meaning in which listeners can *explore* insight adopts the Voice of a knowing Sage who can guide listeners on a journey of self-awareness. A preacher whose intention is to *engage* confessional identity, in ways that permit listeners to come to terms with who they are in Christ, will likely Testify with the formative Voice of the church in contrast to the voice of secular culture. In each case voice identifies a constitutive rhetoric of faith consciousness for both preacher and parishioner.

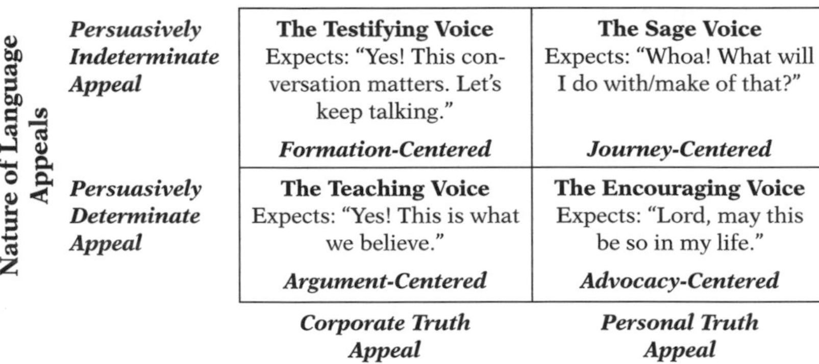

Figure 1.1: A Matrix of Contemporary Christian Voices

This book explores contemporary understandings of the purpose of preaching and the practice of preaching biblical truth embodied in the preaching identity of voice. I explore this notion of a preaching identity in these four contemporary preaching voices in order to help readers discover their own assumptions about the purpose of preaching and how those assumptions are performed in the voice a preacher enacts in sermons.

1. In the Teaching Voice preachers seek to *explain* meaning by making an *argument*. The goal of this preaching is to have listeners affirm the sermonic interpretation of the

text's meaning for the community by saying, "Yes! This is what we believe." This is an argument-centered model of preaching.

2. In the Encouraging Voice preachers seek to facilitate an *encounter* with God/Spirit/grace/empowerment by *advocating* a perspective in a way that listeners will respond by saying, "Lord, may this be so in my life." This is an advocacy-centered model of preaching.
3. In the Sage Voice preachers seek to invite listeners to *explore* possibilities of meaning by offering critical reflection or *analysis* with the intention that listeners would respond, "Whoa! What will I do with (or make of) that?" This is a journey-centered model of preaching.
4. In the Testifying Voice preachers seek to *engage* listeners in a formative conversation with their faith tradition, their culture, and their own identity as followers of Christ by *articulating* possible ways of building community together with others, so that listeners might respond, "Yes! This conversation matters. Let's keep talking." This is a formation-centered model of preaching.

Each of these voices can be clearly distinguished by the assumptions grounded in the nature of its persuasive appeal.

Other categories might be used to distinguish differences in preaching purposes. For example, the list of offices in the early church identified in Ephesians distinguishes apostles from prophets, evangelists, and pastor-teachers (Eph. 4:11). Each of these roles suggests different purposes in preaching. We could turn to ancient rhetorical theory from the biblical era to distinguish judicial, deliberative, and demonstrative speaking purposes. We could even distinguish different kinds of exhortation and advice-giving speech (paranesis, protreptic, diatribe, admonition, rebuke, reproach, consolation, and mediation). Then again, to these ancient distinctions in preaching purposes we could add the modern genres of the sermon as a reflective meditation or a personal narrative. We have a long history of communicating in a variety of different genres, but my interest in voice as a function of preaching's purpose is different from a mere interest in genres of preaching. Rather than exploring stylistic or rhetorical differences in ways people preach, I want to explore four distinctly different expressions of contemporary Christian cultural consciousness as they are embodied in the assumptions that control what preachers want to have happen as a result of people listening to their sermons.[16]

Voice as a Preached Identity

In order to explore what I mean by defining *voice* as an expression of a distinctive set of assumptions that reveal the speaker's cultural consciousness, it may help to clarify how I am using the term differently from others who have tilled some of this same soil. Traditionally, a discussion of the subject of voice in homiletics is treated as an aspect of delivery, one of the five canons of classical rhetorical theory.[17] Or it has also been used as a term to describe the difference between writing sermons that sound like read essays and sermons that sound like dynamic conversation with thoughtful attention to the use of effective schemes and tropes for memorable oral communication.[18] Stephen Webb's recent *The Divine Voice: Christian Proclamation and the Theology of Sound* is related to my interest in voice, since it is a theological *phenomenology* of the oral dimension of preaching.[19] Its interest in

16. Though developed as a means to identify contemporary preaching purposes, the matrix is part of my ongoing project to identify a theory of contemporary Christian discourse. On the need for this theory see Martin J. Medhurst, "Religious Belief and Scholarship: A Complex Relationship," *Journal of Communication and Religion* 27, 1 (2004): 43. Two existing efforts to fill this gap are Charles H. Kraft, *Communication Theory for Christian Witness*, rev. ed. (Maryknoll, NY: Orbis Books, 1991) and Pierre Babin and Mercedes Iannone, *The New Era in Religious Communication*, David Smith, trans. (Minneapolis: Fortress Press, 1991).

17. These canons date from the time of Cicero. They represent the basic divisions in the disciplinary subject matter of oratory. They are *invention, style, arrangement, memory,* and *delivery.* On voice as a dimension of delivery, see Charles L. Bartow, *The Preaching Moment: A Guide to Sermon Delivery* (Dubuque, IA: Kendall/Hunt, 1995).

18. E.g., G. Robert Jacks, *Just Say the Word: Writing for the Ear* (Grand Rapids: Eerdmans, 1996).

19. Stephen Webb, *The Divine Voice: Christian Proclamation and the Theology of Sound* (Grand Rapids: Brazos Press, 2004).

the performative dimensions of voice as an expression of sound is relevant to my inquiry, but this oral dimension of homiletic expression is not what I mean by voice.

Mary Donovan Turner and Mary Lin Hudson are closer to my purpose when they examine voice as a metaphor for the dimensions of interpersonal identity and the construction of a self-concept in homiletic speech. In *Saved from Silence: Finding Women's Voice in Preaching* they explore ways that the act of speaking reveals dimensions of self that are distinctive, authentic, authoritative, resistant, and relational. They are interested in exploring how individuals, especially women, may feel "voiced" by approaches to preaching that invite community and dialogue or, alternatively, "silenced" by approaches to preaching that employ courtroom rhetoric to suppress the voices of others.[20] Their work is important, especially as it identifies rhetoric that marginalizes the voices of difference, but this is still not what I mean by voice.

I am interested in examining how "what sermons are up to" is shaped by the voice that controls the intention of the sermon. I am using the word *voice* to describe something more than mere homiletic articulation in delivery, more than the preacher's ability to write and speak for the listener's ear, and more than a metaphor for the psychological or interpersonal communication of one's "self" revealed in speech. The notion of voice I take up here has to do with the cultural indicators of the implied *identity* of the one who is speaking in a sermon and the cultural identity this voice assumes on behalf of its implied listeners. In this sense I am interested in identifying the implied identity of who is speaking and how this helps create the identities of those who are responding.

This concept of voice is closer to that of a literary critic who employs the term to name the implied identity of an author who tells the story.[21] Voice in this use describes a dialogic experience

20. Mary Donovan Turner and Mary Lin Hudson, *Saved from Silence: Finding Women's Voice in Preaching* (St. Louis: Chalice Press, 1999), 137–39.

21. On uses of literary voice see Peter Elbow's "Introduction: About Voice and Writing," *Landmark Essays on Voice and Writing*, Peter Elbow, ed. (Davis, CA: Hermagoras Press, 1994),

of identity creation between author and audience, sometimes embedded more in the experience than the expression of the story. It answers the question, "Who speaks?" regardless of the point of view of any characters within a tale. Whenever we read a story, even as we become caught up in the world of its characters and their perspectives voiced in the tale, we are also aware of the moral sensibility of the one who invented, ordered, and rendered its characters into a meaningful world. This implied character is also a literary creation akin to Aristotle's notion of a speaker's implied ethos embedded in the way the arguments and the ideas are ordered and rendered in a speech. Wayne Booth refers to this determinate narrative presence as the implied author, but Walter Ong prefers the word voice because it allows him to distinguish between an author's "false voice" and an author's "true voice."[22] For Ong, when an author is in control of this true voice, it becomes an expression, even an extension, of the author's own genuine self or identity. Ong would say that the writer who finds the way to this true voice finds himself or herself.[23]

Applied to preaching, discovery of one's true voice is embodied in three dimensions of preaching identity we saw in the story of Miz Lil and the preacher. First, voice is embodied in the identity assumed by the one who speaks—the preacher. Second, it is embodied in the way this voice calls listeners into its confidence—the way it shapes the identity of the responding listeners. And, third, this embodiment can be experienced as so authentic it can become a third identity—the embodiment of voice as Word of God.

The preacher's voice is the means by which sermonic reality is construed, and therefore "constructed," for listeners. When combined with the content of a particular theology, voice is expressed

xi–xlvii.

22. On this use of voice see Wayne Booth, *The Rhetoric of Fiction,* 2d ed. (Chicago: University of Chicago Press, 1983); Walter J. Ong, *The Barbarian Within, and Other Fugitive Essays and Studies* (New York: Macmillan, 1962), 49–67. Also see the discussion of the terms "Persona, Tone, Voice" in M. H. Abrams, *A Glossary of Literary Terms,* 7th ed. (Boston: Heinle & Heinle, 1999), 219.

23. Here I join Stephen Webb in locating part of the theory that drives my inquiry in the work of Walter Ong.

in the sermonic intention that calls forth different kinds of faith identities from listeners. For example, when a student finishes a sermon in the classroom I ask, "What did you want to have happen as a result of people listening to that sermon?" Students often act as if I asked, "What is the point of the sermon?" They know how to summarize a theological assertion in a focus statement. But asking them, "What did you want to have happen?" invites them to reveal the implicit communicative assumptions of the sermon's intention:

> "I wanted listeners to understand that . . ."
> "I wanted listeners to let God . . ."
> "I wanted listeners to choose . . ."
> "I wanted listeners to care about . . ."

Answers like these tend to reveal the nature of the implicit persuasive appeals embodied in the preacher's sermonic voice. They tend to reveal the preacher's assumptions about *the nature of authority* and *the nature of language*. When a preacher learns how to identify the implicit communication assumptions that shape a "true voice" rather than "false voices," in the words of Walter Ong, that preacher is discovering himself or herself—a voice that expresses that preacher's most authentic expression of naming God and naming grace in a sermon.

In each case, the preaching intention reveals the assumptions that shape the preacher's faith identity and the faith identity that an approach to preaching calls forth from listeners. Depending on how well a preacher functionally understands what makes for coherence in his or her voice, that witness will be experienced either as clear and credible or as the expression of a confused identity, a witness to faith somewhat adrift. In this sense, the preacher's communicative assumptions about the nature of authority and the nature of language are as relevant as his or her theological assumptions in the homiletic dance that makes up the human and divine dimensions of preaching.

Preachers who choose to explore the cultural presuppositions of their preaching voice have begun a process of determining their own anthropology of preaching—the human side of this "homiletic dance." To achieve a full anthropology of preaching they would need to move beyond the question of *cultural presuppositions* to address concerns of an ethic and/or an ethics of preaching relevant to their cultural consciousness. And for this anthropology to become a full homiletic, the preacher would need to develop a personal theology of preaching. Though issues of theology are certainly assumed throughout this book (i.e., my effort to propose an understanding of preaching's purpose broad enough to be inclusive of a variety of understandings and still theologically meaningful), my purpose is to provide readers with resources to identify the cultural assumptions that frame an anthropology of preaching implicit in the voice they take up or the voice they hear in preaching. By addressing questions of excellence in each voice, this book also alludes to the concerns that would be central to an ethic of preaching in each voice.

Discovering the Power of Voice

When sermons begin to consistently connect with listeners, we often say that a preacher has found his or her voice. By this we imply that preachers who are in possession of their voice speak with a clearer sense of purpose and with greater faithfulness to their own convictions about faith. This is why discovering the power of voice in preaching matters. So why do preachers have so much trouble identifying and finding their voice?

There are several responses to this question. The first and most obvious is that they lack understanding of what makes for a culturally and theologically congruent voice in preaching. *Too often preachers are unsure of what they want to happen as a result of people listening to their sermon.* These preachers tend to view their homiletic role as the "answer person," the "psychosocial healer," or the "confessional caretaker." Because of this too many sermons are:

- a mishmash of thoughtful reflections gathered together in the wistful hope that listeners will find the observations helpful;
- a *tour de force* position paper of the kind they used to hand in to their seminary professor;
- an explanatory history lesson with a spiritual lesson tacked on for good measure;
- a collection of answers, appropriately illustrated, directed toward providing advice on how to think or live;
- a motivational guide to better living through Jesus;
- assertions of concern meant to challenge a status-quo understanding;
- pleasant talks about Jesus; or
- "this is who we are" confessional-tradition talks.

The list is easily expanded. But such sermons, focused as they are on delivery of theological content, rarely seek to name God and name grace for others.

If preachers begin with an assumption that they must find ways in the sermon to name God and name grace, then they are forced to think about how what is said should effect a desired response from listeners. Sermons focused only on the delivery of theological content tend to remain abstract rather than offering witness to gospel possibilities. In educational language, preaching focused on the delivery of content tends to operate out of a teacher-centered paradigm of communication rather than a learner-centered paradigm.[24] This distinction in the field of homiletics has typically been discussed as the difference between a subject-centered versus an audience-centered approach to preaching.[25]

24. See Mary E. Huba and Jann E. Freed, *Learner-Centered Assessment on College Campuses: Shifting the Focus from Teaching to Learning* (Boston: Allyn and Bacon, 2000).

25. Thomas G. Long, "And How Shall They Hear? The Listener in Contemporary Preaching," in *Listening to the Word: Studies in Honor of Fred B. Craddock*, Gail R. O'Day and Thomas G. Long, eds. (Nashville: Abingdon Press, 1993), 167–88.

A second reason that preachers have trouble finding their voice is that too often they assume that intentions should vary at different points within a sermon. This makes intuitive sense. At different points within any sermon a preacher is likely to speak as one who teaches, as one who encourages, as a sage, and as one who testifies. So how can a preacher create sermons in which one intention controls the possible response?

Aristotle answered a similar question long ago. He found that most speeches simultaneously address questions of fact, questions of policy, and questions of value. On the other hand, he found that only one of these should be the *organizing* question for any specific speech. Thus, in any speech, *only one question should control the presentation's intention*. Based on this assertion, he argued that the controlling question dictated whether the genre of a speech should be classified as forensic, deliberative, or demonstrative.[26] The same intention applies to discovering one's voice in preaching. In this context we simply change Aristotle's notion of a *controlling question* to the metaphor of *taking a trip*. Thus, in any sermon, all four voices may be along for the ride, *but only one of the voices should be behind the wheel.* The voice that controls the direction of the sermon is the one that shapes the intention. It is this voice that helps the preacher clarify where the sermon will go and what should happen when it gets there.

Preachers who have trouble identifying which intention—which voice—should be behind the wheel of the sermon tend to deliver sermons that end up "going nowhere." Sermons with no clear voice leave listeners confused by what is expected of them in response to having heard the sermon. However, a note of caution is in order here. Consistency of voice does not mean exclusivity of voice. It means that the assumptions about the natures of language and authority of only one of the voices *should control what the preacher desires to have happen as a result of people listening to a specific sermon*. There are ethical implications to all

26. From the time of Aristotle until today speakers have distinguished three kinds of speaking situations and treated most genres as a particular instance of one of three classes of discourse. Aristotle is quite clear in his presentation of this set of distinctions. See Aristotle's *Rhetoric* 1.3.1–4; 1358b.

of this, which is why I move to a discussion of excellence in the concluding section of the chapters on each voice. Beyond this, I will return to the question of ethics as a dimension of identifying one's voice in the final chapter of this book. At this point the reader is invited, first, to explore the textures of each of the voices in the following pages and find either the voice that seems to fit as his or her own preaching identity or, if the reader is a listener of sermons, the voiced identity of the person whose preaching calls forth the reader's own faith identity.

In Service to This High Calling

When I work with preachers I ask them to bring four recent sermons and, together, we analyze each one with the basic question, "What did you want to have happen as a result of people listening to that sermon?" If you are a preacher reading this book I encourage you to take this challenge before you read the remaining chapters. Push past the effort to be defensive or the need to be all things to all people. Try to locate the basic thrust of your preaching identity. In my experience most preachers have a reasonably consistent purpose that controls the intention of their preaching. The purpose of this book is to help you, first, identify that voice and, second, understand the cultural assumptions that drive it, so that you can reach for excellence in preaching.

I am also suggesting that parishioners who regularly listen to a pastor's preaching ministry should be able to identify the desired response of their pastor's sermons. If you listen to sermons instead of preaching them, over the next month of worship experiences focus on the question, "In what way does my pastor hope I will respond as a result of hearing this sermon?" Good sermons are designed and edited to achieve a desired response from listeners. So, you should be able to tell whether the sermon makes its appeal based on a collective agreement about what matters or an appeal to you as a person on a quest for personal understanding or advancement. You should be able to tell whether the preacher speaks with assuredness in making pronouncements about truth or speaks in ways that suggests that truth is more tensional, more a sacred mystery worth working out with others, more about something to think about after the sermon ends. Identifying your pastor's preaching voice will help you to ask questions about what matters to you in your own faith formation. It will also help you to frame questions that let you explore the way your faith can continue to be challenged and encouraged.

In all of this I am suggesting that preachers who understand the relationship between a preaching intention and the intersection of cultural assumptions that make for a congruent voice will likely be able to recognize their preferred preaching identity in the Matrix of Contemporary Christian Voices. Identifying one's voice is the first and most important task in discovering the key to greater authenticity of voice. The second task involves understanding the cultural assumptions about the nature of language and the nature of authority that can liberate a preacher to speak the Word of God to a community with greater power. A preacher who can join this greater insight into the cultural assumptions of a preaching voice with an authentic wrestling with matters of faith in preaching is on a journey to greater excellence in preaching. This book differs from traditional homiletic books by arguing that excellence in voice can be achieved through a consistent negotiation of the assumptions that support a specific voice.

In the chapters that follow I take up each proposed voice, provide a historical-theological context that situates the orientation of its cultural consciousness, identify the natural boundaries of its assumptions, track its expression in current theologies of homiletic practice, and then provide some observations concerning what excellence sounds like in that voice. To help preachers and those who listen to sermons experience the differences between preaching purposes that structure each voice, I have included four sample sermons at the end of each chapter.[27] The sample

27. Readers interested in a similar fourfold analysis of four sermons based on a text in Amos should look at my first effort to frame the argument of this book found in Robert Stephen Reid, "Exploring Preaching's Voices from Ex Cathedra to Exilic," in *The Cry of the Eighth Century Prophets*, David Fleer and Dave Bland, eds. (Abilene, TX: ACU Press, 2004), 135–64.

sermons are all based on Luke 18:1–8, the Gospel text for the Twentieth Sunday after Pentecost in Cycle C. The text is

> [1]Then Jesus told them a parable about their need to pray always and not to lose heart. [2]He said, "In a certain city there was a judge who neither feared God nor had respect for people. [3]In that city there was a widow who kept coming to him and saying, 'Grant me justice against my opponent.' [4]For a while he refused; but later he said to himself, 'Though I have no fear of God and no respect for anyone, [5]yet because this widow keeps bothering me, I will grant her justice, so that she may not wear me out by continually coming.'" [6]And the Lord said, "Listen to what the unjust judge says. [7]And will not God grant justice to his chosen ones who cry to him day and night? Will he delay long in helping them? [8]I tell you, he will quickly grant justice to them. And yet, when the Son of Man comes, will he find faith on earth?" (NRSV)

I find this to be a particularly suitable text for my purpose because it begins with a didactic statement of intention yet ends with a disconcerting question that lends itself to multiple understandings. The sermons at the close of each chapter are meant to serve as exemplars of what I believe to be excellence in the expression of the indicated voice. The decision to identify each sermon as an exemplar of the voice is mine rather than that of the individual preacher.

The four chapters that follow, though shaped by my prescriptive perceptions as to what counts as excellence, are primarily descriptive. Only in the final chapter do I offer prescriptive advice concerning the importance of finding one's own voice as a preaching identity, its relationship to what listeners experience as authenticity of voice, and the significance of that voice in shaping the faith consciousness of listeners.

The Four Voices of Preaching offers a typological exploration of contemporary American perspectives for what counts as the cultural consciousnesses of the preacher whose sermons name God and name grace with the intention of calling forth a response of faith from listeners. My purpose throughout is to assist preachers to achieve greater excellence in preaching by finding their own voice in service to this high calling and to assist listeners who wish to understand how the voice their preacher adopts may be shaping the quality of their own faith.

The Hope

Miz Lil told her pastor, "When you teach, I learn something for the day. I can take it home and, God willing, I can do it." Concerning her pastor's other voice she said, "But when you preach—God is here." Miz Lil knew at least two of her pastor's voices, and she knew them by their preaching intentions. Invariably, when I have the privilege to listen to student sermons, one of my first questions in follow-up is to ask, "What did you want to have happen as a result of people hearing that sermon?" Without clarity of intention it is rare that a sermon will be experienced as authentic.

When the preacher is able to match preaching intention and homiletic theology with a strategy of preaching that is consistent with the presuppositions of both, then the voice the preacher takes up has the potential to be experienced as authentic by listeners. Obviously other factors affect the experience of authenticity, but I have suggested that a preaching identity is embodied in the way sermons reveal the intentionality of voice, in the way that this voice calls listeners into its confidence, and the way that this identity can, at times, be experienced as so authentic, it becomes the embodiment of voice as Word of God. That's what Miz Lil craved. And so do we.

2

Preaching in the Teaching Voice

The story of Eutychus in Acts 20 never fails to delight. On a Sunday in Troas, Paul is preaching well into the night. He has so much to say that young Eutychus, perched on a third-story windowsill, first falls asleep, then falls perilously out the window. Our worst fears are momentarily piqued only to discover that, when Paul joins the crowd downstairs, he embraces the seemingly dead teenager and surprises everyone by declaring that all is well. The young man is then led away to a joyous re-embrace by his family. Of course, it is unlikely Eutychus learned much that evening, having been lulled to sleep by poor ventilation and the seemingly endless talk. Yet, for those who remained, Paul's preaching must have taken on an evanescent quality. More than just plausible argument, this was teaching vindicated by a demonstration of the Spirit's power (1 Cor. 2:4).

The story is also delightful for our present purpose because it employs two words that capture the intersection of preaching and teaching in the primitive church. Twice, before Eutychus took his plunge, Paul is described as *discussing* matters with those gathered. The word *discussing* suggests a kind of dialogical give and take of a teacher. Then, in the aftermath of the Eutychus incident, Luke shifts the word to say that Paul was *homileo*-ing until morning light. Luke uses the same word to describe Jesus' conversation with Cleophus and his traveling companion on the way to Emmaus (Luke 24:27; cf. Acts 24:26). This is the word that the church eventually adopted to describe the act of giving witness to the Good News that in Christ, God was reconciling the world to himself (2 Cor. 5:19).

The history of preaching obviously predates Jesus' and Paul's efforts to persuade others to accept the good news. It would also be anachronistic to assume that our modern concept of the relationship between teaching and preaching remained the same as the expression we find in the pages of Scripture. Our modern concept of the homily as a specific form of preaching took more than twelve hundred years to develop.[1] Yet, from the beginning, the relationship between teaching and preaching makes this the strongest voice associated with sharing the Good News of God's love and forgiveness in Christ Jesus.

A brief history of the relationship between teaching and preaching across the centuries of Western practice can help to highlight the difference between this relationship in the first century BC and its contemporary association. I want to trace how we have moved from the sense of teaching as an interpretive talk to our modern conception of teaching as the presentation of a reasoned argument. By exploring this history we should be able to arrive at a more nuanced understanding of the assumptions that form the cultural consciousness of the Teaching Voice at the outset of the twenty-first century. Following this I describe the essential cultural assumptions of the Teaching Voice and explore its continuum of contemporary practice.

Teaching and Preaching Across the Centuries

By the close of the first century Christian preaching had come to be characterized by a style of *homileo*-ing that exhorted listen-

1. On the difficulty of defining the theory of the homily before 1200 see James J. Murphy, *Rhetoric in the Middle Ages: A History of Rhetorical Theory from Augustine to the Renaissance* (Berkeley: University of California Press, 1974), 298.

ers to live into the moral claims of the gospel while also offering theological teaching.[2] By the second century homilies tended to combine the interpretive form of reasoning we call Jewish midrash (either a literal or figurative reinterpretation of a sacred text for present circumstances) with the rhetoric of Greek forms of argument and paraenesis (exhortation that draws on widely accepted moral truisms not subject to refutation).[3] The result was a distinctive style of proclamation attuned to the needs of the church. The oldest church manual, the *Didache*, begins with a homily offering moral instruction to those about to be baptized and concludes by commending appropriate practice for worship and for church discipline. Justin Martyr reports that in the middle of the second century it was customary for the lector to read from the Gospels and the prophets and then for the presiding elder to give a talk "urgently admonishing his hearers to practice these noble teachings in their lives."[4]

In the Apostolic Church, preaching appears to have been a talk the intention of which was to admonish those who listened to live into the claims of their faith. In his extensive examination of worship in this period Hugh Old finds that the terms for teaching and preaching in the primitive church were often interchangeable,[5] and Roy Osborn adds that by universal custom and conviction the pre-Constantinian church "established preaching as integral and essential to public worship, its major instrument of Christian teaching, motivation, and discipline, as well as of evangelism. Along with the Eucharist, the ministry of the word

2. David E. Aune, *The Westminster Dictionary of New Testament and Early Christian Literature and Rhetoric* (Louisville: Westminster/John Knox Press, 2003), 219.

3. On "The Hermeneutics of Midrash" see Gerald L. Bruns, *Hermeneutics Ancient and Modern* (New Haven: Yale University Press, 1992), 104–23. On the significance of rhetorical strategies of thought in the composition of early Christian homiletics and apologetics, see David E. Aune, *The New Testament in Its Literary Environment,* Library of Early Christianity, Wayne Meeks, ed. (Philadelphia: Westminster Press, 1987).

4. From St. Justin's *First Apology* written in Rome about 150 AD.

5. Hughes Oliphant Old, *The Reading and Preaching of the Scriptures in the Worship of the Christian Church*, vol. 1: *The Biblical Period* (Grand Rapids: Eerdmans, 1998), 235. Dodd's theological argument that the New Testament distinguishes preaching from teaching has not held up under rhetorical investigation of the genre; see C. H. Dodd, *The Apostolic Preaching and Its Developments* (New York: Harper, 1937).

(even when reduced to the briefest of homilies) proved to be the necessary carrier of Christian understanding and devotion."[6]

During the first four centuries of the Christian era, the homily developed in the church as a conversation or a talk with a goal of interpreting or applying the implications of the gospel for either the converted or the unconverted. The character of the audience determined whether the presentation was didactic or evangelistic, and the speaker chose whether the intention was primarily doctrinal, expository, or exhortative. Unless the homily was an exposition, Scripture was employed primarily in quotation or application rather than as a text. The structure of the discourse was idiosyncratic and usually short.[7] Gregory of Nanzianzus had identified three divisions of preaching—moral edification, teaching of dogma, and the celebration of worthy lives—that appear to adapt the speaking intentions of rhetoric's deliberative, judicial, and epideictic genres of speech to Christian preaching.[8] Otherwise, during this period little of rhetoric's "rules of eloquence" were acknowledged as useful for gospel proclamation.

Augustine was the first theologian to argue that Christian teaching is an art that must attend to how its purpose should be accomplished. The church was faced with a seemingly insoluble problem. If the Bible is divinely revealed, then what need is there to defend its doctrines? Teachers should simply assume the truth of their teaching. But how were false teachers and false teachings to be countered? Historically, rhetoric was the field of study that trained people to make arguments primarily in matters where persuasion rather than truth is at stake (i.e., the difference between what Aristotle called artistic or invented rather than inartistic or evidentiary argument). But the theologians had soundly rejected the idea that Christian truth should ever be sullied with rhetoric's

6. Ronald E. Osborn, *Folly of God: The Rise of Christian Preaching*, A History of Christian Preaching, vol. 1 (St. Louis: Chalice Press, 1999), 425.

7. Homilies by educated Roman citizens like Paul were more likely to conduct argument according to the contemporary rhetorical precepts than those by untutored Christian leaders; see Robert S. Reid, "Paul's *Conscious* Use of the *Ad Herennium's* 'Complete Argument,'" *Rhetoric Society Quarterly* 35, 2 (2005): 65–92.

8. George A. Kennedy, *A New History of Classical Rhetoric* (Princeton: Princeton University Press, 1994), 262.

means of persuasion and its strategies of persuasive argumentation. After all, revealed truth needed no assistance from fallible human reasoning. Augustine considered this claim naïve. In *On Christian Doctrine* he asks, "Who will dare to say that truth in the person of its defenders is to take its stand unarmed against falsehood?"[9] He had already defended using the art of rhetoric as a form of reasoning for the interpretation of Scripture that must be adopted and adapted for Christian use.[10] In the last part of *On Christian Doctrine*, devoted to the public expression of Christian teaching, he tears down the artificial wall his predecessors had constructed between the sacred and the secular tasks of defending truth through skilled strategies of argument and eloquence.

His introduction of rhetoric into the business of teaching and preaching is cautious but firm. What matters is the ability of those who hear the gospel to understand its message so that they can apply its truth to their life.

> Therefore the person who is saying something with the intention of teaching should not consider that he has yet said anything of what he wants to the person he wants to teach, so long as he is not understood. Because even if he has said something he understands himself, he is not to be regarded as having said it to the person he is not understood by, while if he has been understood, he has said it, whatever his way of saying it may have been.[11]

For teaching to connect in this way, Augustine argues that a speaker's teaching must be lucid. The teacher should use a subdued style when instructing, seek to delight when offering praise, and be eloquent when exhorting Christians to live faithfully. In all of this, Augustine speaks of the need for the Christian teacher to become an effective communicator. It is clear that he sees no significant distinction between teaching and preaching. Unlike the interests of the secular rhetorical handbooks of his time,

9. Augustine, *On Christian Doctrine*, J. F. Shaw, trans., in *Augustine*, vol. 18, The Great Books of the Western World, Robert Maynard Hutchins, ed. (Chicago: Encyclopedia Britannica, 1952).

10. Augustine, 653 (Book II, Chapter 36), and 655 (Book II, Chapter 40).

11. Augustine, *On Christian Doctrine*, in *The Company of Preachers: Wisdom on Preaching, Augustine to the Present*, Richard Lischer, ed. (Grand Rapids: Eerdmans, 2002), 284.

Augustine's study presents no formal structure for his sermons. Instead, he describes them as "popular discussions, which the Greeks call homilies."[12]

Augustine's work was only one of many that sought to respond to the new era of preaching inaugurated with the conversion of Constantine. The beginnings of Christendom brought about a seismic shift for the role of the homily as it entered a new, more-public era where Christian bishops and Christian preachers were now the true heirs of the rhetorical tradition. Though some bishops initially struggled with making use of the rules of eloquence in proclamation of gospel, the role of rhetoric is readily evident in the judicial strategies of argument church fathers employed in dealing with doctrinal controversies and in the deliberative strategies observable in proceedings such as those of the Council of Chalcedon (450 AD).[13] To the already distinctive genre of the Christian homily, which increasingly became a talk based on the assigned text for a particular Sunday or feast day, the church added the topical and expository sermons. Topical sermons, though biblical in content, were more a sustained argument using biblical texts and strategies of reasoning to sustain a particular claim. A third kind of preaching that became popular in Christendom has been described as *lectio continua*, a continuous interpretive presentation of the teachings of Scripture, what today we would describe as an expository "sermon series" on a specific book of the Bible.

The relationship between preaching and teaching remained strong throughout most of the first millennium of the Christian era, but as the influence of rhetoric grew, its various resources were appropriated in service to the art of persuasion by way of a specific argument. Though Augustine may have urged the re-

12. "Augustine," *The New Schaff-Herzog Encyclopedia of Religious Knowledge*, retrieved at www.ccel.org/s/schaff/encyc/encyc01/contrib/371.htm. His essays are a different matter. See the meticulous analysis of *On Catechizing Inquirers*, regarding his proposal for conducting catechesis according to the Ciceronian principles of a juridical oration, in William Harmless, *Augustine and the Catechumenate* (Collegeville, MN: Liturgical Press, 1995), 123–40, 155.

13. This is the first council for which we have any significant record. See Jaroslav Pelikan, *Divine Rhetoric: The Sermon on the Mount as Message and as Model in Augustine, Chrysostom, and Luther* (Crestwood, NY: St. Vladimir's Seminary Press, 2001), 24–25.

appropriation of rhetoric for making argument in teaching, he still offered no list of commonplace topics, lines of argument, or appropriate subjects for preaching. These additions came later, each one quietly moving the sermon away from simple teaching and more toward the task of making a persuasive argument. For example, Pope Gregory (*c.* 540–604) took up the subject of appropriate subjects for preaching; and five hundred years later, Anselm's contemporary Guibert of Nogent (1053–1124) wrote *A Book about the Way a Sermon Ought to Be Given.* Guibert treats the appropriate motives for preaching and underscores the significance of the "four senses" necessary for the interpretation of Scripture.[14] Elements of the rhetorical tradition had been adapted to preaching, but the basic genre structures of preaching were still dictated by the kind of preaching involved, be it a talk, a topical presentation, or a continuous commentary. The shift that begins to form our more modern distinction between preaching and teaching may best be observed in Guibert's guidance that *moral* instruction is always preferable to *mere* instruction.

Up to the twelfth century, the sermon was primarily an inorganic homily with no formal introduction or divisions.[15] As Taylor notes, by the medieval period preachers clearly assumed that Scripture needed to be embellished in order to make its appeal to listeners, but there was little consensus concerning appropriate sermon form.[16] Educated clergy may have been aware of the standard arrangement divisions for making an argument found in Cicero's *De Inventione* and the anonymous *Rhetorica Ad Herennium*—the two most influential ancient rhetorical textbooks

14. The four senses of Scripture—the literal, the allegorical, the moral, and the anagogical—were originally proposed by John Cassian, Chrysostom's deacon (*c.* 360–430), based on Origin's (*c.* 184–254) hermeneutical principles. Origin believed that the Bible offered three levels of meaning: a corporeal or literal level of meaning; a moral level to be interpreted typologically; and a spiritual or theological level. For a contemporary recovery of the importance of this tradition see Paul Scott Wilson, *God Sense: Reading the Bible for Preaching* (Nashville: Abingdon Press, 2001).

15. Harry Caplan, "A Late Medieval Tractate on Preaching," in *Studies in Rhetoric and Public Speaking in Honor of James Albert Winans*, A. M. Drummond, ed. (New York: Russell & Russell, 1962), 63.

16. Larissa Taylor, *Soldiers of Christ: Preaching in Late Medieval and Reformation France* (New York: Oxford University Press), 228.

of the medieval period—but, without a formal study detailing how to make use of this rhetorical tradition for preaching, the efforts were haphazard at best.[17] During the Renaissance these two rhetorical handbooks became known as *rhetorica prima* and *rhetorica secunda*. They were the essential books of Ciceronian eloquence for anyone who sought to understand the art of rhetoric as applied to preaching.[18]

A full precept-driven appropriation of the rhetorical tradition applied to preaching had yet to be written, but this all changes with *On the Preacher's Art* by Alan de Lille. Written on the eve of the twelfth century, this treatise was the first fully prescriptive work devoted solely to homiletics as an art of preaching. Alan wrote:

> Preaching is an open and public instruction in faith and behavior, whose purpose is the forming of men; it derives from the path of reason and from the fountainhead of the "authorities." . . . Preaching is that instruction which is offered to many, in public, and for their edification. Teaching is that which is given to one or to many, to add to their knowledge. . . . By means of what is called "preaching"—instruction in matters of faith and behavior—two aspects of theology may be introduced: that which appeals to the reason and deals with knowledge of spiritual matters, and the ethical, which offers teaching on the living of the good life. For preaching sometimes teaches about holy things, sometimes about conduct. . . . [Its benefit] is implied in [saying] "whose purpose is the forming of men." [For its source] preaching must be dependent on reasoning and corroborated by authoritative texts. . . . There should be weight in the thought of a good sermon, so that it may move the spirits of its hearers, stir up the mind, and encourage repentance. Let the sermon rain down doctrines, thunder forth admonitions, soothe with praises, and so in every way work for the good of our neighbors.[19]

17. Throughout the medieval period it was assumed that Cicero was the author of both works, with the former fulfilling the promised completion (*De Inv.* 2.178; cf. 1.9) of the latter, supplying the additional treatments of delivery (*Ad Her.* 3.19–27), memory (3.28–40), and, most notably, style (4).

18. Brian Vickers, *In Defense of Rhetoric* (Oxford: Clarendon Press, 1988), 28.

19. Alan of Lille, *The Art of Preaching*, G. Evans, trans. (Kalamazoo, MI: Cistercian Publications, 1981), 16–18.

Notice the clear distinction between preaching and teaching. Preaching is still equated with instruction that speaks of holy things and adjures listeners to behave as people of faith, but its presentation is now dependent on reasoning corroborated by the tradition of authoritative texts. The purpose of preaching is to move the spirits of the hearers by simultaneously stirring their minds and encouraging them to respond by turning away from that which does not work for the good of our neighbors. The remainder of the book offers prescriptive advice on how to present argument in a number of matters reminiscent of the rhetorical handbook tradition of topics.

In the decades after this rhetoric of preaching was written there was an explosion of treatises composed on the subject of preaching. They are filled with advice and rules for homiletic composition, often offering highly structured approaches to the amplification of a theme derived from a scriptural text. Rather than an unstructured conversation about the meaning of a text, sermons were now transformed into strategies of argument intended to explain the internal essence of a text. Precept-driven preaching increasingly satisfied a scholastic desire for ordered thought. The speaker would announce a pro-theme, invite listeners to attend to the seriousness of God's Word, and announce a theme based on either a doctrine or a text. This was followed by a presentation of the argument in three divisions, with each part subdivided by tasks relevant to the development of the argument or the narrative.[20] The Medieval Preaching Tree depicted in Figure 2.1 offers a wonderful pictorial development of the sermon form with its sturdy thesis trunk, three limbs of argument, and three branches per limb defining each of the distinctly different argument tasks assigned to each limb. Jacobus de Fusignano, a Dominican priest writing around 1310, is the author of this organic metaphor that "A Sermon Is like a Tree." The artist who turned this into the visual diagram that comes down to us remains unknown.[21]

By the Reformation, the cultural assumptions that undergird the modern notion of argument in the Teaching Voice were beginning

20. Gillian Evans, "Introduction," in Alan of Lille, *The Art of Preaching*, 5–6.

21. This anglicized version of a Latin folio is reproduced in Otto Dieter, "*Arbor Picta*: The Medieval Tree of Preaching," *Quarterly Journal of Speech* 51 (1965): 130.

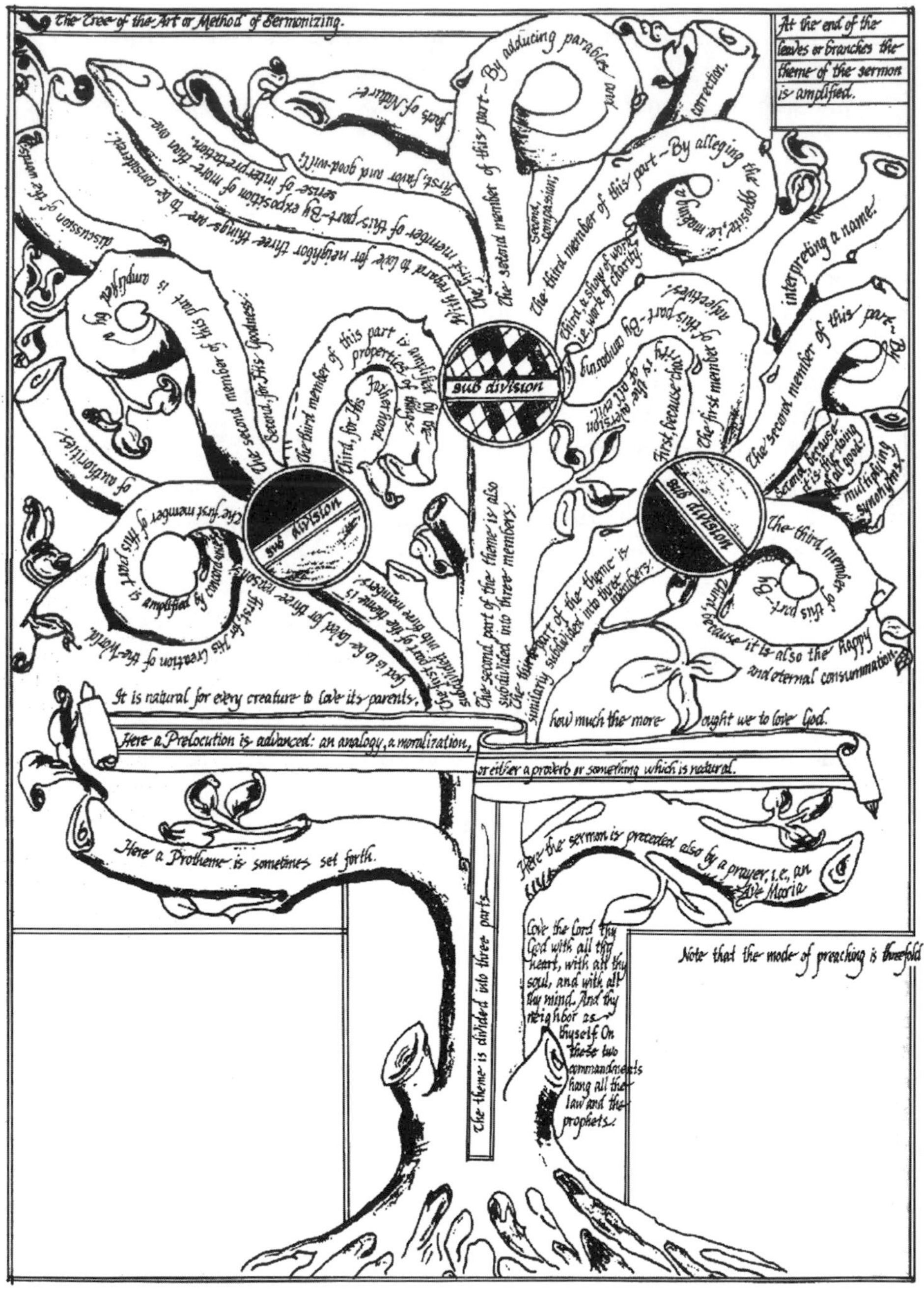

Figure 2.1: The Medieval Preaching Tree

to take shape. This notion was significantly influenced by a flood of homiletical treatises and by a renewed dependence on Cicero's divisions of a deductive rational argument. This kind of argument is a model of reasoning devised as a variation of the logical syllogism. It consists of five parts: a *major premise*, a *proof*, a *minor premise*, a *proof* of the minor premise, and a *conclusion*.[22] By the Elizabethan era this Ciceronian notion of classical argument had been blended with the model of the Complete Argument found in the Ciceronian *Rhetorica secunda* (the *Ad Herennium*) in a rough if unimaginative fashion. The result was a form of preaching in which the standard divisions of a sermon were an introduction, a statement of the proposition, an argument, a confutation of opposing views, and a conclusion. Note that where the Complete Argument employed embellishment as a form of reasoning, this strategy of thought had been replaced with Cicero's notion of *confutation* (arguments that weaken an opponent's case).[23] Alan Herr finds that sermons from this period were generally polemical, conducted in an "atmosphere of acrid disputation . . . hostile to the poise and the assurance which seem indispensable to pulpit oratory of enduring literary value."[24] Although Herr's own romantic-aesthetic judgment dominates this assessment, its essential claim is accurate. Preaching had made a polemical turn in which the goal was to prove a claim often in dispute of someone else's claim.

The basic division of the Puritan Plain Style Sermon varies from the Elizabethan model by expanding the role of the proof of the reason. In this form of the sermon, the preacher:

1. first reads a biblical *text*;
2. then explains the historical circumstances of the *text*;

22. Cicero, *De Inventione*, The Loeb Classical Library, Harry Hubbell, trans. and ed. (Cambridge, MA: Harvard University Press and William Heinemann, 1949), 1.37.67.

23. The five parts of the Complete Argument in the *Ad Herennium* were proposition, reason, proof of the reason, embellishment, and conclusion. See [Cicero], *Ad C. Herennium de Ratione Dicendi Rhetorica ad Herennium*, The Loeb Classical Library, Harry Caplan, trans. and ed. (Cambridge, MA: Harvard University Press, 1954), 2.18.28. For an example of the Apostle Paul's use of this form of reasoning see Robert Stephen Reid, "Paul's Conscious use of the *Ad Herennium*'s 'Complete Argument,'" *Rhetoric Society Quarterly* (2005): 65–92.

24. Alan Fager Herr, *The Elizabethan Sermon: A Survey and a Bibliography* (New York: Octagon Books, 1969), 87–88.

3. defines key words and or unclear references;
4. thematically develops doctrines that arise in the *text* or doctrines logically deducible from it as proofs;
5. provides proof of the reasons for the arguments in the doctrine section especially by way of Scripture citation; and
6. makes practical application of the teaching to general use or to exhort listeners to improve their ways.[25]

Depending on the preaching context or the personality of the preacher, proofs may or may not have taken on a polemical cast of *confutation* and *refutation*. Gone is the *Ad Herennium* notion that embellishment could be an allegorically rich way of elaborating the thematic as part of the structure of an argument (*Ad. Her.* 2.18.28). This is yet another indication of the degree to which preaching in this era had turned away from the ancient "four senses of interpretation" in favor of the presumption that preaching's purpose should be controlled by the dictates of only rational argument as reasoned debate.

For our present purpose what matters is the degree to which the argument model from ancient rhetorical theory had come to dominate the assumptions of the voice a preacher took up in preaching. This is sermon as argument rather than sermon as interpretive talk or interpretive teaching. The goal is to assert the order of a confessional or an interpretive tradition and invite the listener to affirm the correctness of the speaker's interpretation or presentation. Or alternatively, the intention of this sermon structure could be used polemically to challenge an existing order with a view to assert a new order, a new authority. In either case, this becomes the dominant framework for preaching. The simple homily may still have been offered by the country cleric, but it was no match for the authoritative presentation of the sermon as argument that became the form of preaching among the educated.

25. Ronald F. Reid, "Disputes over Preaching Method, the Second Awakening and Ebenezer Porter's Teaching of Sacred Rhetoric," *Journal of Communication and Religion* 18 (1995): 6.

By the eighteenth century, the assumptions that structure the nature of reason and argument in modern culture are cast. The full marriage between homiletics and rhetoric as a union based on belief produced through argument is eloquently detailed by George Campbell in 1760. His *The Philosophy of Rhetoric* is simultaneously one of the most original treatments of rhetorical theory since the classical era and a primer on how to employ this kind of reasoning in making rational argument in sermons. He states that speakers have one of two motives in speaking, either to instruct concerning doctrines not fully comprehended or to prove a position either disbelieved or doubted by listeners. The former seeks to dispel ignorance while the latter serves to vanquish error; where one kind of speaking provides information, the other provides conviction. "Accordingly, the predominant quality of the former is *perspicuity*; of the latter, *argument*." By the former listeners come to know. By the latter listeners come to believe.[26]

Campbell's commonsense rationalism was fully engaged in the academic conversations of its day, embracing rather than fighting the new, philosophical empiricism that structured reasoning in all matters of fact and human affairs.[27] To bring about conviction, it was no longer sufficient for sermons to engage in mere argument. Preachers in this new era had to become adept in the skill of presenting argument as a form of "scientific evidence." When it came to offering good reasons, Campbell concludes that "[t]his, though peculiarly the logician's province, is the foundation of conviction, and consequently of persuasion too. To attain to either of these ends, the speaker must always assume the character of the close, candid

26. George Campbell, *The Philosophy of Rhetoric*, rev. and exp. ed., with critical introduction by Lloyd Bitzer, ed. (Carbondale: Southern Illinois University Press, 1988), 2.

27. For discussions of the impact of Scottish Common Sense Rationalism on contemporary theology, especially conservative theology, see James Barr, *Fundamentalism* (Philadelphia: Westminster Press, 1977), 272–79; Ernest Robert Sandeen, *Roots of Fundamentalism: British and American Millenarianism, 1800–1930* (Grand Rapids: Baker, 1978), 103–31; Jack Rogers and Donald McKim, *The Authority and Interpretation of the Bible: An Historical Approach* (New York: Harper and Row, 1979), 236–60; George M. Marsden, *Fundamentalism and American Culture* (New York: Oxford University Press, 1980), 14–17; and Mark Noll, *The Scandal of the Evangelical Mind* (Grand Rapids: Eerdmans, 1986), 90–93.

reasoner: for though he may be an acute logician who is no orator, he will never be a consummate orator who is no logician."[28]

This model of reasoning had been dramatically shaped by the Enlightenment philosophies of empiricism and rationalism. If Descartes can be thought of as the father of the search for empirical method to whom Campbell is responding, Immanuel Kant can be thought of as the father of the rationalist effort to arrive at a modernist way of knowing. Empiricists claim that sense experience is the true source of information and the basis of forming concepts that lead to knowledge, while rationalists claim that conceptual knowledge can be arrived at independently of sense experience. These two intellectual streams are often referred to as the Enlightenment project's diverse effort to identify the foundations upon which knowledge can be discriminated from mere belief.[29]

Kant's declaration of independence from the church's control of knowledge was formulated in his motto "Dare to Know!" After posing the question, "What is the Enlightenment?" he responded,

> Enlightenment is man's exodus from his self-incurred tutelage. Tutelage is the inability to use one's understanding without the guidance of another person. This tutelage is self-incurred if its cause lies not in any weakness of the understanding, but in the indecision and lack of courage to use the mind without the guidance of another. "Dare to know!" Have courage to use your own understanding! This is the motto of the Enlightenment.[30]

By separating knowledge from belief, the Enlightenment made new kinds of inquiry possible. The gifts of Enlightenment rationality have made technologies available that span from Galileo to Gates, but its most significant accomplishment was the new freedom to leave behind the constraint that traditions could

28. Campbell, *Philosophy of Rhetoric*, 61.

29. See Alasdair MacIntyre, *Three Rival Versions of Moral Enquiry: Encyclopaedia, Genealogy and Tradition* (Notre Dame, IN: University of Notre Dame Press, 1990), 42.

30. Immanuel Kant, "Answer to the Question: 'What is the Enlightenment?'" as cited in Jaroslav Pelikan, *The Melody of Theology: A Philosophical Dictionary* (Cambridge, MA: Harvard University Press, 1988), 69.

impose on an individual's ability to pursue the courage of his or her own understanding.

Of course, there are some who believe that too much was sacrificed in this intellectual casting off of theology's tutelage. Karl Barth assailed the Enlightenment's intellectual project as a system of belief "founded upon the presupposition of faith in the omnipotence of human ability."[31] At this point I choose to postpone the critique of Enlightenment rationalist assumptions about the nature of language until chapters four and five. For now, I am merely interested in noting the Enlightenment's profound effect in shaping the modern concept of teaching as a reasoned presentation of the facts of a matter or a reasoned argument in support of specific claims about a matter.

A second, stylistic change in North American presentational speech during the nineteenth century also redefined what counts as a reasoned presentation of a matter in preaching. Where Campbell's rhetoric of commonsense realism still commended the use of Cicero's grand style to command the passions of a popular audience, by the beginning of the twentieth century this assumption changed dramatically. The nineteenth-century golden age of oratory was left behind in favor of public address composed with simple, declarative sentences. North American listeners went from a nation that valued a speaker's ability to sound like a gentleman to a nation that valued a speaker's ability to sound like an expert. By the beginning of the twentieth century, if speakers wished to have their arguments accepted, they needed to sound like experts; they needed to present arguments that let the "facts" speak for themselves. In his book *Public Speaking*, Dale Carnegie captures this shift of sensibilities:

> An entirely new school of speaking has sprung up since the Civil War. In keeping with the spirit of the times, it is as direct as a telegram. The verbal fireworks that were once the vogue would no longer be tolerated by an audience in this year of grace. . . . A Modern audience, regardless of whether it is fifteen people at

31. For Barth on the Enlightenment see Karl Barth, *Protestant Theology in the Nineteenth Century* (Grand Rapids: Eerdmans, 2002).

> a business conference or a thousand people under a tent, wants the speaker to talk as directly as he would in a chat, and in the same general manner that he would employ in speaking to one of them in conversation. [32]

By the turn of the century, the role of Ciceronian rhetoric, which had become committed to the notion of refined speech as the mark of a gentleman, or the truly educated, was swept away by the middling English of democratic eloquence.[33] For much of the twentieth century preachers believed that their task was to offer clear and cogent arguments on behalf of gospel claims and to present them in ways that let the facts speak for themselves.

Thus, by the modern period, the concept of teaching with relationship to preaching had come to mean something dramatically different from its meaning in the first centuries of the Christian movement. Whether the contemporary preacher wishes merely to instruct or to make a persuasive argument, preaching in the Teaching Voice has become the expression of a cultural consciousness that provides the rhetorical resources either to present or make arguments concerning "the facts." This voice is taken up by those who assume a preacher can and should assert the interpretive meaning of biblical texts as if he or she speaks on behalf of the church or speaks on behalf of some theological community's convictional understanding of the text. The purpose of speaking in this voice is to invite listeners to respond by declaring their agreement with or acceptance of the convictional understanding presented in the sermon.

The Teaching Voice in Preaching

The distinctive element of the Teaching Voice is its assumption that the purpose of the sermon is to affirm truths for a community of faith in a persuasively determinate fashion. Sermons in

32. Dale Carnegie, *Public Speaking* (New York: Pocket Books, 1926), 94.

33. Kenneth Cmiel, *Democratic Eloquence: The Fight over Popular Speech in Nineteenth-Century America* (New York: William Morrow, 1990).

this voice generally operate with objectivist assumptions about the nature of reality and call forth faith in and with the community that stands behind the ordered traditions of this appeal to corporate truth. Sermons in this voice may conclude by calling for a response of some kind, but the controlling intention throughout the sermon is one that invites listeners to affirm the ideas presented as representative of a confessional or an interpretive tradition.

Based on the Matrix of Contemporary Christian Voices, introduced in the previous chapter, the Teaching Voice operates with an assumption that listeners will respond to an objectivist, persuasively determinate appeal rather than an appeal that embraces the ambiguity of indeterminacy. The authority of this appeal invites the listener to affirm or reaffirm the corporate truth of the confessional tradition or theological perspective, to count himself or herself as one who would say, "Yes! This is what we believe. This is what people should believe." It is an argument-centered approach to preaching that assumes the authoritative voice, whether the speaker actively seeks to persuade listeners or merely instructs listeners in the doctrines or affirmations of their heritage (see Figure 2.2).

Nature of Language Appeals	***Persuasively Determinate Appeal***	**The Teaching Voice** Expects: "Yes! This is what we believe." ***Argument-Centered***
		Corporate Truth Appeal
		Nature of Authority Appeals

Figure 2.2: The Teaching Voice

Sermons in a Teaching Voice are distinguished by the controlling intention of helping listeners affirm or reaffirm their faith identity as part of a people who agree on the basic tenets of a confessional tradition or a theological perspective. Its objectivist assumptions make implicit appeals grounded in the listener's belief that reality can be known rationally through logical categories and empirically through the senses. By default, it presumes that human perceptions are basically trustworthy. In addition, it operates with an implicit appeal that listeners will accept the authority of an ordered, tradition-centered way of understanding the world as "a way of knowing" presented in the sermon.

The Teaching Voice serves a vast array of theologies and perspectives. Fundamentalists and old liberals draw on it as a resource equally. Sacramentalists, Lutherans, Mennonites, and Reformed all find its resources useful in helping parishioners reaffirm the beliefs central to these confessional traditions. It also serves those who ground the nature of their appeal to order in the arguments of a particular theological perspective. In other words, this approach can as readily be a voice taken up by a liberationist as it can be the voice of a dispensationalist. It is a voice that unambiguously asserts a specific articulation of how faith should be understood and offers clear explanation of the meaning of specific texts and teachings of the church with regard to the issue at stake.

Sermons offered in this voice present an authoritative interpretation of a text/topic/contemporary thematic. The preacher steps to the pulpit as one who is assured by his or her own conviction of the truth of the gospel—shaped through an understanding of her or his own confessional or perspectival tradition—and interprets meaning for listeners. By virtue of position and/or training, preachers assuming a Teaching Voice tend to speak *ex cathedra*—on behalf of the church—or they speak argumentively, as one making the case that a particular theological perspective should prevail in how one thinks about and understands matters of faith. They speak as persons who have been certified to explain meaning authoritatively, whether their credentials are ordination to a particular confessional tradition or expertise in a particular interpretive or perspectival tradition. Even if a sermon in this voice concludes with an invitation to respond or to take action, the purpose of speaking in this voice is to invite the listener to accept the cultural consciousness implicit in this kind of talk. It is an appeal to construe what counts as the nature of reality out of this voice's sense of assuredness and to construe the center of gravity for the determination of what should count as truth in the external verities of a tradition or perspective rather than by appeal to an internal locus of authority.

The Spectrum of Possibilities

When I have presented this matrix of voices to clergy and to students, they are often disturbed at the idea that so many theologically diverse groups can all be collected under the Teaching Voice. "Who's left?" they ask. It often takes time to help them see I am not arraying the standard assumptions of the old conservative-liberal continuum. Rather, I am addressing the degree of a speaker's *assuredness* in the expression of convictions. This sense of assuredness may provide resources as readily for a Dutch Reformed theology as the theology of a Southern Baptist. What matters is that the preacher speaks out of a sense of assuredness, drawing on the resources of a particular set of cultural and theological assumptions to explain and apply the meaning of a text or the meaning of specific theological teaching.

This assuredness may be expressed as commitment to a core set of beliefs, be they doctrinal, confessional, or merely tradition-centered. It may be expressed as an assuredness in a preacher's style of explaining the meaning of a text verse-by-verse. It may be expressed in the way a speaker takes up the defense of one side of an issue in debate. It may be expressed in the sense of urgency with which a speaker addresses a need for change. It may be expressed in the good reasons a preacher offers justifying the expression of personal convictions in a sermon. What matters in the Teaching Voice is that the speaker assumes some communal set of convictions out of which he or she can speak with assurance in making persuasive appeals.

The nature of persuasive appeals in this voice can vary greatly. For example, sermons in which argument is more implicit may simply name a doctrinal truth and invite listeners to reaffirm their identity as a community of the faithful who would assent to this creedal affirmation. In such sermons, a preacher may:

- begin with an illustration;
- name a doctrinal or theological issue at stake in the text or topic;
- locate that issue in a biblical text or a theological context with reference to the doctrinal or creedal belief of the community;
- draw out the implications of the doctrinal or confessional tradition's belief as it relates to the issue at stake in several points;
- reaffirm the confidence the community has in this confessional tradition as identity "in Christ;" and
- remind adherents to live into the claims of their belief.

One of the tensional divisions of the matrix assumes that preaching occurs in either a persuasively determinate/objectivist voice or a persuasively indeterminate/interpretivist voice. This sermon's structure is persuasively determinate, not because the preacher tries to convince listeners; rather, it is persuasively determinate because the preacher implicitly assumes the objective truth of a particular creedal or doctrinal formulation of faith and structures the sermon to invite listeners to reaffirm this identity as their response. The creedal or doctrinal commitments of a theological tradition are forefronted in this approach to preaching.

If a listener approached a preacher who structured her sermon in this fashion and voiced disagreement with her argument, the preacher might well be surprised. Unless the listener faulted her understanding of the doctrinal tradition or the way she applied it, she would probably be surprised that the person experienced the sermon as an argument. She would likely ask whether that person saw himself as one included in the covenant relationship assumed in her approach to preaching. What makes her sermon an argument is the assuredness with which she assumed her confessional identity or her adherence to a doctrinal perspective when she speaks. To anyone listening who does not share her perspective, the sermon would likely be heard as a rather exclusive set of claims for those who constitute themselves as that kind of Christian.

I was initially trained to preach in this voice by James Daane. According to Professor James Daane all preaching should be incarnational. In good preaching, God speaks and the power of the Word proclaimed will always arouse a reaction of its own accord. Preachers should never seek to make the Word of the sermon persuasively effective with either human strategies or rhetorical techniques. Conversion, we were told, is the work of the Holy Spirit and not the work of the minister. Daane saw no difference between expository and thematic preaching. "Expository preaching is setting forth neither more nor less than the truth of the biblical text."[34] We were taught that sermons should say one thing capable of being stated in a simple proposition that would serve as the primary affirmation of the text the preacher selected. The body of the sermon was to be made up of theological ideas taken from the text intended to serve as "warrants" supporting the basic propositional assertion.[35] These points were always developed as participial clauses (never full sentences, since these would amount to multiple affirmations) introduced by the possessive pronoun "its."[36] We students called them "Three Its" sermons, though we would certainly have been permitted a fourth "its" if the text yielded a further insight.

Daane offers several model outlines of this kind of logical preaching of "valid truths," such as:[37]

Text: John 3:16
Proposition: The Greatness of God's Love
I. Its Costly Expression
II. Its Unworthy Object
III. Its Saving Purpose

34. James Daane, *Preaching with Confidence: A Theological Essay on the Power of the Pulpit* (Grand Rapids: Eerdmans, 1980), 50.

35. Ibid., 65.

36. Ibid., 66.

37. Ibid., 69–72.

Text: Isaiah 55:6–9
Proposition: A Summons to Repentance
I. Its Urgent Character
II. Its Specific Content
III. Its Compelling Inducement

Text: Hebrews 1:1–3
Proposition: Christ: God's Final Word
I. Its Earlier Expression
II. Its Ultimate Form
III. Its Eschatological Significance

These many years later I look with interest to the way Daane used the language of argument theory (logic, proposition, affirmations, warrants, validity, etc.) while always claiming that a sermon should make no effort to persuade and that no argument was being offered. Daane was deeply influenced by Barth's antirhetorical approach to language usage, but it was out of his thoroughly Reformed faith that he would speak *ex cathedra* utterly confident in the truth which his approach to preaching implicitly invited listeners to affirm as the truth of the gospel.

From George Campbell's perspective, one could say that Daane maintains that preaching should only instruct and never argue. As a representative of the Teaching Voice, I would invite readers to see how Daane's incarnational preacher would always speak with a voice of *assuredness* that invites listeners to implicitly affirm the truth of the Word proclaimed as Word of God for the community. This is clearly the Teaching Voice with an emphasis to instruct rather than persuade, but it is still persuasively determinate because the listener is implicitly invited to accept or reject the teaching and the authority by which the preacher declares this truth as a self-evident proposition.[38]

38. My work has been significantly influenced by Lucy Rose, but I differ with her significantly in her assessment of James Daane's homiletic and the manner in which she divides approaches to homiletics that would put Daane in a different approach. For Rose, Daane is one of her key theorists of the kerygmatic approach to preaching. See Lucy Atkinson Rose, *Sharing the Word: Preaching in the Roundtable Church* (Louisville: Westminster/John Knox, 1997), 32,

At the other end of the spectrum of possible expressions of this voice are sermons where the purpose is to make an explicit argument. The nineteenth-century homiletician John Broadus makes the case clearly. He argued that the ability to explain a theological doctrine is insufficient to meet the requirement of facility in preaching. This Baptist theologian was appalled that too much of the preaching he observed in 1870 was but mere assertion, exhortation, and careless argument. So he applied Whatley's *Elements of Rhetoric* specifically to homiletics as "the adaptation of rhetoric to the particular ends and demands of Christian preaching."[39] Unlike Campbell, he contended that preaching, like all public speaking, "should be largely composed of argument."[40] According to Broadus, arguments are offered in sermons to sustain a preacher's judgment, establish truth, and justify a persuasive application of that truth.[41] He wrote, "The chief part of what we commonly call application is *persuasion*. It is not enough to convince men of the truth, nor enough to make them see how it applies to themselves, and how it might be practicable for them to act out,—but we must 'persuade men.'"[42] Broadus believed that every preacher needs to develop the discipline of making clear and cogent arguments as a demonstration of the power of reason in defense of the gospel.

> If averse to reasoning, he should constrain himself to practice it; if by nature strongly inclined that way, he must remember the serious danger of deceiving himself and others by false arguments. . . . But the right to speak with . . . authority will be acknowledged among Protestants, only where the preacher shows himself able to prove whenever it is appropriate all that he maintains.[43]

43, 47–48. On Barth's antirhetorical orientation as a rejection of any need to create a "point of contact" with listeners, see Karl Barth, *Homiletics* (Louisville: Westminster/John Knox Press, 1991), 121–27.

39. John A. Broadus, "Author's Preface to the First Edition," *On the Preparation and Delivery of Sermons*, new and rev. ed., Jesse Burton Weatherspoon, ed. (New York: Harper & Brothers, 1944), 10.

40. Ibid., xii.

41. Ibid., 167.

42. Ibid., 215.

43. Ibid., 168–69.

R. E. O. White contemporized this theology in the middle of the twentieth century by determining that preaching in the context of worship must "focus upon some deeply felt truth, state it, clarify it, justify it from Scripture, illustrate it, make it memorable, apply it, and evoke my response to it. . . . [In this way] the preaching of the gospel is the extension through time of the saving event upon which the gospel rests."[44] In a far more influential homiletic, Haddon Robinson so presumes that preaching is the presentation of an argument that he feels no obligation to justify how argument is to be differentiated from merely informing listeners. He defines preaching as "the communication of a biblical concept, derived from and transmitted through a historical, grammatical, and literary study of a passage in its context, which the Holy Spirit first applies to the personality of the preacher, then through him to his hearers."[45]

Bryan Chapell offers a more nuanced description of this approach that balances the work of argument with the work of the Word by affirming that "Scripture's portrayal of its own potency challenges those who preach to always remember that the Word preached rather than *preaching* the Word accomplishes heaven's purposes."[46] For Chapell expository preaching is best understood as three divine potentialities:

1. As *The Power of the Word*—Preachers should offer expository preaching that attempts to present and apply the truths of a specific biblical passage. It is this presentation of truths of God, proclaimed in such a way that people can see how the concepts derive from Scripture and how they apply to their lives, that should preoccupy the expository preacher's efforts.
2. As *The Authority of the Word*—Because preaching in its essence addresses the perpetual human quest for authority

44. R. E. O. White, *A Guide to Preaching* (Grand Rapids: Eerdmans, 1973), 20.

45. Haddon Robinson, *Biblical Preaching: The Development and Delivery of Expository Messages* (Grand Rapids: Baker, 1980), 20.

46. Bryan Chapell, *Christ-Centered Preaching: Redeeming the Expository Sermon* (Grand Rapids: Baker, 1994), 19.

and meaning, expository preaching should seek to discover and convey the precise meaning of the Word. This *precise meaning* should rule over what the expositor preaches as that individual seeks to unfold what the text *says*.
3. As *The Work of the Spirit*—Technical excellence may rest with the preacher's skill, but preaching's efficacy always resides with God.[47]

White, Robinson, and Chapell are all sensitive to the problem of the preacher who would usurp the role of the Holy Spirit in conversion, but they cast their conviction with Broadus that the purpose of a sermon is to be persuasively determinate in its use of argument that explains, but goes on to prove and persuasively apply biblical truth for listeners.[48]

In many ways, this notion of the sermon as persuasive argument has dominated preaching in the twentieth century. For example, John Killinger describes the difference between his first and second editions of *Fundamentals of Preaching* that makes this point clear:

> When I first wrote this book I placed primary emphasis on what I called the "developmental" style of preaching—the kind that featured carefully formed "points" that move by logical or psychological progression to win an argument or persuade the members of the congregation of the inner truth of a controlling idea, so that, one hopes, they will acquiesce and henceforth attempt to live as much as possible according to that truth.[49]

In his new edition, Killinger continues to present a model of this deductive style of casual argument in preaching he calls the "bread and butter method," which preachers will return to

47. This is an edited summary of Chapell's definition of preaching's three dimensions; Ibid., 22–25.

48. Robinson writes, "Basically ideas expand in line with the broad purposes of the sermon. Just as any statement we make develops through explaining, proving, or applying it, so sermon ideas too demand explanation, validation and application" (116; cf. Chapell, *Christ-Centered Preaching*, 121–23).

49. John Killinger, *Fundamentals of Preaching*, 2d ed. (Minneapolis: Fortress Press, 1996), 5.

time and again. To this he commends adding consideration of a more inductive, or as he calls it a more "conspiratorial," style of communicating. In the latter, ideas build to a claim rather than offering an exposition in support of one.[50] Like the model of preaching proposed by Ralph and Gregg Lewis, this approach "lays out the evidence, the examples, the illustrations and postpones the declarations and assertions until the listeners have a chance to weigh the evidence, think through the implications and then come to the conclusion *with* the preacher at the end of the sermon."[51] However, whether deductive or inductive, offering "evidence" in support of an argument's conclusion still controls this voice in preaching.

Excellence in the Teaching Voice

Nancey Murphy argues that speech that assumes a convictional center can still be open to the complex issues that arise over differing views about the nature of language.[52] What matters is that they operate with a central, paradigmatic core of belief, much like the talk by which scientific inquiry operates. This kind of productive theology would draw on a hard core of convictions related to the historically theological and doctrinal convictions of the community. These convictions, like those of an empirical scientific paradigm, should be able to withstand refutations and sustain inquiry that advances knowledge.[53] Her argument

50. Ibid., 5.

51. Ralph L. Lewis and Gregg Lewis, *Inductive Preaching: Helping People Listen* (Wheaton, IL: Crossway Books, 1983), 43.

52. Murphy does not assume a logical positivist position on the referential nature of language. Instead, she follows McClendon and Smith's dependence on Austin's speech-act theory to develop an intellectually defensible theory of justifying theological convictions. She is also open to discussing "holistic" ways (à la Quine) of understanding the social "wholes" in which language is employed (à la Wittgenstein). See Nancey Murphy, *Anglo-American Postmodernity: Philosophical Perspectives on Science, Religion, and Ethics* (Boulder, CO: Westview Press, 1997), and Nancey Murphy, *Beyond Liberalism and Fundamentalism: How Modern and Postmodern Philosophy Set the Theological Agenda* (Valley Forge, PA: Trinity Press International, 1996).

53. This is Murphy's perspective as summarized by James Wm. McClendon Jr. and James M. Smith, *Convictions: Defusing Religious Relativism*, rev. ed. (Valley Forge, PA: Trinity Press In-

provides an important bridge to similar concerns for order and social solidarity expressed by preachers who have been accustomed to speak in a Teaching Voice and are trying to find their way to speak out of the cultural consciousness of the Testifying Voice's center of gravity.[54] When a preacher speaks out of the convictional center of the Teaching Voice, it tends to solicit from listeners the final affirmation, "Yes! This is what we believe."

Both the Teaching Voice and the Encouraging Voice share the cultural assumption that a preacher should speak with authoritative assuredness in the theological truth of his or her witness to God. The former is distinguished from the latter because it grounds its appeals in concerns to reaffirm a sense of social solidarity provided by a specific theological identity, a doctrinal perspective, a confessional tradition, or the commitment to a specific tradition of dogma. The Encouraging Voice also makes its appeal out of this same sense of assuredness, but it shifts its other cultural presupposition away from making its appeal to order. It makes its appeal to the listener's internal locus of authority and the individual's desire to be transformed by an encounter with God, Spirit, grace, or the holy.

In describing preaching in this voice, Elizabeth Achtemeier writes that most mainline sermons in the twentieth century have tended to distill a specific theological theme from a scriptural text (i.e., "worship, repentance, prayer, the love of God, faith, forgiveness," etc.). Or they have chosen to develop ideas with reference to contemporary topical issues (i.e., "race relations, marriage, war and peace, abortion, crime," etc.) and consider these

ternational, 1994), 191. Murphy identifes McClendon (her husband) and Smith's argument as core to her own convictions about the nature of theological argument (Murphy, *Beyond Liberalism*, 119–22).

54. David Fleer and Dave Bland, "Tension in Preaching," in *Preaching from Luke/Acts*, Rochester College Lectures on Preaching, vol. 1, David Fleer and Dave Bland, eds. (Abilene, TX: ACU Press, 2000), 21–37. Many of the sermons published in the volumes of this sermon series represent an interesting effort by preachers traditionally accustomed to speaking in a Teaching Voice to find their way into the ability to speak in a Testifying Voice. For a provocative effort to bridge the Teaching Voice and the Testifying Voice while maintaining a strong view of the role of evangelism, see Chris Altrock, *Preaching to Pluralists: How to Proclaim Christ in a Postmodern Age* (St. Louis: Chalice Press, 2004).

from a theological perspective. Or, again, thematic sermons may begin with a theological doctrine (i.e., "the judgment of God, the atonement, the sacraments," etc.) and develop ideas about these.[55] She is particularly concerned that thematic preaching can too easily become grounded more in human experience, philosophy, doctrine and creeds, poetry, scholarly findings, personal anecdotes and quotes, rather than the biblical story. However, her concern for excellence in preaching lies more with the starting place of preaching.

Traditional thematic preaching of the type outlined above tends to lock the speaker into static ideas about the text in ways that invariably lead to illustrating meaning with ideas and images drawn from outside the text. Achtemeier wants to invite preachers to allow the points of sermons to emerge from the form and function of the biblical text(s) taken up in the sermon.[56] In this way, the congregation has a stake in the text as its story once again becomes their story by analogy: "By concentrating on the whole text, in its contextual narrative setting, and not some theme abstracted from it, the three aspects of the sermon [its content, form, and function] are welded together."[57] Achtemeier still believes that a preacher must determine a big idea that frames his or her approach to interpreting and explaining the meaning of a text/topic/problem. She argues that good preaching will help the people of God analogically identify with the identity of the people of God as revealed in Scripture rather than imposing meaning from the outside. In this, she is concerned that preaching should reflect the performative concerns of the text itself. Good preaching, she reminds preachers, always invites the contemporary community of faith to see the biblical story as their own story.[58]

55. Elizabeth Achtemeier, *Creative Preaching: Finding the Words* (Nashville: Abingdon Press, 1980), 61–62.

56. Achtemeier strongly urges the pairing of a New Testament text with an Old Testament text in preaching in order to assist listeners in seeing the continuity of their identity as the people of God.

57. Achtemeier, *Creative Preaching*, 69

58. Ibid., 20 and 71. See also Elizabeth Achtemeier, *Preaching from the Old Testament* (Louisville: Westminster/John Knox, 1989), 54–59.

John Stott argues that "bridge-building" needs to be the master metaphor of preaching in order to address the crisis of the anti-authority orientation of contemporary culture; e.g., its unwillingness to listen because of the cybernetic-digital reorientation of listener's attention, its lack of interest in what is said, its loss of confidence in the power of the gospel, and its doubt that gospel matters. He summarizes the principal features of a preaching ministry conceived of as an activity of bridge-building between the revealed Word and the contemporary world in this way:

> Such preaching will be authoritative in expounding biblical principles, but tentative in applying them to complex issues of the day. This combination of the authoritative and the tentative, the dogmatic and the agnostic, conviction and open-mindedness, teaching the people and leaving them free to make up their own minds is exceedingly difficult to maintain.[59]

Only thus will the preacher be able "on the one hand to handle the Word of God with integrity (declaring what is plain, but not pretending that everything is plain when it is not) and on the other to lead the people of God into maturity (by encouraging them to develop a Christian mind, and use it)."[60] In Stott's model of Teaching Voice preaching, excellence takes confidence in the proclamation of gospel without permitting that confidence to legitimate simplistic analysis of the contemporary ills or lack of generosity in the honest efforts of others to name God and name grace.

What unifies these various efforts to define method in preaching is the cultural assumptions they hold in common and how the design of the sermon's intention invites listeners to understand themselves as persons of faith. In other words, sermon forms are designed to present the appeal of a sermon in ways that call forth different faith responses from listeners. I will take this idea up at

59. John Stott, *Between Two Worlds: The Challenge of Preaching Today* (Grand Rapids: Eerdmans, 1982), 178.

60. Ibid.

greater length in chapter six. Some arrangement patterns that, by design, invite preachers to take up the Teaching Voice include:

- Puritan plain style
- argument by points (whether deductive or inductive)
- verse-by-verse grammatical-historical exegesis sermons
- thesis-antithesis-synthesis sermons
- indicative-imperative ethical sermons[61]

The point of raising the issue of sermon designs here is to clarify the relationship between a preaching intention and the cultural consciousness that brings voice to that intention. Let me be clear: the intentions of these designs invite listeners to affirm the interpretation offered as an appropriate application of the text's meaning for the community. When preached with clarity of voice, these designs invite listeners to respond, whether the intention is to instruct or persuade, by saying, "Yes! We agree. This is what we believe."

A Sample Sermon

Craig Blomberg's sermon included here is from his book *Preaching the Parables: From Responsible Interpretation to Powerful Proclamation*.[62] It is organized by three clear points—"three lessons from this passage"—and concludes by reiterating that "At least three lessons, then, emerge in this passage." Blomberg moves with seeming, but well-crafted, ease between interpretation of the meaning, illustrative contemporary implications, and specific challenges for application for his listening community. This is a fine example of traditional expository preaching that makes points.

61. Most of the patterns listed in this and the subsequent chapters can be found in *Patterns of Preaching: A Sermon Sampler*, Ronald J. Allen, ed. (St. Louis: Chalice Press, 1998).

62. Craig L. Blomberg, *Preaching the Parables: From Responsible Interpretation to Powerful Proclamation* (Grand Rapids: Baker Academic, 2004), 169–77.

Pray and Persevere
Luke 18:1-8
Craig L. Blomberg

> You will be appalled by the story I'm about to relate to you. Appalled, that is, if you have any kind of social conscience. The poor black, living on Chicago's South Side, sought to have her apartment properly heated during the frigid winter months. Despite city law in the matter, her unscrupulous landlord refused. The woman was a widow, desperately poor, and ignorant of the legal system; but she took the case to court on her own behalf. Justice, she declared, ought to be done. It was her ill fortune, however, to appear repeatedly before the same judge, who, as it turned out, was an atheist and a bigot. The only principle by which he abode was, as he put it, that "blacks should be kept in their place." The possibilities of a ruling favorable to the widow were, therefore, bleak. They became even bleaker as she realized she lacked the indispensable ingredient necessary for favorable rulings in cases like these—namely, a satisfactory bribe. Nevertheless, she persisted.
>
> At first, the judge did not so much as even look up from reading the novel on his lap before dismissing her. But then he began to notice her, just another black, he thought, stupid enough to think she could get justice. Then her persistence made him self-conscious. This turned to guilt and anger. Finally, raging and embarrassed he granted her petition and enforced the law. Here was a massive victory over "the system"—at least as it functioned in his corrupted courtroom.[63]

The story I have just told you was written by David Wells, for many years now a professor of theology at Gordon-Conwell Seminary in Massachusetts. But in 1979 when he published this article in *Christianity Today*, he was still a professor at Trinity Evangelical Divinity School, where I was a young seminarian. Wells continues by stating what you may have already guessed: "In putting the matter like this I have not, of course, been quite

63. David Wells, "Prayer: Rebelling against the Status Quo," *Christianity Today* 23 (1979): 1465.

honest. For this never really happened in Chicago (as far as I know)"—though I might add plenty of such things did happen a generation ago under the infamous machine of the senior Mayor Daley. Wells adds, however, "Nor is it even my 'story.' It is a parable told by Jesus (Luke 18:1–8) to illustrate the nature of petitionary prayer."

The story Wells has sought to update or contemporize originally appeared in Luke 18:1–8. Luke introduces the passage with the explanation, "Then Jesus told his disciples a parable to show them that they should always pray and not give up" (v. 1). Then he goes on to quote Jesus' words in verses 2–5:

> In a certain town there was a judge who neither feared God nor cared what people thought. And there was a widow in that town who kept coming to him with a plea, "Grant me justice against my adversary." For some time he refused. But finally he said to himself, "Even though I don't fear God or care what people think, yet because this widow keeps bothering me, I will see that she gets justice, so that she won't come and attack me!" [NIV]

Jesus then applies this short parable, in verses 6–8:

> Listen to what the unjust judge says. And will not God bring about justice for his chosen ones, who cry out to him day and night? Will he keep putting them off? I tell you, he will see that they get justice, and quickly. However, when the Son of Man comes, will he find faith on the earth? [NIV]

Oftentimes we have to update the parables, just as Dr. Wells did, in order for us to feel their original force or shock value. There is a key aspect of interpreting the parables that remains in dispute among the commentators. To what extent should they be considered allegories (point-by-point comparisons between literal and symbolic realities), or do they simply make one main point? It seems to me that in many cases a good compromise between these two extreme approaches is to read the parables through the eyes of each of the main characters and look for one lesson from each of these fictitious individuals.

This story obviously contains two explicit characters, the widow and the unjust judge. But there is a third character lurking in the background throughout this story as well, and that is God himself. He appears within the parable, when Jesus has the judge admit that he does not fear God. And he appears again, as Jesus applies the parable, as someone eager to dispense justice and bring about an age of complete righteousness when Christ himself, the Son of man, returns at the end of the age. It seems to me, then, that we can learn as many as three lessons from this passage by focusing, in turn, first on the widow, then on the judge, and finally on God himself.

The widow's circumstance in this story, particularly as portrayed in verse 3, creates a serious obstacle to her receiving justice. We're not given very many details about this woman except that she is described as a classic victim, a paradigm of helplessness in the ancient Middle Eastern world. Widows, like orphans, are presented throughout the Bible as poignant examples of the dispossessed. What little we are told about this particular woman suggests that she is destitute and has no male friend of any kind in a position to help her. Women, you see, went to court only if there was no man to plead their case. And we read here in verse 3 that this was a widow in a village who repeatedly kept coming to this judge with a plea, "Grant me justice against my adversary." She does have one advantage that men did not enjoy, precisely because she was in such a position of powerlessness. She could repeatedly return and even badger representatives of the judicial system, though in normal cases there was little chance of her receiving justice. A man, however, would quickly be evicted or perhaps even locked up if he behaved in such a way. But apart from these slender details, everything else about the woman's case is guesswork. Property disputes were commonly taken to local judges like this one, particularly disputes having to deal with inheritance. Maybe that's what the widow needed help with, especially if her husband had just recently died and there was a dispute over settling his estate. But whatever the specific situation, Jesus is clearly portraying a case of an individual who has all the odds stacked against her.

Somewhat uncharacteristically, Luke tells us one of the lessons of the parable right up front in verse 1, that Jesus intends to encourage his disciples always to pray and not to give up—*persevering prayer*, we might call it today. But immediately when we focus on the widow, we find someone whose position and circumstances seem to provide a great obstacle to such perseverance. They could easily have led to her being demoralized, giving up, and not continuing to come back and demand a fair shake.

If this parable is an illustration about persevering in prayer, then I would venture to say we need to pay careful attention. Persistence in prayer is not something contemporary Americans are very good at. All the recent studies suggest that American Christians today, even those in volunteer or paid ministry, often do not have regular times of daily prayer. Or if they do, they involve two, three, perhaps five minutes, hardly enough time to say much to God or hear much from him. From my own experience, as I have shared prayer requests with close friends, it often seems fairly obvious from subsequent conversations that they have not prayed for me, certainly not long enough for them to remember it. We take a significant portion of time praying for one another in our Sunday school class. But again, I'm afraid that, despite my repeated pleas, only a faithful minority of the class members actually take home and consistently pray for the things we've shared on Sundays. There are, however, antidotes to this malaise. There are cultures throughout the world that prove very faithful in public and private prayer. There are periods in church history when even Western Christians have distinguished themselves by this practice. For some folks today it may require setting aside a regular time each day, perhaps writing it on our calendars, telling other people, if there are conflicting appointments or pressures on our schedules, that we are already booked, which would be true. Perhaps it requires doing what I have found very helpful in the last couple of years, after a lifetime of hearing of others who have done so, and that is to make lists in different categories, one day praying for foreign missionaries whom we know and support, another day for colleagues at the seminary, a third for a small collection of students whom I have committed to pray for, a fourth day for friends and events elsewhere in the United States, another day for the international scene, another day for church friends and events, and so on, with certain things such as family members being a priority almost every day. Perhaps for you it means simply writing down on a notepad or a Palm Pilot every time you promise to pray for someone and then going back and consulting those notes. Perhaps it means stopping for a few moments as you receive prayer requests by email, as I often do, and just lifting those items up immediately to the Lord before you continue to type on your computer. It is possible, even in the frantic pace of contemporary American life, to make prayer a priority.

But what may be even harder is to persevere, to persist in prayer when no answer seems forthcoming. God hasn't granted our request, but he hasn't obviously closed the door either, and what we pray for certainly seems to us like a good thing that he would want to give us. The classic example is prayers for the salvation of a close friend or family member. Jesus' parable, with its audacious model of the persistent widow, suggests that we are simply to keep at it. It's interesting that while most people who make professions of faith do so as children or young adults, the second most common time people are particularly receptive to the gospel is during times of illness, especially in old age, as they realize they may be nearing death. I have several friends who have prayed for parents or other relatives throughout their whole lives and then rejoiced as those parents made commitments to Christ as very elderly people. We simply have to persevere and keep at it.

But persistence need not be limited to prayer. The woman's faithfulness in doing what she believed reflected God's just priorities encourages us to persevere in every aspect of Christian life and ethical living. In an age when commitment and loyalty seem to mean less and less in society as a whole, and at times even in Christian circles, there is a crying need for people to commit to staying in one community, in one church, in one ministry, even when opportunities may arise for them to go elsewhere, simply for the sake of providing continuity and stability in the lives of those around them when so much else is transient and changing. I watched my father turn down opportunities to leave the public school system in which he taught his entire career. And I watched the enormous doors of influence open up for him as he became very well known in a medium-size community in the state of Illinois, teaching the children and ultimately a few grandchildren of some of the first students he taught as a young man. I've been privileged to watch just the tail end of the life of a similar model, Dr. Vernon Grounds, the former president and current chancellor of Denver Seminary, who came as a young man in his thirties to be a professor, then became the academic dean, soon advanced to the presidency, and has now remained with one institution for more than fifty years, continuing a remarkably active ministry of counseling, teaching, and public speaking as an eighty-eight-year-old. He built a school and developed a reputation, along with a network of friends and influences that would have required him in certain ways to start all over again had he jumped from one location to the next. I don't want to be so presumptuous as to say I know God is calling me to stay in Denver until and beyond my retirement. But the longer I'm here, going on seventeen years now, the easier it is for me to imagine doing so.

The widow's model of perseverance should challenge us in the area of faithfulness to our spouses, for those who are married, and to our wedding vows, even if marriage turns out to be less, perhaps even far less, than our youthful idealism once dreamed it might be. One of the statistics that profoundly affected me as I decided to commit my life to the Lord, as a teenager in the early 1970s, was that, of avowedly evangelical, born-again Christians, only one in fifty marriages ended in divorce,[64] whereas nearly one in three overall in the United States in the early seventies fell apart.

64. The information about one in fifty evangelical marriages dissolving came from a talk by Jimmy DiRaddo, a Campus Life Illinois State Christmas Conference speaker in Champaign, Illinois, in December 1972. Even if the statistics might have represented overly round numbers (though more likely they seem extreme because "evangelical" was not nearly as popular a term for self-identification prior to 1976 and *Time* magazine's "Year of the Evangelical"), the contrast with current trends remains striking.

Today the statistics are almost identical, one in three, or even a little bit more, for Christian and non-Christian alike. I know that the world has changed in thirty-two years, but it has not changed *that* much. People are simply reneging on their promises. That's why we need an organization like Promise Keepers to challenge us to faithfulness once again. The college Christian group that I was a part of has largely remained intact and kept in touch by a series of reunions for twenty-five years now, and, while we've lost touch with a few people, and while one or two marriages have fallen apart, more than 95 percent of our couples have stayed together, and most have even flourished. Faithfulness is possible, even at the beginning of the twenty-first century, if people are willing to be true to their commitments.

Finally, the most significant area in which we need without exception to be absolutely sure we remain faithful is that of our relationship to God, even when the Christian life seems harder than we ever imagined it could be, even when all those around us are calling us to abandon our standards and our values, even if our job is on the line because of our Christian faith, even when "everybody" is doing "it," including apparent Christians, but we know that whatever "it" is violates God's revealed will in Scripture.

It is interesting that the area this particular parable illustrates, however, was *perseverance in the arena of social justice*, and that leads us to the story's second character, a quite unjust figure—the judge.

We learn about him primarily in verses 2, 4, and 5. He is described as one who neither feared God nor cared what people thought. Whatever the widow's complaint was that required a court of law, it was highly ironic that the very place in which she should have found justice only compounded her problem. The judge is not concerned about what the Lord thinks or with the fact that one day he will have to stand accountable before him, nor does he seem to have any scruples about how the public looks upon him. This man is obviously involved in an elaborate system of bribery, as not a few officials throughout the Roman Empire were in the first century. People in numerous Third World countries today can often relate very closely to the corrupt system described here. Sadly, even in the United States, stories of corrupt officials in various walks of life are becoming more common.

In many ancient contexts community opinion would have shamed a public figure into right behavior, even if the threat of divine judgment wouldn't. But this man has steeled himself against public opinion. Nevertheless, the woman's perseverance eventually gets to him. Initially he simply refuses to hear her, as verse 4 states. But in time he recognizes, despite his wicked character, that he should dispense justice. The woman is getting very annoying. The widow keeps "bothering" him—the word that Jesus uses in verse 5. Thus, not because he is committed to providing justice for all but simply to be rid of her, he grants her request. The imagery of the last part of verse 5 reads literally "so that she won't come and give me a black eye." But the language is almost certainly metaphorical, just as today we might speak of somebody who "gives us a headache." That doesn't mean they've necessarily punched us in the face. But to be rid of this increasingly aggressive and annoying woman, despite his initial unwillingness, the judge will grant her justice.

I wonder how much of our praying, or of our Christian activity more generally, is directed against social injustice. Do we read the news, including Christian news, so that we can pray for world events, including religious developments? Are we outraged by the injustice in the Middle East? There's plenty to go around on all sides, though it's interesting that in all the overt hostility between Jews and Arabs, the Palestinians, whom many Americans don't even realize are a different ethnic group from Arabs, are caught in the middle. By the way, most Christians in Israel today are Palestinians. And those who are Christians are doubly harassed, both by the Jewish leaders and by fellow Palestinians who are Muslims and can't tolerate their profession of Christian faith. For almost our entire married life, Fran and I have been supporters of Bethlehem Bible College, the only Christian higher educational institution indigenous to the country of Israel. Most of its students and staff are Palestinians, but few Americans have ever heard of it, though the college is doing a great work.

Or what about those portions of the world, and there always are several, that teeter on the brink of famine? Today it's twelve million people in southern Africa, especially Zimbabwe and neighboring countries, where a food shortage is compounded by the economic policies of corrupt governments that have wrought havoc with once relatively stable farming economies. Are you aware of those issues? Do you pray for them? Do you give to help meet the needs? Or what about the daily murders and assaults and rapes in *our* streets in the United States, including the Denver metro area? Our country suffers an incredible number of murders because we have more ready access to guns and firearms than any developed country in the world. Oh yes, I know those wonderful slogans by the NRA and other folks that "guns don't kill, people do." But it's also true that people without guns kill far, far fewer people than those with guns. Isn't it fairly astonishing that five years after Columbine the Colorado State Legislature still has not been able to pass any significantly stiffer gun control laws? Isn't it time conservative Christians dramatically change their attitudes on these kinds of issues?

Would you consider choosing (or creating) a church, at least in part, on the basis of how much a priority it gave to addressing these issues of justice at home and abroad? Can we move beyond our typically narrow set of social issues—abortion and homosexuality, prayer in the schools, creation versus evolution, and so forth? Why don't we hear equally as much talk in our American evangelical congregations about the persecuted churches and peoples in the world, including persecuted Christians? Why don't we hear at least as much an appeal for Christians to eat out less, to waste less food and less gasoline, to stop going into such enormous debt with money that could be better spent? How much of our prayer time personally and in church focuses on the injustices of the world? In most cases the answer is precious little. But there's nothing preventing us from changing. And Jesus' parable demands that we do so.

The widow, then, is obviously a model of one of the most helpless categories of human beings in her world who needs justice. But the judge is by no means an obvious model of divine justice. In his case, Jesus' logic is what is called "from the lesser to the greater" or a "how much more logic." In other words, if a certain principle is true for fallible and even evil human beings, how much more must it be true with a perfect and good God? In this case, *God wants far more readily or quickly to grant his people justice* than the corrupt judge wanted to. And that leads us to the final character and to Jesus' concluding words in verses 6–8.

The Lord said, "Listen to what the unjust judge says. And will not God bring about justice for his chosen ones who cry out to him day and night?" The implied answer is, "of course." "Will he keep putting them off?" The implied answer is "of course not." "I tell you, he will see that they get justice, and quickly." And yet the ultimate dispensing of perfect justice will come only when Christ returns and human freedom to work evil and to choose to fight God's purposes is forever abolished. Thus the parable ends with the haunting question, "However, when the Son of Man comes, will he find faith on the earth?"

God is the ultimate standard or model of justice and righteousness, a major theme repeated throughout both the Old and New Testaments. The inadequacies of the helpless and the inequities of injustice among God's people will all be dealt with on Judgment Day. Some prayers, however worthy, will remain unanswered until then, but eventually all wrongs will be righted.

But can we really believe that promise, twenty centuries after Jesus spoke these words, and the world continues as corrupt as ever? This was a question that was raised even just one generation after Christ's death. And the most direct and the most encouraging answer found anywhere in Scripture to the problem of the delay of the end of the world as we know it appears in 2 Peter 3:8–9. There Peter writes, "But do not forget this one thing, dear friends: With the Lord a day is like a thousand years, and a thousand years are like a day. The Lord is not slow in keeping his promise, as some understand slowness. Instead he is patient with you, not wanting anyone to perish, but everyone to come to repentance." The reason God has not brought the end of the world and the righting of all wrongs more quickly is because, when he does, the door will forever be closed to even one more person responding and coming to him in faith.

The key issue is not if we can make sense of God's delay. We can. The key issue is the one Jesus poses in the last half of verse 8, which forms the conclusion and the climax of this passage. Even though from our perspective it seems like a long delay, will Christ, the Son of Man, find faith when he returns? That is to say, will he find his followers persisting in their faith, however long and arduous the wait is?

At least three lessons, then, emerge in this passage: First, pray perseveringly, work perseveringly, with optimism, confident that God much more gladly than the judge in this passage often does want in this life to grant us answers to our requests. Second, consider the helpless, and the injustice of this world that they experience, as a larger topic for your prayer life and for your actions, which often give those prayers feet. Finally, recognize that, even in those areas in which God does not in this age grant us our requests, he remains eager to grant justice but has good reasons for his delay.

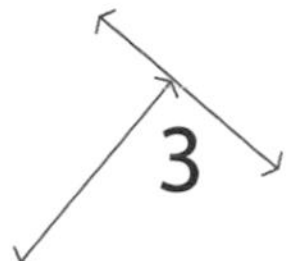

Preaching in the Encouraging Voice

When the Baptist seminary in Greenville, North Carolina, reopened after the American Civil War, only one student registered for Dr. Albert Broadus's class in homiletics, and that student happened to be blind. The meticulous lectures Broadus prepared for this student's instruction served as the basis of *A Treatise on the Preparation and Delivery of Sermons*, which appeared in print four years later. The book went through numerous editions with two significant revisions over the next fifty years and was, without question, the most influential textbook for North American Protestant homiletics during this period. In the first half of the twentieth century various homiletics textbooks were produced, but most of them were simply variations on or supplements for the basic Broadus text. The most significant evolution in preaching theory of this era was actually introduced by a brilliant practitioner—Harry Emerson Fosdick. Instead of an argument-centered approach, Fosdick modeled the power of an advocacy-centered approach to preaching in the Encouraging Voice.

To a generation increasingly unfamiliar with this giant of the pulpit, the author of the most authoritative biography on Fosdick writes, "To understand Fosdick's commanding position in twentieth-century religious history, it is crucial to recall his influence in the realm of homiletics. He was, for weal or woe, clearly the era's leading homiletician, and the example of his preaching guided the preparation and delivery of the sermons of much of Protestant ministry."[1] Sermons by Fosdick were the most emulated or outright borrowed of any in the century. Though he wrote no textbook on preaching, he discussed the essence of his approach in a smattering of popular articles.[2] In essence he argued that people do not come to church to learn about Bible history or the details of doctrines. They come because they are beset with problems and concerns of modern living and are willing to listen to discover whether God can help.

Fosdick found the standard topical approach to preaching, in which a preacher identified a theme from the text and explained its meaning to listeners, inadequate to speak to the felt needs of listeners. Sermons must capture the attention of listeners by creating identification with their life situations and problems and then explore how Scripture and faith can address these felt needs. He wrote, "Start with a life issue, a real problem, personal or social, perplexing the mind or disturbing the conscience; face the problem fairly, deal with it honestly, and throw such light on it from the spirit of Christ, that people will be able to go out able to think more clearly and live more nobly because of that sermon."[3] He adapted the basic problem-solution public speaking speech design, with its explicit intention to call people to action, and applied it to preaching. By 1944 Halford Luccock cited Fosdick as the progenitor of this approach to preaching,

1. Robert Moats Miller, *Harry Emerson Fosdick: Preacher, Pastor, Prophet* (New York: Oxford University Press), ix.

2. The primary text is an essay, "What Is the Matter with Preaching?" *Harper's Magazine* 47 (July 1928): 133–41. The essay has been reprinted in *What's the Matter with Preaching Today?* Michael Graves, ed. (Louisville: Westminster/John Knox Press, 2004), 7–19. Other sources for Fosdick's theology of preaching include articles variously titled "Learning How to Preach," "If I Only Had One Sermon to Preach," "The Christian Ministry," and "Personal Counseling and Preaching"; see Miller, *Fosdick*, 341.

3. Cited in Halford E. Luccock, *In the Minister's Workshop* (Nashville: Abingdon Press, 1944), 51.

stating, "What is popularly called 'life-situation preaching' is being so widely and so often practiced today that to discuss it at any length seems like carrying a very superfluous cargo of coals to Newcastle."[4] It was a revolution that reoriented homiletics to the needs of the listener based on an emerging awareness that people come to church not to be reminded of who they are, but hungry to discover who they can become.

Preaching that occurs in the Encouraging Voice is controlled by an intention to speak in such a way as to make it possible for an individual to experience the transforming power of God/Spirit/grace/the holy. Where the Teaching Voice invites listeners to reaffirm the role of communal *tradition* and *social solidarity*, the Encouraging Voice invites listeners to respond as individuals who long for personal *transformation*. Both voices are firmly shaped by and centered in the worldview that assumes preaching should be grounded in the rationality of making arguments or interpreting the meaning of faith with assuredness, but the Encouraging Voice shifts its interest to the individual and the personal need of that individual who longs to experience hope in God.

In this chapter I explore the implications of the Encouraging Voice that presumes the Enlightenment assertion of the individual's right to discover his or her own way in realizing the personal empowerment of this faith. Study after study has shown that we are a nation of individualists who continue to value personal autonomy over communal accountability.[5] This emphasis on individualism has led to an increasing willingness to tolerate uncertainty as a rebellion against order and to encourage a view

4. Luccock, *Workshop,* 50. See Charles F. Kemp, *Life-Situation Preaching* (St. Louis: Bethany Press, 1956); Lionel Crocker, ed., *Harry Emerson Fosdick's Art of Preaching: An Anthology* (Springfield, IL: Charles C. Thomas Publisher, 1971); Edgar N. Jackson, *How to Preach to People's Needs* (Grand Rapids: Baker, 1972); Edmund Holt Linn, *Preaching as Counseling* (Valley Forge, PA: Judson Press, 1966).

5. See Robert Nelson Bellah, Richard Madsen, William M. Sullivan, Ann Swidler, and Steven M. Tipton, *Habits of the Heart: Individualism and Commitment in American Life* (New York: Harper and Row, 1986); Paul Leinberger and Bruce Tucker, *The New Individualists: The Generation after the Organization Man* (New York: HarperCollins, 1991); Anthony Giddens, *Modernity and Self Identity: Self and Society in the Late Modern Age* (Cambridge, MA: Blackwell Publishing, 1991); and Robert D. Putnam, *Bowling Alone: The Collapse and Revival of American Community* (New York: Simon and Schuster, 2000).

of spirituality that requires individuals to negotiate their own understanding of sacred experience. I want to trace the relationship between these social phenomena in this chapter as a way of explaining how the Encouraging Voice makes its appeal to the cultural consciousness of the individual in existential isolation—an approach to preaching that in the words of H. Grady Davis orients preaching to answer the question, "[H]ow does the text come alive from a basic statement of truth about God to the living existential person-to-person relationship?"[6] Following this I unpack the assumptions of the contemporary expression of the Encouraging Voice and its continuum of practice.

The Appeal to the Individual

In the previous chapter I noted how the Enlightenment project came to solidify the modern notion of argument as a rational presentation in which facts are established by the way claims are made and supported. In this chapter I return to this idea to discover how contemporary appeals to the individual are shaped by the way we moderns construct our identities. As we shall see, a good deal of contemporary preaching makes its appeal to individuals whose sense of self is remarkably different from that of the people to whom Calvin or Luther once made their appeals. Preachers who make appeals out of this modern cultural consciousness are invariably aware that many listeners desire to be transformed, whether by faith, by education, or perhaps just by discovering the three-step secret to being successful in whatever concerns them. Add to this the effect of radical individualism identified as such a dominant force by many sociologists over the last two decades, and we begin to understand the drive to be "relevant" faced by contemporary preachers who want to discover how "to connect with listeners."

Why does individualism matter so much in the American context? In *Cultures and Organizations: Software of the Mind*,

6. H. Grady Davis, *Design for Preaching* (Philadelphia: Fortress Press, 1958), v.

Geert Hofstede and his son Gert Jan Hofstede find that the United States scored the highest of seventy-four different national cultures in the individualism index. Using data from a massive international survey they identified five distinct dimensions that distinguish national cultures. Of these five—hierarchy, identity, gender, truth, and virtue—*identity* describes the tensional relationship between tendencies toward individualism or collectivism that help explain whether people relate better in low or high context situations and whether they are primarily oriented to particularism or universalism. The Hofstedes offer the following definitions of the poles of the *identity* dimension:

> Individualism pertains to societies in which the ties between individuals are loose: everyone is expected to look after himself or herself and his or her immediate family. Collectivism as its opposite pertains to societies in which people from birth onward are integrated into strong cohesive in-groups, which throughout people's lifetimes continue to protect them in exchange for unquestioning loyalty.[7]

Notice that they define individualism primarily in terms of personal autonomy and the way its exercise affects issues of loyalties.

In proposing my Matrix of Contemporary Christian Voices I am not suggesting that these two tensions be superimposed on the American context. American culture is simply too committed to the individualist perspective to suggest that collectivism as defined by the Hofstedes is a real option within our culture. Instead, with Robert Bellah and his associates, I suggest that prior to the emergence of what they call radical individualism, North American culture drew on the resources of a biblically religious and classically republican worldview that was combined with an innate sense of the individual to make up the traditional North American identity. This worldview provided the cultural glue of social solidarity that served those who came of age during

7. Geert Hofstede and Gert Jan Hofstede, *Cultures and Organizations: Software of the Mind,* rev. and exp. 2d ed. (New York: McGraw-Hill, 2005), 76.

World War II and its aftermath, the people Tom Brokaw has called The Greatest Generation.[8] To understand the symbolic boundaries that shape the way preachers make appeals to the generations that have come of age after this cultural sensibility, we need to have a better understanding of what individualism is and how it functions as a basis of appeal in the contemporary North American context.

Self Matters

What am I going to do? How should I act? Who should I be in this situation? What do people expect from me? How will this differ from expectations in my other roles? These are questions average people in late modernity find themselves asking on occasion.[9] I regularly have students take Mark Snyder's "Self-Monitoring Scale" to discover whether they are the kind of person who can become whatever the situation needs and calls for them to be—a high self-monitor—or whether they are low self-monitors—good old-fashioned "Popeyes" who "are who they are and that's all that they are" regardless of the situation. The students find themselves torn between the idea that high self-monitors tend to be what high-profile national employers look for, while low self-monitors tend to be a better long-term risk for a marriage partner.[10] Obviously, this is a reductionist interpretation of Snyder's scale, but it never fails to help students in the class recognize just how different the conceptions of what counts as a "self" may be and how malleable this concept is to social forces.

The notion of the self is not just a modern invention, but as a massive literature already indicates, our modern notion of individualism grows out of a centuries-old movement toward deeper and deeper interiorization of consciousness of the human

8. Tom Brokaw, *The Greatest Generation* (New York: Random House, 1998).

9. Giddens, *Modernity and Self Identity*, 70.

10. See http://pubpages.unh.edu/~ckb/SELFMON2.html for Snyder's Self-Monitoring Scale and a description of what it measures.

psyche.[11] In his study, *Sources of the Self: The Making of the Modern Identity*, Charles Taylor describes the effect of the influence of the Enlightenment in the further development of the modern cultural construct of individualism and its relationship to self-concept in three senses. These influences include (1) the way a modern person prizes his or her own autonomy, including a sense of natural rights, (2) the premium moderns place on the self-exploration of their feelings concerning life's meaning and purpose, and (3) a reframing of the ancient quest for the good life as a consequence of fulfilling the moral obligations of personal commitment.[12] Taylor describes these aspects of modern identity as the powers of disengaged reason released to pursue the courage of its own self-understanding.

This is not to say that people are modern simply because they can think about themselves. We are moderns, according to Taylor, because we still understand what it means to be someone taken up by these three influences. In the same way that medieval Catholic feudalism provided lord and peasant alike with a unified worldview that made it impossible for them to imagine any other way of living in relationship to others, modern culture operates with a set of unspoken suppositional beliefs that are nearly invisible to us. Yet these assumptions structure what we believe about the nature and goal of living purposefully and what counts as the morally acceptable ways of socially interacting with one another. We may find it difficult to understand how people once lived into the sense of self that fueled medieval feudalism or the sense of self that made possible the seventeenth-century notion of the divine right of kings. Many of us even have a difficult time understanding why contemporary Middle Eastern clerics and insurgents prefer the ordered world of Islamic hierarchies to the implicit individual freedoms that would come about with the implementation of democracy. Whether it's strange notions from

11. See Robert W. Hanning, *The Individual in Twelfth-Century Romance* (New Haven: Yale University Press, 1977); Walter J. Ong, *Hopkins, the Self, and God* (Toronto: University of Toronto Press, 1986).

12. Charles Taylor, *Sources of the Self: The Making of the Modern Identity* (Cambridge, MA: Harvard University Press, 1989), 305.

our own past or divergent intellectual impasses in our war-torn present, we generally assume that people have always pursued lives much like ours and have always had similar dreams and aspirations. We rarely see our own self-concept as an artifact of our particular cultural moment. To understand, it may help to unpack Taylor's three influences.

Autonomy and Natural Rights: One of the more significant beliefs that emerged from Enlightenment thought is the assumption that human freedom was initiated by God, who established self-responsibility and human dignity. In particular, Deist philosophers came to believe in a God who designed creation to operate with established laws of providential order for the good of rational creatures. This God was then bound to let creation operate without further interference. The Deist view of the universal benevolence of natural design was eventually combined with the idea of the free, self-determining subject. It was a philosophical perspective that placed humans and human purposes at the forefront and laid seed to the modern egalitarian ideal of fair dealings with one another as a social virtue. In all of this, freedom is determined as both a good and a natural right leading to a moral imperative of universal justice. Since we tend to think that the non-autonomous individual lacks a sense of significance as a consequence of not being a free, self-determining subject, we too easily forget that our belief in the relationship between autonomy and natural rights has been profoundly shaped by the Enlightenment assumption that the only fully significant life is one that is self-chosen.

Feelings and Personal Meaning: By the eighteenth century, modern German romantic idealism had begun to influence the notion of the rational self by recovering personal feeling as a valuable experience of knowing that serves as a bridge between reason and sensibility. This expressivist worldview invited individuals to trust their own natural feelings and trust their feelings toward nature without. In this sense,

> Nature that can move and awaken our feelings is no longer tied to us by a notion of substantive reason. It is no longer seen as

> the order which defines our rationality. Rather we are defined by purposes and capacities we discover within ourselves. What nature can do now is awaken these: it can awaken us to feeling against the too pressing regulative control of an analytic, disengaging, order-imposing reason, now understood as a subjective procedural power.[13]

In this new era, where identity freed from nature by a disengaged reasoning can be defined by inner impulses, human sentiments can now find value in ways that they had previously been socially and ethically marginalized. In other words, romanticism embodies the notion that truth is within us and that we are in touch with this truth only if we are in touch with our feelings.[14]

This sense of romantic idealism also holds that we are only truly able to be in touch with our feelings when we are able to get back to that which is most natural—nature itself.[15] Though we no longer look at culture through the sentimentality of the romantic era, this expressivist response is still with us whenever we have the urge to get back in touch with nature, or the urge to heal the division between rationality and our feelings. Though these beliefs once had deeply religious motivations, they are more diffuse today. They occur as unfocused beliefs about our need to nurture a quality of wholeness and a need to get back to some less complex or less complicated way of realizing what matters in our lives.

The Quest for the Good Life: By the eighteenth century modern romantic idealism had also begun to influence the notion of the self in ways that focused on how each individual is uniquely different and original. This originality was thought to be so determinative that for each person there is a best way to pursue the good life. All individuals have an obligation to live into their

13. Taylor, *Sources of the Self*, 301.

14. For a far more nuanced understanding of the romantic movement (1775–1830) and its continuing implications for the contemporary dialogue between modernist and postmodernist cultural perspectives on what counts as "the real," see Charlene Spretnak, *The Resurgence of the Real: Body, Nature, and Place in a Hypermodern World* (New York: Addison-Wesley Publishing, 1997), 131–80.

15. Taylor, *Sources of the Self*, 368.

originality or carry with them a sense of failure for not having lived up to their potential.[16]

These three sources of the modern self make expressivist concern for experience and personal feelings morally crucial.[17] By the end of the eighteenth century the modern individual had become someone autonomously responsible for his or her own life and charged with the responsibility of living into his or her own potential. This modern individual had been cut free from the security of a communally defined identity and must now balance a disengaged reason and the creative sensibilities of an inner life in order to imagine a life worth living.[18] These trajectories of social thought function as sources of the modern self; they shape "what it means to be me" for the modern individual.[19]

The Individual in Search of Transformation

From the Enlightenment's newly disengaged ability to reason coupled with German romantic idealism I turn now (by way of Hegel's dialectical view of history) to Marx's theory of dialectical materialism. As part of Marx's argument that history has produced the situation of modern man's sense of alienation, he concluded that the notion of the modern individual is an *ideological* artifact of the influence of two historic social movements in seventeenth-century England. The first of these movements was the emergence of capitalism's market system, which forced

16. Ibid., 375.

17. Ibid., 305.

18. Ibid., 503.

19. Taylor notes, "Individualism has in fact been used in two quite different senses. In one it is a moral ideal. . . . In another it is an amoral phenomenon, something like what we mean by egoism. The rise of individualism in this sense is usually a phenomenon of the breakdown, where the loss of a traditional horizon leaves mere anomie in its wake, and everybody fends for themselves—e.g., in some demoralized, crime-ridden slums formed by newly urbanized peasants in the Third World (or in nineteenth century Manchester). It is, of course, catastrophic to confuse these two kinds of individualism, which have utterly different causes and consequences" (Charles Taylor, *The Ethics of Authenticity* [Cambridge, MA: Harvard University Press, 1991], 125–26n. 17). Taylor's book offers an important critique of sociological readings that tend to view our overarching contemporary cultural consciousness as a deviant expression of an ideal to which we must find our way back if we are to have a good society.

buyers and sellers to compete as individuals in an economic system of supply and demand. It created an economic climate that privileged the notion of individual property rights and the dismantling of the traditional solidarity groups that blocked free trade. The second movement was Puritanism's displacement of Catholic and Anglican religious traditions with a religion of private faith and personal accountability for public morality. Puritans rejected the teaching that salvation could be mediated by the church through the sacraments and that clerics could, by virtue of their ecclesiastical offices, functionally dispense forgiveness of sins. They taught that salvation was personal, between God and the individual only, and that each individual was accountable only to God. For Marx, this privatization of religion led to an increasing sense of alienation from the responsibilities of social solidarity. Marx believed the cultural force of the intersection of these two social movements created the modern crisis that leads to a sense of personal alienation and existential isolation.

Most contemporary sociologists have accepted Marx's argument concerning these social forces that led to the emergence of the individual and individualism.[20] The most significant alternative is Michel Foucault's argument that individualism actually developed in the eighteenth and nineteenth centuries as a result of the modern propensity for cultural classification schemes and the underlying social arrangements that were developed as responses to this urge to classify. Whether in the strict arrangements of military regiments, in the way physicians began treating individuals medically, by the way we came to incarcerate individuals in prison cells, by the way work arrangements became increasingly specialized, requiring expertise for each division, Foucault believed that the modern notion of self is a creation of such cultural urges.[21]

20. See Robert Wuthnow, *Meaning and Moral Order: Explorations in Cultural Analysis* (Berkeley: University of California Press, 1987), 194–98.

21. This is Wuthnow's wonderfully succinct summary in *Meaning and Moral Order* (303–4) of the studies of Michel Foucault: *Madness and Civilization: A History of Insanity in the Age of Reason* (New York: Random House, 1965); *The Birth of the Clinic: An Archaeology of Medical*

Whether one favors the argument of Taylor, Marx, or Foucault—they are not mutually exclusive—what remains uncontested is the overwhelming social influence of this modern conception of the individual as a person possessing inherent rights, who is free to act and has responsibility to act in matters of choice. Of course this freedom entails moral obligations to other persons as a kind of implied social contract.[22] There is also agreement that, unlike their predecessors, modern individuals must learn to juggle multiple notions of their *social*, *cultural*, and *interpersonal* sense of self that will vary with kinds of relationships and with roles assumed. Some theorists believe that this fracturing of the self has functionally led to an increasing fragmentation of agreement concerning the values that support our implied social contract.

This is the finding of Bellah and his colleagues in *Habits of the Heart*. Their highly influential study charts what they believe is the increasingly debilitating effect of a radical individualism in American culture. This fragmentation of selves is only imaginable, they conclude, because the American character has become defined by this radical individualism:

> It is true that we are all children of specific parents, born in a particular locality, inheritors of those group histories, and citizens of this nation. All of these things tell us who we are in important ways. But we live in a society that encourages us to cut free from our past, to define our own selves, to choose the groups with which we wish to identify. No tradition and no community in the United States is above criticism, and the test of the criticism is usually the degree to which the community or tradition helps the individual to find fulfillment.[23]

They argue that the preexisting biblically religious and classical republican vision of American culture is increasingly being

Perception (New York: Random House, 1975); *Discipline and Punishment: The Birth of the Prison* (New York: Vintage, 1979).

22. Wuthnow, *Meaning and Moral Order*, 199–200.

23. Bellah et al., *Habits of the Heart*, 154.

driven to the periphery of significance by this consuming culture of narcissistic utilitarianism and expressive individualism. They suggest that these influences are symbolically brokered by the professions of manager and therapist—roles that provide modern individuals overwhelmed by the moral complexity of a bureaucratized technological culture with language that permits them to negotiate a particular segment of life as a world that can be both manageable and privately fulfilling.[24]

Habits of the Heart is a profound assessment of our contemporary situation, but it offers a critique that presumes a negative assessment of our current cultural trajectory. There is a clearly implied argument in *Habits* that the negative public consequences of this radical individualism could be restored if North Americans would but recover the social capital that could lead us back to the era defined by the biblically religious and classically republican worldviews. In this sense, *Habits of the Heart* represents a longing to return to the world of order, the world of corporate integration and social solidarity that was previously described by the Teaching Voice's cultural consciousness in the Matrix of Contemporary Christian Voices. It represents a longing to reconstitute a social world in which the Teaching Voice (or, as will become apparent, the Testifying Voice) would once again provide the dominant resource for cultural cohesion.[25]

Yet on reflection many people would not elect to return to the affiliative connectedness of this society. Modern individuals live in a world full of choices that let them determine their own destiny, determine the convictions that shape their choices, and develop their own sense of conscience and obligation toward others. A host of contemporary rights unavailable to our

24. Ibid., 50–51. See also Robert Nelson Bellah, Richard Madsen, William M. Sullivan, Ann Swidler, and Steven M. Tipton, *The Good Society* (New York: Random House, 1991).

25. Bellah and his colleagues seem to long for a return to the same classical republic that Richard Weaver desires in his essay "The Spaciousness of the Old Rhetoric" in *The Ethics of Rhetoric* (Chicago: Regnery/Gateway Press, 1953), 164–85. It is the same concern that one hears in Allan Bloom, *The Closing of the American Mind* (New York: Simon and Schuster, 1987). Taylor is appreciative of Bellah's assessment but questions his prescriptive orientation; see *Sources of the Self*, 508–9. Leinberger and Tucker argue that this approach is an idealistically nostalgic conception of historical analysis that is unlikely to prove corrective (*New Individualists*, 381–87).

predecessors allows us to determine the shape of our own lives. Those rights are both defined and defended by the legal and political systems we support. We no longer fear being sacrificed to the demands of the sacred orders of Christendom's previous control of culture. *Kant won*. And whether religious or secular, few individuals today would choose to turn back the clock and surrender their personal sovereignty to the pre-Enlightenment tutelage of a benevolent dictator.

Congregations once functioned more as resource centers for "mutual caring and sharing, the collective enactment of religious rituals, or the cultivation of moral obligations through actual experiences of bonding and reconciliation."[26] In the same way, denominationalism once functioned to provide its members with a constitutive identity of social solidarity.[27] Christians once thought of themselves primarily as Lutherans, Catholics, Baptists, or Methodists. But much of this has shifted since the 1950s. The foci of preaching, evangelism, and discipleship-socializing ministries in many contemporary congregations is directed toward the empowering of individuals to live with their feet in two worlds—in modern culture and a community of faith adapting to it.[28] For many of these congregations their denomination still matters, but it matters less.

In *After Heaven: Spirituality in America since the 1950s*, Robert Wuthnow draws out specific implications of this tension by describing one pole of contemporary religious practice as a *dwelling-oriented spirituality*. He argues that this has been increasingly supplanted by an individualist *seeking-oriented spirituality*. In the former, people of faith derive their sense of spiritual identity from a metaphysic that provides cohesion and makes them feel secure in their denominational or their confessional identities. But this way of experiencing spirituality has increasingly been

26. Robert Wuthnow, *The Restructuring of American Religion: Society and Faith Since World War II* (Princeton: Princeton University Press, 1988), 55.

27. For an application of the argument of this book to interpreting the constitutive denominational identity of being Baptist see Robert Stephen Reid, "Being Baptist," *Rhetoric and Public Affairs* 7, 4 (2004): 587–602.

28. See Wuthnow, *Restructuring*, 274–76.

giving way to one in which spiritual seekers "negotiate among competing glimpses of the sacred, seeking partial knowledge and practical wisdom."[29] These seekers are as likely to find inspiration from counseling centers, popular authors, New Age guides, self-improvement seminars, or self-help groups as they are to find it in the church.[30] In this context, preachers find themselves competing with these diverse sources of the "spiritually inspiring" in making their appeals to listeners.

Dwelling-oriented spirituality locates its identity in the security of a more fixed institutional self, finding this identity in sacred space. *Seeking-oriented spirituality* negotiates its identity through the promise of transformation, finding it in the search for sacred moments and sacred experience.[31] Wuthnow explores the motives of this seeking-oriented spiritual identity as a negotiation of three basic desires:

- a desire for personal discipline to be achieved through spiritual techniques;
- a desire to experience miracles and mystery as portals of the sacred experience; and
- a desire to trust one's own quest to realize the inner self by remaking oneself.

Each of these motives reveals a deep spiritual desire to be transformed.

A third orientation may be emerging, one Wuthnow describes as *practice-centered spirituality*. I will return to the significance of this proposal in discussing the Testifying Voice in chapter five. What is particularly helpful in Wuthnow's general positioning of these tensions of religious cultural consciousness is the reminder

29. Robert Wuthnow, *After Heaven: Spirituality in America since the 1950s* (Berkeley: University of California Press, 1998), 3.

30. See Robert Wuthnow, *Sharing the Journey: Support Groups and America's New Quest for Community* (New York: The Free Press, 1994). See also Robert D. Putnam, Lewis M. Feldstein, and Don Cohen, *Better Together: Restoring the American Community* (New York: Simon and Schuster, 2003).

31. Wuthnow, *After Heaven*, 3–4.

that theorists must be careful in privileging critique, because critique is always offered from some perspective that assumes its own superior vantage point. Potshots across the divide are as readily found in scholarly as in popular literature. For example, much of the current literature on "worship wars" and appropriate styles of worship tends to assume the standard of either dwelling or seeking spirituality and then becomes "knockers" of the other perspective by becoming "boosters" of the superiority of their own. Such arguments are meaningful only for the insiders who already share the perspective or for the naïve who cannot see that the arguments originate from a presumptive posture that either privileges order and social solidarity over change and transformation, or vice versa.

At this point I wish to position Wuthnow's dwelling-oriented spirituality and his seeking-oriented spirituality as the spiritual equivalent of a theoretical tension that sociologists Gibson Burrell and Gareth Morgan proposed. In *Sociological Paradigms and Organizational Analysis* Burrell and Morgan provide a matrix intended to array differences that amount to paradigms of theory for conducting sociological analysis of organizations. In looking across the complex set of assumptions that orient different approaches to social theory, Burrell and Morgan realized that most social theory could be accounted for as an expression of four paradigms that can be identified if one bisects the standard objectivist-subjectivist orientations in theory production with a second discrimination between theories concerned with regulation's preference for order and theories concerned with radicalism's preference for transformation.[32] Wuthnow's juxtaposition of dwelling-centered and seeking-centered spiritual practices has obvious correlation to the theoretical orientation identified by Burrell and Morgan's second tension. For my purpose, the perspectives of both studies are at the core of my proposal of the

32. Gibson Burrell and Gareth Morgan, *Sociological Paradigms and Organizational Analysis: Elements of the Sociology of Corporate Life* (Burlington, VT: Ashgate Publishing, 1979), 21–37. Their four paradigms are Functionalist Sociology (e.g., Social System Theory), Interpretive Sociology (e.g., Phenomenological Sociology), Radical Humanism (French Existentialism), and Radical Structuralism (e.g., Contemporary Mediterranean Marxism).

Matrix of Contemporary Christian Voices. Just as Burrell and Morgan are able to locate most theory within their typology of orientations, my purpose here is to use a similar proposal to array theoretical distinctions among proposals for homiletic practice. Wuthnow's study helps put legs on theory to demonstrate how it functions as real practice in the culture. The alert reader might grasp at this point that with *The Four Voices of Preaching* I am proposing a communication theory, demonstrable across the practice of homiletics, that can be generalized to a general theory of contemporary Christian discourse—a concern for which the present book serves as a specific case.[33]

The Encouraging Voice in Preaching

The distinctive element of the Encouraging Voice is its assumption that the purpose of the sermon is to invite individuals to affirm truths directed to them in a persuasively determinate fashion. Sermons in this voice generally operate with objectivist assumptions about the nature of reality. Encouraging Voice preachers shape sermons with the intention that listeners feel renewed hope, stronger faith, a desire to recommit, etc. They view preaching as an event in which listeners have the opportunity to meet the living God, have an encounter with grace, an encounter with the holy, renew their zeal to let the Spirit of God be released to effect some work of grace in their lives, or simply celebrate what God is already doing in their lives. The preacher speaks as one who encourages the listener to experience the personal meaning of truths made apparent based on that listener's awareness of his or her own existential need. Preaching in this voice invites listeners to conclude "Lord, may this be so in my

33. On narrative voice as communication's "Silent Speech," Ricoeur finds that, "Point of view [in narrative] answers the question, 'From where do we perceive what is shown to us by the fact of being narrated?' Hence, from where is one speaking? Voice answers the question, 'Who is speaking here?' . . . [N]arrative voice is the silent speech that presents the world of the text to the reader." Paul Ricoeur, *Time and Narrative*, vol. 2, K. M. Laughlin (Blamey) and D. Pellauer, trans. (Chicago: University of Chicago Press, 1985), 99. This notion of voice is at the heart of identifying a theory of communication's cultural consciousness that speaks to us.

life" or "Thank you, God, for making this possible in my life." It is an advocacy-centered approach to preaching in which the preacher offers a clear depiction of the life the listener is invited to embrace or accept as a response to God and the possibilities of grace (see Figure 3.1).

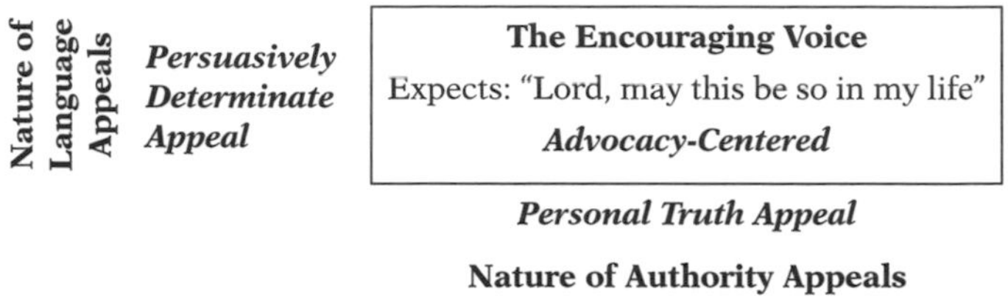

Nature of Language Appeals	*Persuasively Determinate Appeal*	**The Encouraging Voice** Expects: "Lord, may this be so in my life" ***Advocacy-Centered***
		Personal Truth Appeal
		Nature of Authority Appeals

Figure 3.1: The Encouraging Voice

Encouraging Voice preachers may still raise concerns of order and solidarity relevant to dwelling-centered Christianity in their sermons. As I stated earlier, at various points in a sermon a preacher may take up the concerns of the Teaching Voice, the Encouraging Voice, the Sage Voice, or the Testifying Voice, but only one of the voices should "be behind the wheel"—in charge of the sermon's purpose. Encouraging Voice preaching that would be clear about its intention will be characterized by persuasively determinate appeals that intersect with appeals to personal rather than corporate truth concerns. It is an advocacy-centered rather than an argument-centered approach to preaching. Just as Wuthnow would say that what appeals to people oriented to dwelling-centered spirituality is significantly different from what appeals to seeking-centered spirituality, so it is that sermons in the Encouraging Voice will have the concerns of the latter in view more than the concerns of the former.

Like the Teaching Voice, the Encouraging Voice serves an array of theological perspectives and is identified primarily by its assumption that the appeal should be directed toward individuals who wish to be transformed by an encounter with the sacred or transformed by their celebration of what God is doing in their midst. This approach certainly includes what has often been referred to as therapeutic preaching, invitational preaching, and celebratory preaching. Sermons in this voice may be overtly persuasive in the way they tease out implications from the biblical text to be applied to listeners' lives, or they may simply identify the possibilities of God's grace and conclude with an implicit invitation for listeners to avail themselves of the sacred. Either way, this voice assumes a persuasively determinate approach to the Nature of Language Assumptions. The controlling sensibility of preaching conducted in this voice is the hope that listeners will accept the possibilities of transformation identified in the preaching event. Sermons offered in this voice generally present an interpretation of a text/topic/contemporary thematic, but this interpretation is secondary to a design that invites listeners to avail themselves of the sermon's sacred possibilities.

The Spectrum of Possibilities

J. Randall Nichols cogently observes that "[i]ndividualization, privatization, and psychologization of the gospel are the handmaidens of preaching for conviction. A listener stands convicted—and stands alone; the verdict is an inner one—between you and your God; the response is subjective—you feel guilty, and maybe your attitude changes."[34] This preaching for personal transformation is obviously far from Karl Barth's notion of the divine commission to preach the gospel and the gospel only, but those who take up the Encouraging Voice are less concerned with standing with dogma and tradition and more concerned with finding effective ways to speak a relevant word. Preaching to convince may be an orientation more indicative of one end of the spectrum in this voice, but whether overt or artful, the intention of preaching is to speak in a way that facilitates an encounter with God/Spirit/grace/the holy. It is a voice concerned with speaking a relevant word that identifies a problem or point

34. J. Randall Nichols, *Building the Word: The Dynamics of Communication and Preaching* (San Francisco: Harper and Row, 1980), 13.

of need common among listeners and then provides a clear word of faith that invites a faithful response.[35]

In *Design for Preaching* H. Grady Davis penned the first major homiletic that tried to account for this shift in preaching's purpose. He called for preachers to attend to an organic unity between the preaching of biblical texts and the functional intention of the texts in their original setting. In the process he expanded the genres of preaching beyond proclamation and teaching to include the pastoral use of exhortation as *therapeuein*. "The immediate concern of therapeutic speech," he wrote, "is to remedy or improve the existing condition of the hearer."[36] Davis sought to move the sermon out of the distanced third-person presentation of historical information or doctrine to become something vitally centered in the truths that inspired continued devotion to faith. He envisioned preaching that would vary its forms (to encourage, to correct, to inform, to lead, to inspire, to challenge, and even to sing its truths) to connect the generic form of the text to the substance of the communication in the sermon. For example, if the sermon text is a parable, then the preacher may need to ask how to communicate its concern parabolically or risk assuming that the parable's substantive content can be separated from its active form.

He argues that those who are called to preach must be concerned about the form of their preaching for three reasons.

- "The first has to do with the purpose of preaching. The aim of preaching is to win . . . a response to the gospel, a response of attitude and impulse and feeling no less than of thought. Since form does its work immediately and at deeper levels than logic, persuades directly and silently as it were, form has an importance second only to that of thought itself."

35. For overt arguments on preaching's persuasive purpose see the collection of essays that first appeared in *Leadership Journal*: James D. Berkley, ed. *Preaching to Convince* (Waco: Leadership/Word, 1986).

36. Davis, *Design*, 127.

- "The second reason is the exceedingly complex nature of people who hear the Word of God. . . . The Word of God is a call to . . . broken and divided selves who stand giddily on the edge of life. It is a call to both mind and heart at once and equally. At such a time, the form which strikes directly and silently below all rational defenses may make the difference between a hearer's redemption and despair."
- "[And] a third reason why the form of [the] message should be of special concern to the preacher is the Character of God's Word itself. . . . If the form of what we say has the immediate and almost automatic power to repel or attract, and do its work on levels of response that lie below the arguments and counterarguments, then the very nature of the gospel, as well as the nature and conditions of mankind, requires us to be concerned with form."[37]

Davis's homiletic clearly assumes that the purpose of preaching is to persuade, to win a response from the listener, but this is a homiletic designed to reach the experiential-expressivist inner self while it also makes appeal to a modern reason now disengaged from the automatic assumption that church truth *is* to be accepted as given truth without question.

This same appeal to the expressivist individual's inner self is clearly evident in the homiletic theology of Ian Pitt-Watson. Instead of "winning a response," Pitt-Watson wants preach ing that by its very design invites response to God. He writes, "Preaching is God speaking through us who preach"[38] Thus, "Instead of telling people what to do, authentic biblical preaching helps people to do it. Authentic biblical preaching is about action enabled by insight, imperatives empowered by indicatives, ethics rooted in theology, 'what we ought to do' made possible by what God has done."[39] Pitt-Watson challenges the kind of preaching presented exclusively in a Teaching Voice—preaching

37. Ibid., 4–8.
38. Ian Pitt-Watson, *A Primer for Preachers* (Grand Rapids: Eerdmans, 1986), 14.
39. Ibid., 22, 66, 100.

in conceptual propositional terms at the expense of the inner experience of felt truths. By way of an intriguing rhetorical play on words he finds that "[t]he truth we preach must be a truth *not just thought, but also felt and done . . . not just felt, but also thought and done;* and . . . *not just done, but also thought and felt.*"[40]

Pitt-Watson regularly uses the rhetorical trope of a play-on-words to make his points. (E.g., "In preaching, the *whole* person is addressed by the *whole* truth. The gospel is most clearly heard when we speak *whole*heartedly, heart to heart, with hearts that not only feel, but also think and act.")[41] Preaching in this voice challenges speakers to push beyond propositional preaching that separates mind from body with sermons that invite listeners to act upon truth proclaimed, inviting commitment to or recommitment of one's faith. The invitation to respond may be explicitly made or implicit to the design of the sermon, but the sermon is considered incomplete if it does not seek to invoke some kind of response of faith. "We may or may not move from our seats, but in some way our response to the Word must involve some change in the way we think and feel and act, some change in the way we see ourselves and one another and God."[42] This is preaching that advocates transformation or change made possible by dependence on a relationship of empowerment made possible through an encounter mediated by the Word of God. This appeal to transformation is the controlling intention that makes Pitt-Watson's homiletic clearly identified with an advocacy-centered approach to preaching.

It should come as no surprise that Pitt-Watson's sample sermon brief is organized as a basic call-to-action, problem-solution speaking design. First he identifies a problem with an inadequate conception of faith both by those in the story in the text and then in the lives of contemporary people. He then identifies the solution, which requires that the people in the text should have trusted God and that today's listener should trust God in this same

40. Ibid., 98–99 (italics his).

41. Ibid., 101.

42. Ibid., 65.

way.[43] The problem-solution strategy of organization, whether in preaching or in public speaking, is designed to accomplish one intention—to call listeners to take action in support of the solution offered.

If Davis represents one end of the persuasive spectrum (sermon as "winning a response") and Pitt-Watson is the middle (sermon as "invitation to respond"), Paul Wilson envisions a homiletic where the speaker advocates on behalf of the grace of God rather than making an argument. For Wilson, preaching can become a medium through which a listener can experience the grace of God. His *The Four Pages of Preaching* serves equally as a proposal for conducting homiletic exegesis as it does a strategy of sermon design. The preacher's task, according to Wilson, is to explore the tension between trouble and the potential of grace in Scripture, and identify commensurate applications of this trouble and the possibilities of grace available for listeners today. Unlike Pitt-Watson's, Wilson's homiletic is a text-centered rather than a theme-centered approach to preaching. He varies the traditional problem-solution design by proportionally subdividing the problem section into then-now divisions and the solution section into a similar then-now format—hence four pages. In each move, Wilson is also concerned to have the preacher find ways to image the ideas so as to create identification with contemporary listeners.

For Wilson, the solution is invariably finding one's way to the grace already made possible by God. He writes, "The purpose of the sermon is to invite people into faith; the purpose of faith is service to the gospel of Jesus Christ. From faith issues actions; thus the sermon points listeners toward their active ministries in the world."[44] In *The Practice of Preaching*, he states,

43. Ibid., 78–80. Pitt-Watson's sermons would invariably follow the problem-solution design since he suggests that, once a theme has been identified as the truth to be preached, the preacher should "invert the theme" in order to identify the problematic expression to be remedied by the truth proclaimed (81).

44. Paul Scott Wilson, *The Four Pages of Preaching: A Guide to Biblical Preaching* (Nashville: Abingdon Press, 1999), 205–6.

> In the finest sermons we feel renewed hope, stronger faith, and recommitment to mission. More simply stated, we experience God. For this reason we claim that preaching is an event in which the congregation meets the living God. When we use the word event in this way, we mean an action, an occurrence, something that happens in a moment of time in the lives of the hearers. When we say this is a divine event we acknowledge that, through preaching, God chooses to be encountered. Since this encounter effects a new relationship with God of reconciliation and empowerment, we may also acknowledge preaching as a salvation event.[45]

Good preaching makes possible an *event of encounter* with God that is quite literally an act of grace. The intention of this approach to preaching is to leave the listeners with a stronger and deeper faith commitment to doing God's work.

When preaching fails to accomplish this end it is often because the preacher has failed to identify what is at stake in the sermon in one of six points. Wilson argues that preachers need to identify:[46]

- one **text** from the Bible to preach;
- one **theme** sentence arising from the text;
- one **doctrine** arising out of that theme statement;
- one **need** in the congregation that the doctrine or theme sentence addresses;
- one **image** to be wed to the theme sentence, and
- one **mission**.

However, this approach does not assume that the identification of theme and doctrine should be confused with *the meaning of the text.* Wilson notes that prior to Davis's *Design for Preaching* and Craddock's *As One without Authority*, preachers assumed that texts could be reduced to and summarized by a propositional statement as if the statement was coterminous with the meaning of the

45. Ibid., 20–21.
46. Ibid., 38.

text: "That earlier process essentially flattened the biblical text by reducing it to one idea that represented the whole. Nowadays, we understand that the selected idea is not the text in a nutshell but is one significant idea in the arena of authentic meaning of a text, without at the same time being a fully adequate statement in and of itself."[47] It is this focus on preaching possible meanings and implications of the text as the well-focused facilitation of an encounter with God/Spirit/grace/the holy, whether directed or implied, that is indicative of excellence in preaching in the Encouraging Voice.[48]

Some contemporary black preaching also occurs in this voice. In *They Like to Never Quit Praisin' God*, Thomas states that the genius of African-American preaching arises from profound anguish and suffering, in which the African-American preacher sought not to give answers to the problem of suffering and evil in life, but to help people experience the assurance of grace in God. This has always been

> an assurance to the people that God was with them, in and through the suffering, and would ultimately liberate them from the suffering. The focus was not on cognitive explanations, but an experience of the transforming, sustaining, and saving power of God in the midst of suffering and evil. The African American sermon was designed to celebrate, to help people *experience the assurance of grace* that is the gospel.[49]

This form of preaching helps listeners discover how the power of gospel assurance is the solution to whatever problems they face, and that the embrace of this assurance is cause for celebration.

Thomas believes that in the best of African-American preaching, the appeals to both cognitive and emotive logics are designed

47. Paul Scott Wilson, *God Sense: Reading the Bible for Preaching* (Nashville: Abingdon Press, 2001), 35.

48. Though Wilson offers a rich definition of preaching, the key word may well be "In the *finest* sermons . . ." Readers can readily imagine the obverse of this definition: sermons so toxic that "[m]ore simply stated, we experience Evil." Wilson's definition implies a theology of excellence which, in turn, entails an ethic of preaching.

49. Frank A. Thomas, *They Like to Never Quit Praisin' God: The Role of Celebration in Preaching* (Cleveland: Pilgrim Press, 1997), 3.

to move the sermon through the problem-solution design to the distinctive culmination of this celebration of God's gospel purposes with the goal to influence personal behavior.[50] Though it would be an overstatement to assume that all black preaching must move to celebration—not every subject evokes this response—Joseph Bethea still maintains that "[a]uthentic black worship is celebration." Black people celebrate the sovereignty of an almighty God who can do anything and their combined ability to survive in a hostile environment.[51] In this sense, black preaching often concludes with a call to *celebrate* the reality of living into a world of trust in God and living into the utter confidence in the good news of the gospel.

Traditionally, black preaching has found its source of empowerment in the "church as refuge" model of preaching and worship, where black people gather to experience a refuge from racism through preaching of gospel that identifies them as people of worth. Cheryl Townsend Gilkes has characterized this function of black church worship as a "collective therapeutic experience."[52] Preaching in the context of this kind of worship becomes a function of pastoral care that demonstrates the value of life in relation to God and one's neighbor while also nurturing personal coping skills, a sense of personal worth, and a belief in the promise of personal liberation both here and now as well

50. Ibid., 88–89. See also Henry H. Mitchell, *Celebration and Experience in Preaching* (Nashville: Abingdon Press, 1990); and Henry H. Mitchell, *Black Preaching: The Recovery of a Powerful Art* (1970; 1977; Nashville: Abingdon Press, 1990). Thomas invites preachers to break out three aspects of strategy to frame the sermon's final celebration move. First, *What truth of the gospel concerning God's control or purpose shall we celebrate?* Second, *How shall we celebrate this good news?* Third, *What materials or resources of celebration shall we use?* (84–106).

51. Joseph B. Bethea, "Worship in the Black Church," *Duke Divinity Review* 43 (Winter 1978), 44–53. Anthologized in *Border Regions of Faith: An Anthology of Religion and Social Change*, Kenneth Aman, ed. (Maryknoll, NY: Orbis, 1987), 208–15.

52. Cheryl Townsend Gilkes, "The Black Church as a Therapeutic Community: Suggested Areas of Research into Black Religious Experience," *Journal of Interdenominational Theological Center* 8 (Fall 1980): 29–44. Excerpted in Aman, *Border Regions of Faith,* 197–207. The refuge model of the church assumes that a congregation must reach out to the marginalized members of a community if it is to draw on Jesus as the model of its ministry. This is the church as a countercultural relocation of the basis of community from the center of society to its margins. At its best it gives an empowering voice to the marginalized. The drawback is that success can mean loss of the model's continued purpose and source of identity.

as in the fulfillment of God's kingdom purpose.[53] In this sense, black preaching identifies a human problem, announces God's redemptive solution, and culminates in a celebration of communal identity that communicates (1) the inherent worth of the individual, (2) the potential for the individual to realize his or her growth and development in relationship with God, (3) the primacy of community of faith as the place to experience caring and supportive relationships, and (4) the power of God to help individuals realize their conscious and unconscious aspirations through a community willing to act on its faith.[54] It invites listeners to move from a sense of personal shame, regardless of whether it is inspired inappropriately by one's culture or as an appropriate response to true biblical sense of sin, and discover a sense of self-worth in being the people of God.[55]

Black preaching is a particularly complex instance of preaching in the Encouraging Voice in that its initial problem-solution sermonic moves are typical of the advocacy-centered approaches to preaching. On the other hand, the sermonic move of celebration often transcends the therapeutic to invite listeners to celebrate their role as the "insiders" in the corporate solidarity of being a people who know that God's truth is already realized in the conviction of the community. The preacher shifts the sermonic intention from making an appeal to the individual to respond to God's call to expressing an intention for the listener to take refuge in the social solidarity of the community that knows the truth of the grace revealed in the sermon.

Depending on the way the preacher places emphasis on this appeal, the sermon can be controlled either by the Teaching Voice or the Encouraging Voice. In the black preaching tradition, this shift of intention has been traditionally embodied in ways that can keep the sermon from becoming a muddle of mixed

53. Dale P. Andrews, *Practical Theology for Black Churches: Bridging Black Theology and African American Folk Religion* (Louisville: Westminster/John Knox Press, 2002), 34–37.

54. Cf. Edward P. Wimberly, *Pastoral Counseling and Spiritual Values: A Black Point of View* (Nashville: Abingdon Press, 1982), 32.

55. See Edward P. Wimberly, *Moving from Shame to Self-Worth: Preaching and Pastoral Care* (Nashville: Abingdon Press, 1999).

preaching intentions. I will discuss a similar tension in the next chapter when I take up the expression of black preaching in the Sage Voice. At this point, the specific example of diversity in the expression of this preaching tradition should serve as a reminder that the Matrix offers a "typology of" rather than a "container for" preaching's different voices. Here I will simply state that black preaching controlled by an intention that focuses primarily on individualistic concerns, and responding therapeutically by providing God's invitation to experience redemption, would be an expression of the Encouraging Voice. The controlling feature of black preaching in the Teaching Voice would be a dominant sermonic appeal to the order and social solidarity of the community. As we shall see in the next chapter, black preaching operates out of the Sage Voice when its voice of assuredness shifts to a voice of ambiguity, when its interpretation of the text or thematic focuses more on sermon as the people's story rather than offering authoritative explanations of the meaning of the text.

Excellence in the Encouraging Voice

Celebrating vindication by God has been an empowering experience in black preaching, providing a continuing expression of communal identity in solidarity with the eternal purposes of God. Dale Andrews warns, however, that in the post–civil rights era, where black preaching has begun to embrace more of the values of white American individualism, where personalism functions as a kind of religious personal fulfillment, black preaching may need to find new ways to identify a prophetic black church ecclesiology that renegotiates the function of the refuge model of preaching for a new day.[56] The alternative would be an approach to preaching that is more style than substance in its call to celebration. Excellence in black preaching will find a way to

56. Andrews, *Practical Theology*, 67–88. Andrews identifies the modern concept of individualism versus a traditional conception of the black church as a tensional trajectory that is merely a specific case of the larger tensional discussion I provide in this chapter.

hold the communal validation of self-worth in tension with the cultural drive to realize personal fulfillment.

What Andrews has identified as the need to define the appropriation of the "prophetic" black church ecclesiology necessary to reconcile this set of competing trajectories is also at the heart of the issue concerning excellence in the diverse expressions of the Encouraging Voice.[57] Preaching in this voice is always in danger of making its appeal to what Christopher Lasch has labeled *The Culture of Narcissism* (the title of his 1979 book). In the name of being relevant it can become an embrace of an emotive, therapeutic spirituality empty of the real substance of the gospel.[58] Lasch argues, "The contemporary climate is therapeutic, not religious. People today hunger not for personal salvation, let alone for restoration of an earlier golden age, but for the momentary illusion of personal well-being, health, and psychic security."[59] He concludes, "In a dying culture, narcissism appears to embody—in the guise of personal 'growth' and 'awareness'—the highest attainment of spiritual enlightenment."[60]

Much like Bellah, in his concern to challenge the consuming culture of narcissistic utilitarianism and expressive individualism, Lasch intended his study to be an assault on the preoccupations of "the culture of competitive individualism, which in its decadence has carried the logic of individualism to the extreme of a war of all against all, the pursuit of happiness to the dead end of a narcissistic preoccupation with the self."[61] This is a preoccupation with a totalized self. The danger of preaching that aligns its appeals with this preoccupation is that it surrenders all sense of the content of the gospel in an effort to connect with the needs of this preoccupied self in existential isolation. In other words, the danger of this voice is in making totalized persuasive appeals

57. Ibid., 106–28.

58. See Philip Rieff, *The Triumph of the Therapeutic: Uses of Faith after Freud* (New York: Harper and Row, 1968); Rodney Hunter, "Preaching Forgiveness in a Therapeutic Age," *Journal for Preachers* 28, 2 (2005): 25–32.

59. Christopher Lasch, *The Culture of Narcissism: American Life in an Age of Diminishing Expectations* (New York: Warner Books, 1979), 33.

60. Ibid., 396.

61. Ibid., 21.

to the individual. It would be an approach to preaching that surrenders all the concerns of dwelling-oriented spirituality in the name of connecting with seeking-centered spirituality. It functionally justifies a consuming culture of narcissistic utilitarianism thoroughly rooted in experiential-expressivist individualism.[62]

What might this look like in preaching? In an attempt to identify the problem of communicating the gospel to modern spiritual seekers, Robert Duffett recently challenged communicators to come to terms with the necessity of connecting the content of the Christian faith with the real circumstances in which people live in our post-Christendom culture. He argues that this kind of preaching identifies ways that preaching must address the inner life needs of post-Christendom spiritual seekers:

> Those who speak to seekers need to be authentic and speak with heart, soul, and passion. Unlike churchgoers in the past, seekers know that ministers and Christian communicators struggle with doubt and pain. Therefore, a seeker message does not pretend that the speaker is above the pain. Rather, the speaker shows how the resources of the Christian faith and church help him or her as well as seekers to deal with pain, questions, and problems.[63]

His primary concern is that preaching must transcend Christian platitudes and the kind of Christian talk that was acceptable in a day when church attendance was the norm. Otherwise it sounds like the durable model of life-situation preaching that has been around for more than half a century.

In 1953 Andrew Blackwood began his homiletics textbook *Expository Preaching for Today* by stating,

> [T]he wise interpreter begins with a human need today, and chooses a passage that will enable him to meet this need. Whatever the description, expository preaching worthy of the name

62. In chapter five I will note a number of theorists who totalize the communal approach and suggest that all appeals to individualism are sub-gospel. Totalizing in either perspective can become fetishizing.

63. Robert G. Duffett, *A Relevant Word: Communicating the Gospel to Seekers* (Valley Forge, PA: Judson Press, 1995), 45.

> affords pleasing variety. The content and the form of such pulpit work ought to vary according to the human need in view, the Bible passage in hand, the personality of the man in the pulpit, and the spirit of the day in which he preaches.[64]

Note how Blackwood has virtually made human need the essential resource of preaching rather than the message of the gospel itself. In the commendable effort to identify a post-Christendom homiletic, Duffett's proposal risks letting life-situation preaching become his totalizing hermeneutic. The chief indictment of this approach to preaching is the danger of displacing the Word of God with a word of wisdom.

Harry Black Beverly Jr. argues that life situation sermons

> fail to deal adequately with the contemporary situation of man or to serve the Gospel. A Christian sermon begins, not with a problem, but with a Word which reveals and speaks to man's problem. Fosdick is indeed right in wishing to speak a word to the peculiar situations of his times but he is wrong in starting with the occasions and situations themselves. Only an expository sermon has a Word to speak to the times; any other type of preaching only offers words of human wisdom which may or may not be wiser than the words they hear outside of the church of Christ and may never be God's own Word to the situations.[65]

This is always the danger of life-situation preaching, but this is a critique that assumes the classic Barthian, order-centered concern for sacred tradition versus Fosdick's transformation-centered concern with individual need. Beverly would likely offer the same critique of the Sage Voice's interest to offer insight to the individual on a personal journey of faith. In fact it may even

64. Andrew Watterson Blackwood, *Expository Preaching for Today* (New York: Abingdon-Cokesbury, 1953), 13. This appears to be a conflation of topical preaching, which takes its subjects from theology or social circumstances, and seeks to enjoin it to a verse-by-verse approach to preaching. For a contemporary effort to recover the value of traditional topical preaching see Ronald Allen, *Preaching the Topical Sermon* (Louisville: Westminster/John Knox, 1992).

65. Harry Black Beverly Jr., "Harry Emerson Fosdick's Predigtweise, Its Significance (for America), Its Limits, Its Overcoming" (Ph.D. diss. Basel University, 1965); as cited in Miller, *Fosdick*, 340–41.

be a critique of the twentieth century's shift in attention from the priority of the subject matter to the priority of the listener. What is needed for excellence in this voice is the challenge to seek gospel balance between attention to the life situation and the gospel reality. Notice how Wilson maintains this balance by requiring that the identification of the need be in proportional balance to five other preaching concerns.

There are other dangers in life-situation preaching. Preachers can be readily lured into the temptation to become a resident life-situation expert, capable of offering a three-step plan to help listeners discover how to have a better . . . whatever the psychosocial issue of the day is. The illusion of this approach to preaching is to make it appear as if the self-help-like answers have been teased out of the biblical text. A second temptation is to allow the quest to be relevant to become an end rather than a means, where the needs of the listener overdetermine the content of the message.[66] Bill Hybels argues that today's preacher must begin with the utilitarian assumption that she or he is "speaking to the secularized mind." He writes, "Unchurched people today are the ultimate consumers. We may not like it, but for every sermon we preach, they're asking, *Am I interested in that subject or not?* If they aren't, it doesn't matter how effective our delivery is; their minds will check out."[67] Marshall Shelly, the *Leadership Journal* editor of the book in which Hybels' essay appears, chose this statement to serve as a frontispiece for this essay. But the only thing that really has changed between these contemporary calls to life-situation preaching and the call to life-situation preaching that dominated the first half of the twentieth century is the fact that its contemporary expression, in the hands of people less capable than Hybels, has had a tendency to totalize the issue of relevance for preaching in the "hypermodern" context.

66. On therapeutic preaching see Davis, *Design*, 127–38; Wayne E. Oates, *The Christian Pastor* (Philadelphia: Westminster Press, 1977), 118–20; J. Randall Nichols, *The Restoring Word: Preaching as Pastoral Care* (New York: Harper and Row, 1987), especially 66–91.

67. Bill Hybels, "Speaking to the Secularized Mind," *Mastering Contemporary Preaching*, Marshall Shelly, ed. (Portland, OR: Christianity Today/Multnomah, 1989), 31.

A word of caution is needed here. I am not arguing that Encouraging Voice preaching that privileges seeking-centered concerns is wrongheaded. Nor am I arguing that either Duffett's or Hybels' versions of a therapeutic homiletic are guilty of totalizing relevance. By Duffett's own admission, his homiletic lacks the elements that would make it a full theology of communication and ministry to seekers.[68] And Hybels' essay is identifying the kind of preaching that brings seekers into initial contact with the gospel message as a fresh Word of faith amidst a culture drowning in self-help messages. The danger, in the hands of those who are even more gifted as motivational speakers, is that their well-meaning life-skills messages tend to overwhelm the gospel message. The danger, in the hands of those less skilled than these practitioners, is that the need to be relevant at all costs too often replaces gospel testimony that names God and names grace.

When relevance and revelation are in balance, sermons in the Encouraging Voice can become an advocacy of life's wisdom, sifted by gospel testimony. John Claypool provides a model of excellence in this voice by asking and answering a series of questions in the conclusion of his 1979 Lyman Beecher lectures:

> What is it we are attempting to do when we stand up to preach? We are trying to participate in the restoring of a relation of trust between human creatures and the Creator. Why do we do this? Not to get something for ourselves, out of need-love, but to give something of ourselves in gift-love. How do we do it? By making available as witnesses what we have learned from our woundedness for the woundedness of others. When do we do this? At times and in ways that are appropriate to another's growing as a farmer nurtures a crop. To do this is to participate in the extension of the gospel in our time. Could anything be a higher joy? I think not.[69]

This is a theologically astute, seeking-sensitive approach to preaching that invites listeners to turn away from narcissistic

68. Duffett, *A Relevant Word*, xiii.

69. John R. Claypool, *The Preaching Event* (Waco: Word Books, 1980), 135–36.

need-love and participate in gift-love even as it invites preachers to become, in Henri Nouwen's famous phrase, wounded healers.[70] Relevance, by itself, is an inadequate motive for an ethic of responsible preaching in the Encouraging Voice. It can be a means, but preachers must beware that is does not become an end.

Preaching in the Encouraging Voice occurs when the design of preaching invites an active response to experience transformation from listeners and the preacher assumes a voice of assuredness in providing a gospel answer to a problem or concern identified. Patterns of preaching that invite preachers to take up this voice include:

1. The Four Pages of Preaching;
2. Problem-Solution-Celebration;
3. Journey to Celebration;
4. Ogilvie's "Christian Motivated Sequence,"[71] and
5. Sermon as Jigsaw Puzzle.[72]

The distinctive element shared by all of these strategies of composition is their assumption that the persuasive intention of preaching is to facilitate an encounter between the listener and God/Spirit/grace/the holy.

Whether the sermon focuses on a felt need or is a celebration of the grace God has already made possible, the preacher's ability to speak on behalf of his or her own experience of life and faith in connecting this to an identifiable individual need or concern is the basis of appeal that authorizes authenticity in this approach.

70. Henri Nouwen, *The Wounded Healer* (New York: Harper, 1985).

71. What I have termed the "Christian Motivated Sequence" (Identification-Interpretation-Implications-Implementation-Inspiration) is Lloyd Ogilvie's updated version of Fosdick's preaching design; see Lucy Lind Hogan and Robert Reid, *Connecting with the Congregation: Rhetoric and the Art of Preaching* (Nashville: Abingdon Press, 1999), 125. For Ogilvie's perspective on preaching that addresses felt needs, see Lloyd John Ogilvie, "It's Time to Listen," *Reformed Liturgy and Music* (now *Worship*) 21, 2 (1987): 92–96. On the relationship between the Introductory "Identification" move and the effectiveness of preaching, see Ogilvie, "Introducing the Sermon," in *A Handbook of Contemporary Preaching*, Michael Duduit, ed. (Nashville: Broadman, 1993), 175–87; reprinted in *Preaching* 8 (March–April 1993): 16–22.

72. For succinct explanation of most of these sermon designs see Ronald J. Allen, ed., *Patterns of Preaching: A Sermon Sampler* (St. Louis: Chalice Press, 1998).

These strategies of arrangement all invite the listener to respond or imply a call to action by their very design. They invite listeners to say, "Lord, may this be so in my life" or "Thank you, God, for making this possible in my life." Sermons in the Encouraging Voice invite listeners to experience the transformation of reconciliation with God and of empowerment made possible by the extension through preaching of the grace of God.

A Sample Sermon

If the sermon that makes points invites listeners to assent to the argument, a sermon that employs a problem-solution design calls for action—it invites a more visceral response that longs to see a claim or a hope fulfilled. Paul Wilson's model of sermon movement, *The Four Pages of Preaching*, takes the old problem-solution speech design beyond mere form to embody four biblical and theological tasks in preaching—to help listeners experience the trouble, conflict, sin, or brokenness in the biblical story as something they can also relate to in their own lives and then experience the expression of grace in the story's resolution as grace that is yet available to them today.[73]

In John Rottman's sermon, "While We Wait," listeners are invited to find themselves in the world of the story and discover that its resolution acknowledging the power of prayer can be their resolution as well. After a brief introduction that situates the issue at stake for listeners, readers can readily see the four moves of trouble then and now, and God's gracious response then and now.

While We Wait
Luke 18:1-8
John Rottman

When I was about twelve years old I became David Bush's helper and heir apparent to our neighborhood newspaper route.

73. Ibid., *Four Pages*, 16–18.

Learning the paper route was an "on the job training" kind of deal. Dave did one side of the street and I did the other.

After a few days, I noticed that almost every afternoon Dave stopped at Mrs. Sneed's house and knocked at the door. Since I didn't want to get too far ahead and because I was a bit nosy I would cross the street, stand a few feet away, and watch what he was doing. Apparently, the Sneeds were past due paying for their newspapers and Dave was trying to collect. "Yeah," Dave told me one day, "they're almost two months behind. They won't pay, and I don't know why." The Sneeds had a brand new car and a swimming pool.

They also always had an excuse. "I don't have any money at the moment." "Do you have change for a fifty?" Or they would send one of the kids to say that their mother wasn't home right now. Dave tried time and time again with no luck. He threatened to stop delivering their paper. Once he even tried to embarrass them into paying by pasting a big sign on their front door that said "PLEASE PAY UP"—signed, THE PAPER BOY. I admired his persistence. Dave never stopped trying.

Now the widow woman in our Bible reading from Luke 18 exhibits a similar level of determination. She is no quitter. After all her trying and failing. Countless daily trips to this judge. No satisfaction. No luck. She keeps right on trying.

Everyone in the village knew her situation. I heard that she and her husband had owned this lovely little vineyard. The property adjoined the house. No big operation, but the wine sold well and they lived comfortably off the proceeds. But then her husband had become ill. She'd nursed him until he died, but with no family to help, the ordeal left her both physically and emotionally exhausted. In her grief she took what little money she had left, closed up the house, and went to visit her only sister two weary days' journey north.

She'd stayed longer than she'd planned. At first she'd simply been tired and too grief-stricken to think about leaving. In fact it wasn't until she heard her sister and brother-in-law arguing about her one evening that she realized that it was long past time for her to return home. So she left.

Upon arriving home, the first thing she noticed was a big fence that someone had built between her house and her vineyard. Odd. And the next day when she went to investigate, she discovered that some rude overseer had kicked her off her own land. So the very next day she had gone to the judge to straighten things out. "This wealthy neighbor has robbed me of my vineyard," she said, "land that belongs to me and my late husband." The judge told her, "I'll certainly look into the matter," but as she left he shook his head scoffing.

She waited a full week before making a second visit. But then the judge was unable to see her. The next time he was "still looking into it." And the next. Other times there were awkward moments during which he seemed to be waiting for something. But she had no money and he had hundreds of ways of stalling her. Yet she still persisted in her increasingly hopeless cause. Her land-grabbing neighbor had no right to it. And she needed the money so badly now. But these visits to the judge seemed more and more pointless. She kept on asking for justice, but it certainly seemed that nothing was going to change. Why bother?

Now as Christians, my guess is that many of us at times have asked the "Why bother?" question about prayer—especially when it comes to some of the big issues in our lives. We've asked and asked and asked, but nothing changes. Or we've seen others ask. But nothing seemed to come of it. Some of us have pretty much given up on prayer. We continue to ask for the more small-ticket items, food, restful sleep, nice day, but we have crossed off most of the big-ticket items like the scandal of abortion killing thousands of tiny innocent babies. Nothing changes. So why pray for that? Drug violence and the robbery and addiction that come with it. What can you do? Friends and neighbors who don't know Jesus Christ or care about God. Why bother with praying about such things? Nothing much ever really changes anyway. Maybe it would be more honest to quit setting ourselves up. Stop putting God on the spot. Embarrassing God with all our asking and setting ourselves up for disappointment.

I'm sure the widow in Jesus' story more than once must have considered the possibility of just giving up. Nothing ever seemed changed.

But then one day, right out of the clear blue, everything changed. Seems several of the judge's social acquaintances had begun to kid him at a cocktail party about this widow who always seemed to be hanging around his court. "Some cases are just too complex, even for a judge of your caliber," one said with a wink. People were talking. And so, to stop their embarrassing jibes, the judge decided that the easiest thing to do was to act. So one morning, with a simple sweep of the pen, the judge handed back the persistent widow her vineyard. More than that, he generously assessed damages against her no-good neighbor and collected them on the spot. Ah, sweet justice. An answer to prayer.

And the Bible says that Jesus told this story to teach his disciples that they must always pray and never give up. "Hmmm," you might say to yourself. "You mean to tell me that God is like that judge in the story? He really doesn't care about us, but if we embarrass him enough or bug him with our prayer, he just might do something for us now and again?"

"No," says Jesus.

> Look at that unjust judge. If even an aloof, unjust judge will act to save his reputation, how do you expect God will behave when his very own children pray to him? Don't doubt for one minute that the just and loving judge of the whole universe will make everything right for his chosen ones who cry out to him night and day. Will he keep putting them off? Of course not. He will see to it that they get justice.

And yes, God's reputation is all tied up with the well-being of his people.

I remember when my seven-year-old, son, Eric, went out for his first cross-country run with other elementary school kids. My wife, Marilyn, took him, and when they got home she told me about some of the parents. "You should have seen some of them," she said. "Not only did they go to the meet, they were screaming and shouting, 'Run, Jimmy! Faster, Brittany, faster!' They were really getting into this running stuff." Maybe some of you have parents like that. It can be embarrassing.

I suppose we parents sometimes act like that because so much of our own identity is often wrapped up in our kids. We love them, sacrifice for them, and want for "all the world" to see them do well. We often feel that our reputation as parents is in some sense wrapped up with how well our children do. So, maybe a good parent isn't *that* involved, but a good parent does identify heavily with his or her kids and then acts to do everything they can for them.

Now, our heavenly Father has identified heavily with us. We are his children, his chosen ones. God has gone so far as to actually become human like us in the person of Jesus Christ. And then he suffered and died on the cross for us, so that we might be forgiven. God cares deeply about us—how we are doing, how we feel. God cares more deeply than any parent has ever felt for any child. That much.

And while it may not seem like the day will ever come . . . the day is coming when God will bring justice for us and all those who belong to Jesus. No more hunger. No more loneliness. No more sickness. No more death. The day is coming soon when God will take us, his children, into his arms and personally wipe away every tear from our eyes. And whether that day comes for you in the day you die or on the day that Jesus returns, it will come like a wonderful bolt out of the blue. The deep joy of God's making all that is wrong right again.

"Well, God, why not do it now?" you might ask. "We live in a world so full of violence, sickness, hunger, and death. Why not come make it all right, right now? End the chemotherapy, eradicate AIDS, put the funeral parlors out of business, stop the violence, change all the disheartening stories in the papers into good news."

Well, Jesus doesn't give us satisfying answers to that "why" question. Why not now? We don't know. Perhaps part of the answer has something to do with God's ongoing work in this world. God is still saving people, offering forgiveness. As long as life on earth continues, God continues to rescue people from eternal death and hell. Perhaps God delays final justice so that someone you love, a friend, or maybe even someone here this morning, has the opportunity he or she needs to repent and to get right with God. God is so gracious, patient, not wanting anyone to perish. And so we wait, too.

But while we wait, God gives us prayer as a way of all the while holding us in relationship with him. Isn't that what Jesus means when he turns the question back on us, asking whether the Son of man will find faith on earth? Prayer is our expression of faith in God. And when we pray, it is as if God brings us for a moment up onto his lap, wraps his arms around us, and whispers to our hearts that he loves us deeply. You may not understand sometimes, he says, but I cared for you enough to suffer and die for you. I still care for you more than you can know. You are right to bring these concerns to me. Trust me now, I will not let you down or let you go. You're my son, you're my daughter.

And God sometimes uses the occasion for prayer to deliver real life signs, little hints of the good things that he has planned for us. After all, God is alive and active here in our world, today, even now—saving, healing, and routing evil. There have been times I have joined members of my own congregation in praying for healing and seen God use our prayer as an opportunity to heal—miraculous healing as a sign of that great and final healing that God has planned for us and for our world. Prayer is such a great gift. So God invites us to pray always, and do not lose heart.

In the name of the Father, the Son, and the Holy Spirit.

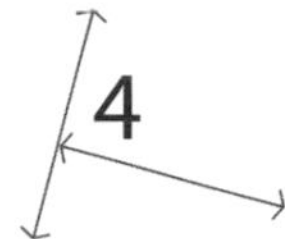

4 Preaching in the Sage Voice

In a masterful analysis of the changing American religious landscape published in 1955, sociologist Will Herberg concluded that

> [t]he picture that emerges is one in which religion is accepted as a normal part of the American Way of Life. Not to be—that is, not to identify oneself and be identified as—either a Protestant, a Catholic, or a Jew is somehow not to be an American. It may imply being foreign, as is the case when one professes oneself a Buddhist, a Muslim, or anything but a Protestant, Catholic, or Jew, even when one's Americanism is otherwise beyond question.[1]

His assessment must be viewed in the context that it occurs within but a year or two of the search for communist-traitors by the House Committee on Un-American Activities (HUAC) and in the immediate aftermath of the addition of "under God" to the American Pledge of Allegiance. To an unprecedented degree in

1. Will Herberg, *Protestant-Catholic-Jew: An Essay in American Religious Sociology* (1955; Garden City, NY: Anchor, 1960), 257–58.

our history, according to Herberg, to be Protestant, Catholic, or Jew was simply an alternative way of being American. In the middle of the twentieth century, antireligious prejudice had all but disappeared. Not to self-identify with one of these three faith traditions might be the basis of suspecting true disloyalty.

Fast-forward a decade and a half to the summer of 1969. I was nineteen that year, and Americans were just waking up to the fact that Herberg's book had documented a monolithic moment of Christendom's cultural, not its permanent, status. Somewhere during that "summer of love" an understanding of our new pluralism was born amidst the race riots and the antiwar protests and the general rejection of religion's restraints. I raise memory of this cultural moment because there was a revolution brewing in homiletics as well, and some of its concerns were deeply tied to this era of turmoil. I was personally unaware of this homiletic revolt because I was out of country—in Southeast Asia at the behest of President Johnson—just a young Christian too busy trying to figure out how to believe in my country and still believe in God to be aware of changes in theology.

Yet the best philosophers and theologians of this era seem to have been able to listen to the questions rising up from this reversal of cultural commitments, had even seen its forces amassing far earlier. There was a growing recognition among good minds and young hearts that the old answers no longer worked. Something about the very way people accepted what counted as "facts" was also changing. In *The Uses of Argument* Stephen Toulmin had shifted reasoning's metaphor from the logic of mathematical certainty to the historical character of argument in jurisprudence. Thomas Kuhn had published *The Structure of Scientific Revolutions* in the first years of the 1960s. Peter Berger and Thomas Luckman published their groundbreaking study in the sociology of knowledge, *The Social Construction of Reality*, in 1967. This was followed a year later with Berger applying similar insights to the study of religion in *The Sacred Canopy*.[2]

2. Stephen Toulmin, *The Uses of Argument* (Cambridge: Cambridge University Press, 1958); Thomas S. Kuhn, *The Structure of Scientific Revolutions* (Chicago: University of Chicago Press, 1962); Peter Berger and Thomas Luckman, *The Social Construction of Reality: A Treatise in the*

With regard to homiletics Don Wardlaw writes that, with the erosion of biblical theology's notion of history, rationalist assumptions about objective revelation in Scripture had begun to collapse.

> By the mid-1960s the philosopher Paul Ricoeur was leading conversations in hermeneutics that focused on the way language functions in consciousness. Enlightenment notions about the static nature of words gave way to the tensive or dynamic actions of language. Scholars like Ernst Fuchs and Gerhard Ebeling spoke of language performing or intending meaning. Metaphor with its offspring—parable, simile, narrative, and myth—took on new importance in hermeneutics and biblical studies.[3]

When it comes to making use of the New Hermeneutic for a New Homiletic, David Randolph needs to be credited as a prescient theorist who fired the shot across the bow announcing an insurrection in homiletic theory. He grasped that sermons structured as theological arguments (e.g., "Faith: its power, its purpose, its promise") were not going to work in a generation that was rising up to say "No!" to the comfortable uniformity of a previous generation's religion. For Christianity to continue to speak its timely message, it would have to find a new voice. In fact, if there is anything that dates Randolph's book, *The Renewal of Preaching*, it is the contemporaneity and urgency of this concern with the events of 1969, the year of its publication. Given what Randolph has to say on the subject of identifying the concern as the first task of preaching, this only makes sense. On one hand the book is about a subject—the renewal of preaching—even as it is also embedded in the *eventfulness* of the cultural moment that gave rise to its concern. Randolph had organized *The Renewal of Preaching* around the affirmation that "[t]he genius of preaching as it is here understood is its *eventfulness*. What is

---

Sociology of Knowledge (Garden City, NY: Doubleday, 1966); and Peter L. Berger, *The Sacred Canopy: Elements of a Sociological Theory of Religion* (Garden City, NY: Doubleday, 1967).

3. Don Wardlaw, "Homiletics and Preaching in North America," in *Concise Encyclopedia of Preaching*, William H. Willimon and Richard Lischer, eds. (Louisville: Westminster/John Knox Press, 1995), 248.

crucial for homiletics is not so much what the sermon 'is' as what the sermon 'does.'"[4]

Gerhard Ebeling's New Hermeneutic provided Randolph with a theological means to rescue homiletics from its exile and captivity in argument theory and restore it to its central place as the fruition of theology properly conceived. In the three decades since Randolph's original proposal, the shape of the new paradigm in preaching has become well defined. It represents a radical shift away from the rationalistic and propositional logics of argumentation and advocacy as the basis of sermon invention and arrangement. A variety of new compositional strategies have been offered as alternatives that give serious attention to what occurs in the event of preaching, especially in shaping the affective experience of the sermon for listeners, focusing on what the sermon does for them. Turning from traditional assumptions of argument in homiletics, preaching in the Sage Voice came to embrace more indirect logics of reasoning rooted in the poetics of metaphor, story, parable, and narrative indirection.

In this chapter I explore the implications of the Sage Voice that continues the presumption of the priority of preaching appeals made to individuals. My interest here will be to explore how this kind of appeal assists individuals in their narrative quest for personal *meaning* rather than their personal desire to experience God/Spirit/grace/the holy. I also examine the assumption of an interpretivist orientation to the nature of language appeals characterized by preaching that is nourished more by faith's questions than by its answers. I wish to trace the intellectual currents that foster a homiletic more interested in what the sermon may do and even undo, in the *experience* of the receiving audience, than in the pointed content of the truths it conveys.[5] Following this

4. David James Randolph, *The Renewal of Preaching* (Philadelphia: Fortress Press, 1969), vii. Portions of the introduction to this chapter are an adaptation of "An Introduction to the Reissue of *The Renewal of Preaching*," which David invited me to supply for *The Renewal of Preaching in the Twenty-first Century* (Babylon, NY: Hanging Gardens Press, 1998), i–xii.

5. This was the essence of the argument that Bullock, Fleer, and I made in our essay that sought to identify the productive unity characterizing the approaches to preaching that had come to be called the New Homiletic; see Robert S. Reid, Jeffrey Bullock, and David Fleer, "Preaching

I will unpack the assumptions of the contemporary expression of the Sage Voice, its continuum of practice as expressed in the writings of contemporary theorists, and, finally, look at an exemplar of good sermonic practice employing this voice.

The Interpretivist Orientation in Preaching

We currently have a plethora of "posts": post-liberal, post-structuralism, post-Marxism, post-literate, post-industrial, post-Christendom. Of the lot, the concept of the postmodern appears to traverse more disciplines and, for this reason, appears to be the designation that has emerged, for better or worse, as the broadly accepted covering term of the emergent cultural consciousness. What is common among all of these theoretical assessments is a similar prefix and suffix corralling a specific descriptor. In this case the descriptor, modernism, represents a fusion of Descartes's, Bacon's, and Locke's projects that represent a commitment to the primacy of method, the domination of nature, and the sovereignty of the individual (the latter is discussed in the previous chapter). That POSTmodernISM has an ISM, like its predecessor, modernISM, simply suggests that it purportedly represents some agreed upon system of ideas, even if the agreement is only in critique. The prefix POST, as Brian McHale suggests, is better understood to suggest the notion of historical consequence rather than some kind of temporal posteriority.[6] If it meant nothing more than historical succession, it could as readily mean something like after-modernism, new and improved modernism, or even modern-er modernism.[7] The notion of historical consequence assumes that some kind of shift or divide has occurred that changes the underlying philosophical presuppositions of the dominant way of understanding the middle term. And it is this

as the Creation of an Experience: The Not-So-Rational Revolution of the New Homiletic," *The Journal of Communication and Religion* 18, 1 (1995): 1–9.

6. Brian McHale, *Postmodernist Fiction* (New York: Methuen, 1987), 5.

7. See Christine Brooke-Rose, *A Rhetoric of the Unreal: Studies in Narrative and Structure, Especially of the Fantastic* (Cambridge: Cambridge University Press, 1981), 345.

divide that is at the heart of the tension I identify as the concern over the Nature of Language Appeals in my proposal of a Matrix of Contemporary Christian Voices.

Notice that I say it represents a tension concerning the assumptions about the Nature of Language Appeals rather than a tension about the Nature of Truth Appeals. The postmodern has shifted questions of truth to prior questions about the relationship between the function of language and human conceptions of truth. One need not look far to see popular postmodern discussions of contemporary disillusionments with the cultural systems that contain and constrain us.[8]

As in the last chapter, a set of existential questions helps draw out the implications of this distinction. We might say that modernist understanding came to be dominated by epistemological concerns, with questions like, "How can I interpret this world of which I am a part? And what am I in it? What is there to be known, who knows it, and how do they know it? How certain is this knowledge, how reliable is its transmission, and what are its limits?" Postmodernist understanding, on the other hand, foregrounds a different set of concerns that have arisen as a *consequence* of questioning the epistemological assumptions behind the modernist questions (i.e., the lack of distinction between subject and object, etc.). Instead of asking questions of how we know what we know, it asks prior ontological questions about the relationship of the knower to the process of understanding itself: "What is a world? What kinds of worlds are there? And which world is this? How are worlds constituted by my talk, by the talk I hear, and the discourse I read? How am I ordering the world I project when I use language? What is to be done in such worlds? Which of my selves is to do it?"[9]

8. For example, the dialogues *qua* novels of Brian McLaren, *A New Kind of Christian: Tales of Two Friends on a Spiritual Journey* (San Francisco: Jossey-Bass, 1999) and *The Story We Find Ourselves In: Further Adventures of a New Kind of Christian* (San Francisco: Jossey-Bass, 2001). I have argued elsewhere that popular evidence of the emerging postmodern culture and postmodern sensibilities is readily found among parishioners; Robert S. Reid, "Postmodernism and the Function of the New Homiletic in Post-Christendom Congregations," *Homiletic* XX, 2 (Winter 1995): 1–13.

9. Adapted from McHale, *Postmodernist Fiction*, 9–10.

For those who have yet to make the jump over this language divide it may help to pause and reflect on the hermeneutic complexity of our own use of language as we preach. As a motive for speaking, what I have called the Teaching Voice has always been an important way of teaching gospel truth. But it would be naïve for someone talking about teaching or preaching today to assume that the person speaking is telling the truth as if what they are saying can be self-evidently established as facts. We do not simply inject ideas about truth into another through speech. Contemporary communication theory would quickly disabuse anyone of the notion that the process of communication could be this simple.

According to I. A. Richards, who was writing during the second quarter of the twentieth century, whenever people talk to others they have to juggle four different verbal tasks with every word they speak. They must communicate the *sense* of the word, how they *feel* about the word, what their *attitude* is about the audience's need to care about the word, and what implied *outcome* they desire from the audience who heard this word. You might think this is rather a heavy load to be carried by each word a person speaks. Then you realize that there are some words that readily work this way: "Fire!" "Stop!" "No." So Richards wants us to ponder the question, "What if the fine distinctions we put into giving voice to words like these are also in play with every other word we say?" Words like "what," "if," "the," "fine," "distinctions," "we"—well, you get the idea. When you think about it, you already knew that humans are incredibly adept at following even the slightest nuance in shades of meaning speakers give to words. This is why the best preachers work so hard at crafting just the right words and just the right way of conveying these words as they prepare their sermons.

Three hundred years before Jesus, Aristotle argued that all communication is an interplay between:

- the formative intentions of our arguments (*logos*),
- our belief in the one speaking (*ethos*),
- our passions (*pathos*), and

- what we wish to accomplish with the way we use these "means of persuasion" (*speech objective*).[10]

If you read closely you can see that Richards's concern for the *sense, feel, attitude,* and *expected outcome* of each word spoken noted above is simply dressed-up Aristotle for a new era. But then Richards adds to this model by suggesting seven tasks listeners must engage in order to make sense of what is said. He argues that for listeners to comprehend a speaker's words, what is communicated must be experienced as:

- *indicating* a focus of attention,
- *characterizing* the quality of this focus,
- conveying the implications of how the words should be *realized*,
- implying a positive or negative *valuation* of the words,
- suggesting whether the words are meant to *influence* the listener,
- *controlling* the interplay of these various intentions, and
- *purposing* the appropriate choice of words to achieve the specific intention for speaking.[11]

If we do the math, these are four speaking tasks that interact with seven listener tasks just to depict what happens with any specific

10. On the *speech objective* Aristotle writes, "The species of rhetoric are three in number; for such is the number [of classes] to which the hearers of speeches belong. A speech [situation] consists of three things: a speaker [relates to *ethos*] and a subject on which he speaks [relates to *logos*] and someone addressed [relates to *pathos*], and the objective of the speech relates to the last (I mean the hearer). Now it is necessary for the hearer to be either a spectator or a judge, and [in the latter case] a judge of either past or future happenings." Aristotle's *Rhetoric* 1.3.1–4; 1358b, Kennedy's translation. Bracketed comments on *ethos, pathos,* and *logos* are mine; other bracketed translation elaborations are Kennedy's. George A. Kennedy, *Aristotle on Rhetoric: A Theory of Civic Discourse, Newly Translated, with Introduction, Notes, and Appendices* (New York: Oxford University Press, 1991).

11. Richards developed these ideas across his career. For a clear discussion of this model see Keith Jensen, "I. A. Richards and His Models," *Southern Speech Communication Journal* 37 (Spring 1972): 304–12, and I. A. Richards, *The Philosophy of Rhetoric* (1936; New York: Oxford University Press, 1965).

word spoken. Multiply this by all the words communicated in a verbal interaction, add the additional mediating features from the standard message transmission model of encoding and decoding messages (e.g., noise, feedback, etc.) and we become amazed anyone ever understands anything that gets said.

A more recent definition describes communication as "a continuous, complex, collaborative process of verbal and nonverbal meaning-making."[12] This definition assumes that all the negotiations listed above matter but argues that humans live in language that is also shaped by our cultural assumptions and the various identities we adopt in different contexts. Instead of viewing communication by the default *hypodermic syringe* model of injecting ideas into listeners, or the interactive *billiards* model of the complex sender-receiver model of communication, this definition adopts a nonlinear perspective that understands communicative negotiations more like a *soup.* Since we all live in language, communicating occurs in a *language soup.* Only a television-style CSI technician could ever dream of isolating all the elements that affect the way individuals construct meaning from what gets said and what is heard. Acceptance that people live in *language soup* is acceptance of Heidegger's claim that "language is the house of being" and Gadamer's claim that "being that can be understood is language."[13] This is the shift in understanding human acts of communication from epistemologically linear ways of trying to provide an account disclosure of being to the more storied ways of ontology's relocation of human meaning in the *experience* of language.

When we preach, we must first understand the text before we can hope to have a congregation understand what we wish to

12. See John Stewart, Karen E. Zediker, and Saskia Witteborn, *Together: Communicating Interpersonally—A Social Construction Approach* (Los Angeles: Roxbury, 2005), 23.

13. Martin Heidegger, *On the Way to Language*, Peter D. Hertz and J. Stambaugh, trans. (San Francisco: HarperSanFrancisco, 1982); Hans-Georg Gadamer, *Truth and Method*, 2d rev. ed., J. Weinsheimer and D. G. Marshall, trans. (New York: Crossroad, 1991), 474. On the soup metaphor see John Stewart, ed., *Bridges Not Walls: A Book about Interpersonal Communication*, 8th ed., (Dubuque, IA: McGraw Hill, 2002), 123–24.

communicate about its meaning and implications. This undertaking of *understanding* involves the interpreter's ability, first, to personally take up the structuring that is performed by the text, and then to express this in a performance that is aligned with this purpose for modern listeners. For Paul Ricoeur, the theologian who shaped so much of this hermeneutic turn to language for theologians in the 1970s, the interpreter's task is to find the questions to which the text offers an answer, to reconstruct its symbolic and cultural codes by attempting to reconstruct the expectations of the text's implied receivers, and to accept that such an inquiry can be conducted only within the constraints of the world of questions and expectations that the modern reader brings to the text.[14] Thus, for an interpreter of texts influenced by Ricoeur, "[t]he merely historicizing question—what did the text say?—remains under the control of the properly hermeneutical question—what does the text say to me and what do I say to the text?"[15]

Notice how this view of interpretation treats coming-to-understanding as an experience one undergoes rather than the more static notion of interpretation as something provided by another for you. This distinction is central to the phenomenological preference of ambiguity over assuredness in preaching. Martin Heidegger states the idea clearly:

> To undergo an experience with something—be it a thing, a person, or a god—means that this something befalls us, strikes us, comes over us, overwhelms or transforms us. When we talk of "undergoing" an experience, we mean specifically that the experience is not of our own making; to undergo here means that we endure it, suffer it, receive it as it strikes us and submit to it. It is this something itself that comes about, comes to pass, happens. To undergo an experience with language, then, means to let ourselves be properly concerned by the claim of language, by entering into and submitting to it.[16]

14. Paul Ricoeur, *Time and Narrative*, 3 vols., Kathleen McLaughlin (Blamey) and David Pellauer, trans. (Chicago and London: University of Chicago Press, 1984–88), III:174.

15. Ibid., III:175.

16. Heidegger, *On the Way*, 57.

In the original German of his text, Heidegger's argument implicitly contrasts this view of experience as the difference between *erlibnis* and *erfahrung*. *Erlibnis* refers to an experience one *has*—a word that assumes the difference between a knowing subject and the object of its perception typical of representational ways of thinking. *Erfahrung* refers to an experience one *undergoes*—an expression that views meaning as a participative event of coming-to-understanding. In other words, Heidegger is arguing that to experience something means to reach for something by going its way. To undergo an experience with something means that in order to attain something we meet we must let its appeal to us do something to us, transforming us into what it is, transforming us into itself.[17] This is the conception of language as performing or intending that was taken up into the theology of the New Hermeneutic of Fuchs and Ebeling.

This shift from representational explanations of meaning to explanations of meaning as a process of coming-to-understanding has placed the nature of language appeals at the center of contemporary philosophy and is having a powerful influence on how we think about and interpret the Scripture we preach. Sandra Schneiders succinctly summarizes the implications of this approach to interpretation by noting:

> Scholars are coming to realize that the locus of revelation for the contemporary Christian is not the events behind the texts, nor the theology of the biblical authors, nor even the preaching of the texts in community, but the texts themselves as language that involves the reader. The focus of interest is not so much on what produced the biblical texts as on what the texts, when fully engaged, produce in the reader. Thus, the positivistic objectification of the text which resulted inexorably in the dilemma of the subject-object paradigm of understanding by analysis has begun to give way to a hermeneutical paradigm of understanding by participative dialogue. Interpretation, in other words, is not a matter either of dominating the texts by method or by submit-

17. Ibid., 73–74. On the distinction between *erlibnis* and *erfahrung* see the translator's preface in Gadamar, *Truth and Method*, xiii–xiv.

> ting to the text in servile fideism, but of entering into genuine dialogue with it as it stands. Through this dialogue reader and text are mutually transformed. The reader is transformed not by capitulation but by conversion; the text is transformed not by dissection but through multiple interpretations to which it gives rise by its surplus of meaning, but which can only be actualized by successive generations of readers whose interpretations enrich the texts themselves.[18]

From this perspective traditional exegesis has about it a modernist lust for certainty that emulates the scientific, while interpretivist "dialogue with a text" would be more interested in readings in front of the text than in excavations to get at what is beneath it.

What would this look like? Dialogic interpretation of a text would begin by affirming the necessity of considering the way in which a text has been interpretively and theologically received by a variety of living communities across the centuries. This means that dialogic exegetes choose to attend to interpretations that the original author(s) could not have anticipated, after-the-fact meanings that are amplified, and innovative readings that emerge out of expectations of interpretive communities. For example, New Testament readings of Old Testament texts represent clear instances in the trajectory of this practice as they take up the interpretation of previous sacred texts as a tradition of meaning relevant for their own living community. This approach suggests that there is an irreducible plurivocity possible in interpreting biblical texts rather than accepting a single, standard univocal effort to get at authorial intention. The latter, according to Ricoeur and André LaCocque, cuts the text off from its ties to a living community such that "the text gets reduced to a cadaver handed over for autopsy."[19]

18. Sandra M. Schneiders, "Does the Bible Have a Postmodern Message?" in *Postmodern Theology: Christian Faith in a Pluralist World*, Frederic Burnham, ed. (San Francisco: HarperSanFrancisco, 1989), 61–62.

19. André LaCocque and Paul Ricoeur, *Thinking Biblically: Exegetical and Hermeneutical Studies*, David Pellauer, trans. (Chicago: University of Chicago Press, 1998), xii. Not all Sage Voice homileticians would embrace the idea that the plurivocity of the text and the plurivocity of dialogic readings should be accepted to this degree. It many ways it represents a perspective

The hermeneutic phenomenology of Paul Ricoeur (and Hans-Georg Gadamer) explores the role of presuppositions in the process of understanding and provides an explanation of how assumptions that audiences bring to engaging discourse effects their *experience* of its meaning. For Ricoeur, "Language is not a world of its own. It is not even a world. But because we are in the world, because we are affected by situations, and because we orient ourselves comprehensively in those situations, we have something to say, we have experience to bring to language."[20] Meaning, like experience, Ricoeur argues, is endlessly capable of new interpretations.

His project in the three-volume work *Time and Narrative* was to explore the question of whether a structure of temporal experience existed capable of integrating historical and fictional narrative. He concluded that these two narrative approaches make possible the connection between narrative identity and inquiry into the nature of language taken up into personal identity (and by extension into community identity). For Ricoeur, personal identity is only intelligible in the temporal dimension of human existence. Thus, the human conception of personal identity is primarily a narrative identity, because narrative provides the primary set of signs and symbols by means of which meaning is mediated and appropriated in human existence.[21] This is akin to the notion that being is disclosed through language and the "language soup" theory discussed above. Readability in narrative identity is conferred by means of the stories people tell about themselves—this because there is a pre-narrative quality of human experience by which personal identity becomes a function of "an activity and a desire in search of a narrative."[22] His conclusion

---

that assumes the development of doctrine more at home in a sacramental than traditional Reformed interpretive theology.

20. Paul Ricoeur, *Interpretation Theory: Discourse and the Surplus of Meaning* (Fort Worth: Texas Christian University Press, 1976), 20–21.

21. Ricoeur, *Time and Narrative*, III:244–49.

22. Paul Ricoeur, "Life: A Story in Search of a Narrator," in *Facts and Values: Philosophical Reflections from Western and Non-Western Perspectives*, Martin Nijhoff Philosophical Library, no. 19, M. C. Doeser and J. N. Kraay, eds., J. N. Kraay and A. J. Scholten, trans. (Dordrecht [Netherlands]: Martin Nijhoff, 1986), 129; emphasis his.

in this matter is aptly summarized in the title of a recent essay: "Life: A Story in Search of a Narrator."

In one of his most recent works, *Oneself as Another*, Ricoeur proposes that an individual conceives of the identity of the self as "the speaking, acting, character-narrator of its own history."[23] Selves refigure their lives continually by all the truthful or fictive stories they can imagine and speak.[24] In other words, the "self" of "self-knowledge" is a narratively situated subject, and for that reason Ricoeur rephrases Socrates' famous aphorism from the *Apology*: it is the *unnarrated* life that is not worth living.[25]

What matters in considering this leap into the narrative quality of experience, the hermeneutics of the self, and the phenomenological claim that being occurs in language, is to grasp that once this leap is made, a person shifts to viewing himself or herself more as someone always in process rather a fixed entity. In preaching oriented to this way of understanding personal identity, the listeners are invited to join the preacher on a journey in which they *undergo* an experience of coming-to-understanding together. Speaker and listener collaborate as they imagine a different way of being in the world and, having imagined it, discover that the encounter with this world has already taken them up into its possible world of meanings.

The Sage Voice in Preaching

The distinctive element of the Sage Voice is its assumption that the purpose of the sermon is to affirm truths directed to the person in a persuasively indeterminate fashion. Recall that the Matrix distinguishes preachers who speak with the voice of assuredness in a persuasively determinate manner from preachers

23. Paul Ricoeur, *Oneself as Another*, Kathleen Blamey, trans. (Chicago and London: University of Chicago Press, 1992), 291.

24. Ricoeur, *Time and Narrative*, III:246.

25. Ricoeur, "Life: A Story," 130; See also Ricoeur, *Time and Narrative*, III:247; and *Oneself as Another*, 178.

who relish the voice of ambiguity and speak in a persuasively indeterminate manner. Preaching in this voice invites listeners to ask, "Whoa! What will I do with that?" Or, "What will I make of that?" It does not presume to tell listeners what they should or ought to do with it. The resolution belongs to the listener. Sermons in this voice operate with interpretivist assumptions about the nature of reality and call forth an individualistic identity for listeners. In speaking in this more oblique manner, the preacher takes on the role of a Sage, whose concern is "to communicate with people who after the sermon is over will have to continue thinking their own thoughts, dealing with their own situations and being responsible for their own faith."[26] Fred Craddock notes that Walter Bruggemann says, "The power of the prophet is to bring up what God's people already know, turn it in their faces, maybe slightly like a prism, and they say, 'Whewww! Have we been saying we believe that?' Preaching not only makes deposits in the bank of the mind and hearts of the people, but it also writes checks on what's already there."[27] It is a journey-centered approach to preaching in which preachers see their own interpretive and homiletic task as attempting to perform *intentions* aligned with the argument strategies of a biblical text (see Figure 4.1).

Nature of Language Appeals

Persuasively Indeterminate Appeal

The Sage Voice
Expects: "Who! What will I do with/ make of that?"
Journey-Centered

Personal Truth Appeal

Nature of Authority Appeals

Figure 4.1: The Sage Voice

26. Fred B. Craddock, *As One without Authority: Revised and with New Sermons* (St. Louis: Chalice Press, 2001), 124. Originally, *As One without Authority: Essays on Inductive Preaching* (Enid, OK: Phillips University Press, 1st ed. 1971, 2d ed. 1974); 3d edition was Abingdon Press. The Chalice reprint includes gender-neutral revisions.

27. From the audiotape of a presentation at the Whitworth Institute, Spokane Washington, 1992. Compare similar ideas in Fred B. Craddock, *Preaching* (Nashville: Abingdon Press, 1985), 45, 160.

Both the Sage and the Testifying Voices share a basic social constructivist perspective that meaning is collaboratively arrived at as part of the "language event" of preaching. Language appeals become an interpretive grid through which this constructed world and worldview are shaped. Contemporary theorists who adopt the Sage Voice view the function of preaching as an opportunity for the listener to *experience* an event of coming-to-understanding—whether by way of response to appeals, by way of narrative resolution, by way of narrative image, or by way of circled indirection.[28] The nature of the authority appeals of the preacher in this approach resides with his or her credibility in communicating both a wrestling with the performative concern of the text and a concern aligned with this intention that invites listeners to imagine gospel-centered ways of being in the world today. If considered in terms of appeals negotiating the social-solidarity versus the personal transformation tension, we shall see that the Testifying Voice has a locus of external authority, while the Sage Voice, like the Encouraging Voice, makes its appeal to a locus of internal authority.

The Spectrum of Possibilities

Sage Voice approaches to preaching have often been called the New Homiletic or the New Homiletics, though this term has also been used to refer to some approaches I will treat as occurring in the Testifying Voice. I first heard the term New Homiletic in a presentation by Fred Craddock in Spokane, Washington, in the summer of 1992. It referred to the way Richard Eslinger had described Craddock's approach to preaching in *A New Hearing: Living Options in Homiletic Method*. Eslinger had classified the preaching methods of Charles Rice, Henry Mitchell, Eugene Lowry, and David Buttrick by this phrase. Eslinger had con-

28. Traditionally, Protestant liberal theology placed primary emphasis on the role of experience in understanding gospel, and its newer, more progressive theologies have placed emphasis on existential experience of narrative knowing. See Donald McKim, *The Bible in Theology and Preaching: How Preachers Use Scripture* (Nashville: Abingdon Press, 1994), 40–51, 100–14.

trasted several "new" approaches that were distinctly different from the "the old homiletic" of three points and a poem.[29] Of course David Randolph had already introduced the term two decades before drawing the language of the New Homiletic from the New Hermeneutic.[30] In either case, the phrase New Homiletic was slipping into discussions of homiletic method, as a comparative to the older, argument model of preaching. The two most salient features of the various homiletics that make up this voice are its concern for performative "concretion" of sermonic intention and its relocation of meaning in the narrative quality of experience rather than rational consideration of argument.

The Performative Concern

I was at the conference in Spokane to listen to Fred Craddock, whose book *As One without Authority: Essays on Inductive Preaching* had first galvanized this shift away from dependence on preaching centered in the rationalist deductive model of argument. Like Randolph, Craddock also made productive use of Ebeling's New Hermeneutic in his approach to preaching. What he originally called a process of inductive preaching tended to move the claim to the end of the presentation while arraying sermonic material that was more concrete and particular than abstract and argumentative. A decade after *As One without Authority*, he reconceived this process in *Overhearing the Gospel* as a process of indirection in preaching. It is an approach to preaching in which the theme or focus is indirectly developed by circling the subject rather than by aiming for it in a linear progression of argument points.[31]

29. Richard Eslinger, *A New Hearing: Living Options in Homiletical Method* (Nashville: Abingdon Press, 1987), 13–14.

30. The origin of New Homiletic as a formal phrase describing a movement within homiletics probably belongs to Thor Hall, who sought to expand Randolph's use of the term beyond an appropriation of the New Hermeneutics for preaching. See Thor Hall, *The Future Shape of Preaching* (Philadelphia: Fortress Press, 1971), xvii.

31. Fred B. Craddock, *Overhearing the Gospel: Preaching and Teaching the Faith to Persons Who Have Heard It All Before,* Lyman Beecher Lectures of 1978 (Nashville: Abingdon Press, 1978).

Craddock's first concern is to suggest that preachers speak in such a way that they help listeners *undergo* the same process of coming-to-understanding that the preacher traveled in her or his own journey in discovering the meaning of a text. His second reason for emphasizing this inverted reasoning process was to shift the responsibility for the sermon's conclusion to the listeners: "If they have made the trip, it is their conclusion and the implication for their own situations is not only clear but personally inescapable."[32] By circling around the concern of a text the preacher avoids a direct run at the insight, permitting the listeners to discover the power of what it is that they have said they believe all along, such that "what is *often* heard is *finally* heard."[33] The purpose of this kind of preaching, for Craddock, is to make the revelation of God present and appropriate to listeners. It is the proclamation of an event and a participation in it, simultaneously reporting on revelation while also participating in its unfinished task. The preacher reports with honesty but also with the immediacy that makes the ancient claims of the text alive to the present moment of the gathered listeners.[34]

In shifting the description of his method from inductive to indirection Craddock made use of Sören Kierkegaard's style of writing, which involved the reader in the choices that lead to the desirable conclusion. He discovered that Kierkegaard regarded direct communication as the appropriate mode for transferring information in fields like history, science, and related disciplines, while indirect communication was the preferred "mode of eliciting capability and action from within the listener, a transaction that does not occur by giving the hearers some information."[35] This is a process of permitting readers or listeners an *experience* of overhearing the speaker's own efforts to consider and reject possible understandings of meaning until a final insight is discovered.

32. Craddock, *Without Authority*, 48–49.

33. Craddock, *Preaching*, 47.

34. Ibid.

35. Craddock, *Overhearing*, 82. On Kierkegaardian indirection see Roger Poole, *Kierkegaard: The Indirect Communication.*, Studies in Religion and Culture (Charlottesville: University Press of Virginia, 1993).

All of this occurs while the listeners are on this same journey, making decisions at each juncture whether to collaborate with the speaker on the journey to possible destinations of this train of thought. In this sense, the experience of listening is the governing situation in the communicative event.[36] The various junctions and disjunctions of the sermon, as with Stanley Fish's image of a self-consuming artifact, become steps on a ladder that serve no other purpose than to provide a means to make the next step.[37] Thus, Craddock's progression of thought seems to move forward with tentative linkages,

> "It seems . . . but still . . ."
> "Of course . . . and yet . . ."
> "Both this . . . and this . . . yet in a larger sense . . ."
> "Certainly it isn't the case that . . . however . . . so perhaps . . ."
> "You have heard it said . . . but . . ."[38]

His most succinct statement of this process of sermon composition is in *Best Advice for Preaching*:

> I find it helpful to write in the center of a sheet of paper my theme or focus sentence. This is the message, distilled and drawn from study of the text. As Luther said, "First the flower, then the meadow." Then I circle this statement with related material drawn from related texts, theological reflection, news reports, observations, experience, congregational life, history, biography, general reading, and so on. Lines are drawn from these sketched pieces (to be fleshed out later) to the central message, like spokes in a wheel. Any material that does not connect with the message, no matter how good it seems, is eliminated from this sermon, but saved for another time. Next, I list these items in no particular order and begin the process of arranging them as they will appear in the sermon. I usually arrange and re-arrange four or five times.[39]

36. Ibid., 121.
37. Ibid., 130–32.
38. Craddock, *Without Authority*, 123.
39. Fred Craddock, *Best Advice for Preaching*, John S. McClure, ed. (Minneapolis: Fortress Press, 1998), 69.

Craddock's phenomenological interest in guiding listeners in creating their own event of meaning, combined with the implicit existential appeal of this approach, makes it an excellent example of what I refer to as preaching in the Sage Voice.[40]

This same existentialist appeal to the individual is characteristic of David Randolph's model of preaching in *The Renewal of Preaching*. Randolph challenged preachers to wrestle with the intention of the text in order to find a way to communicate a purpose analogously aligned with the text's *concern*. Following Ebeling, he argued that the goal of preaching "is not so much to understand the text as to understand *through* the text."[41] A text is not to be approached as an archeological excavation site to discover a theme, but as a speech event, "which discloses its meaning through its relationship to its context, to the faith, and to us."[42] Randolph presses the question, "What is the text doing?" in order to get preachers to discover the performative "to do" of the text and then attempt to preach a "to do" aligned with it.

Aside from identifying the text's *concern*, Randolph challenged preachers to think of a sermon based on a scriptural text in terms of its *confirmation(s)*, its *concretion*, its *construction*, and its style of *communication* in delivery. He rejects the approach to preaching that would dictate how parishioners should apply the message to their life this week: "There is no plan with any such claims to be found in Christian preaching, at least not where that preaching has found its greatest impact. For the goal of Christian preaching is not reconstruction but repentance."[43] Here is Randolph's clearest call for preachers to attend to the "to do" of what they hope will happen as a response to their preaching. The existential question for Randolph, and here he differs from Craddock, is for the preacher to determine what decisions, responses, or applications are called for by the sermon. Randolph's preacher must be very clear about this in the design of the sermon or nothing *concrete* will happen as a result of people listening to the message. It is

40. Craddock, *Overhearing*, 130.
41. Randolph, *Renewal*, 38.
42. Ibid., 49.
43. Ibid., 80.

this existential appeal, inviting a response of a seeking-oriented spirituality rather than a dwelling-centered spirituality, that identifies this as an approach oriented to the individual rather than inviting an affirmation of a tradition of faith.

The concern of both Craddock and Randolph to identify the performative "to do" of the text and identify a concern that aligns with it was echoed by other homileticians and theologians, such as Clyde Fant, Milton Crum, and Leander Keck.[44] In a highly influential book of essays from the early 1980s, *Preaching Biblically: Creating Sermons in the Shape of Scripture*, Don Wardlaw noted that the controlling question had become, "What does it mean for sermon form to embody and express God's word in Scripture?" He then posed the question, "If preaching intends to reenact in the lives of preacher and hearers the saving acts of God in Christ as witnessed in Scripture, how does the preacher shape the reenactment so that it approximates as closely as possible Scripture's reality?"[45] This concern for sermon intentions to be shaped by the performative concern of the text can be found among some theorists in all the voices, but it is perhaps the most salient feature of preaching in the Sage Voice.

The Narrative Concern

The second most common feature of preaching in this voice is its general concern with story and narrativity. Three trajectories are of interest here. The first is to note the narrative self-understanding of black preaching. The second is to note the general emergence of story preaching. The third is to consider how identifying the performative concern of Scripture led to preaching that plots a journey rather than structures an argument.

44. Clyde E. Fant Jr., *Preaching for Today* (New York: Harper and Row, 1975); Milton Crum Jr., *Manual on Preaching* (Valley Forge, PA: Judson Press, 1977); and Leander Keck, *The Bible in the Pulpit: The Renewal of Biblical Preaching* (Nashville: Abingdon Press, 1978).

45. Don M. Wardlaw, "Introduction: The Need for New Shapes," in *Preaching Biblically: Creating Sermons in the Shape of Scripture*, Don M. Wardlaw, ed. (Philadelphia: Westminster Press, 1983), 22.

Black congregations in North America believe that preachers need to be able to "tell the story," by which they mean "tell our story." Their historic and present experiences of oppression have created a deep identification with biblical liberation narratives such as the Exodus journey, stories of exile, and the New Testament's Gospel narratives that validate the dignity of the individual. Even the writings of Paul are often treated as an autobiography of struggle. As James Evans finds, "In the African-American religious community the Bible continues to be read as a unified text whose central thrust guides the interpretation of the individual parts." Scripture is never atomized to explain historical details when the story of struggle is so paramount, which is to say that "African-American Christians have generally refused to dismember the biblical text without first remembering the biblical story."[46] In this sense, they treat Scripture much as the early church did, taking it up to explain and give meaning to the story-shaped world of their present reality. This is an instance, in the language of Ricoeur, of interpreting meaning in front of the text rather than behind it.

David Buttrick observes that laughter plays a vital role in the way black congregations interpret the gospel. They laugh in the face of opposition because they know how the story ends. "Black congregations, socially denied, abused, and discriminated against, identify with a savior who was also put down and nailed up by people who were in charge of the world. But if Christ has been raised by the power of God, then oppressed believers will also be raised up—it's a sure thing!"[47] In community the true story resounds when the preacher is faithful in telling the story. This is why celebration is in order at the close of so much black preaching. When the preacher has guided listeners, without nailing down their expected response, through the journey from oppression, to freedom, to a celebration of the vision of

46. James H. Evans, *We Have Been Believers: An African-American Systematic Theology* (Minneapolis: Fortress Press, 1992), 45–46.

47. David G. Buttrick, "Laughing with the Gospel," in *Sharing Heaven's Music: The Heart of Christian Preaching, Essays in Honor of James Earl Massey*, Barry L. Callen, ed. (Nashville: Abingdon Press, 1995), 130.

God's new order already realized in the life of the congregation, then the preacher has served as a sage who interprets the way. In describing this black, story-shaped approach to interpretation of text, Henry Mitchell observes that "[w]hen Black preachers are most persuasive, they are apt to seem more to plead out of passion than to argue out of logic. They seek to guide the hearers in an experience, rather than overwhelm them with intellectual evidence."[48] Black preachers are more inclined to "probe the depths" than to make an argument. Hence, the Bible is more likely to be used as a homiletical sourcebook than the basis of doctrinal or ethical authority.

For Mitchell, preaching that calls forth faith makes its appeal to the intuitive and emotive consciousness of individuals because the intuitive realm is affected more directly by an *experiential* encounter.

> The term *experiential encounter* is used to denote a homiletical plan in which the aim is to offer direct or vicarious encounters with experiences of truths already certified as biblical, coherent, and relevant. Sermons are reasonable and relevant sequences of Biblical affirmations planted in or offered to the intuitive consciousness of hearers, by way of what may be called homiletical coworkers with the Spirit.[49]

This experiential dimension of black preaching is central to its expression in either its Encouraging Voice or Sage Voice expression. Of course black preaching also can make an appeal to communal order, but it tends to be an appeal to solidarity borne out of an identity as a people who share a specific American cultural experience, both specific and ongoing.[50] The struggle to overcome

48. Henry H. Mitchell, *Black Preaching: The Recovery of a Powerful Art* (reissued; New York: Harper and Row; Nashville: Abingdon Press, 1990), 114.

49. Henry H. Mitchell, *Celebration and Experience in Preaching* (Nashville: Abingdon Press, 1990), 25.

50. Cleophus LaRue argues that the heart of black preaching, that which shapes its primary characteristic, is its absolute belief in the all-powerful sovereign God, its sociocultural self-understanding of marginalization and struggle, and the attention of the black pulpit to five central domains through which black listeners historically have learned to process the gospel: personal

social and political marginalization has provided a unique context where preaching that would normally be dominated by intentions directed to individuals, and to their concern for personal transformation, can also take on communal concerns that speak to issues of justice and parity typical of the Testifying Voice. However, black preaching moves to the Testifying Voice only when its preaching reaches beyond the experiential claims of the refuge model, which focuses on a culturally distinct identity (discussed in the previous chapter) and invites listeners to inhabit a more decentered notion of Christian identity that is actively engaged in or responding to the new pluralism of contemporary religious culture.[51]

The theology that supports a more *narrative* understanding of identity both for black and for white preaching is the indicator of its expression in a Sage Voice. Story may have taken longer to assume center stage among white than among black homileticians, but academic discussion of its function in preaching developed in response to the emergence of narrative theology in the 1970s. Since the mid-1970s a number of theorists have urged preachers to develop the imaginative, aesthetic skills to become masterful storytellers as they preach, while others have been urging preachers to explore how image, metaphor, and musicality can unlock the literary-aesthetic qualities of the text through the power of a preacher's imagination.[52]

For example, Thomas Troeger challenges preachers to develop an image grid that translates idea-centered preaching into scene-

---

piety, care of the soul, social justice, corporate faith concerns, and institutional congregational concerns. See Cleophus J. LaRue, *The Heart of Black Preaching* (Louisville: Westminster/John Knox Press, 2000), 126.

51. See the significant analysis of narrative in black preaching by Richard L. Eslinger, *The Web of Preaching: New Options in Homiletic Method* (Nashville: Abingdon Press, 2002), 103–50.

52. Thomas E. Boomershine, *Story Journey: An Invitation to the Gospel as Storytelling* (Nashville: Abingdon Press, 1988). William J. Bausch, *Storytelling: Imagination and Faith* (Mystic, CT: Twenty-Third Publications, 1984); Bausch, *Yellow Brick Road: A Storyteller's Approach to the Spiritual Journey* (Mystic, CT: Twenty-Third Publications, 1999); Bausch, *In the Beginning, There Were Stories: Thoughts about the Oral Tradition of the Bible* (Mystic, CT: Twenty-Third Publications, 2004). For a useful summary of the emergence of narrative theology and black theology and their influence on homiletics, see McKim, *The Bible*, 125–36, 150–58.

centered stories to be telecast to listeners. [53] For Troeger, as for many preachers in the Sage Voice, the task of preaching is to help listeners discover gospel realities in the pattern of meaning in their lives:

> Throughout our lives we keep looking for a pattern, a meaning that flashes now and then into sight but finally keeps eluding us. We assume that our experience is parabolic, that it will illume our ambiguities, that what has already happened holds the clue to what will happen or might happen or ought to happen if only we knew the right way to act.

This kind of preaching provides direction to the ambiguity listeners experience by helping them discover how the various convolutions of their lives actually form into a pattern of meaning.[54] Patricia Wilson-Kastner writes,

> Narrative-centered preaching centers on a fundamental biblical reality: God's self-revelation is not given to us through abstract propositions of systematic theology, but through the story of God's relationship with human beings in their history. All theology is reflection on this story and our participation in it. Therefore, effective preaching is narrative preaching (storytelling) sharing in the medium and the message of biblical revelation. Narrative preaching of course concerns itself primarily with plot—the sequence of events as arranged by the author—and characters, motivations, and conflicts.[55]

By the mid-eighties, story approaches to preaching were hailed by many "as the most appropriate mode for the discovery of the self and the experience of God" in preaching.[56] Perhaps the

53. Thomas H. Troeger, *Imagining a Sermon* (Nashville: Abingdon Press, 1990), 39–47; see also Paul Wilson, *The Four Pages of Preaching: A Guide to Biblical Preaching* (Nashville: Abingdon Press, 1999), 82–88, who employs the metaphor of filming the moves of a sermon as a director imagines the scenes of a film. See also Thomas H. Troeger, *Ten Strategies for Preaching in a Multimedia Culture* (Nashville: Abingdon Press, 1996).

54. Troeger, *Imagining a Sermon*, 90.

55. Patricia Wilson-Kastner, *Imagery for Preaching* (Minneapolis: Fortress Press, 1989), 12.

56. Richard Lischer, "The Limits of Story," *Interpretation* 38 (1984): 26.

most formative presentation of this argument was articulated by Steimle, Niedenthal, and Rice.[57] They argued that most existing models of preaching are partial views that tend to invite practitioners to see themselves as "a charismatic personality, or as an omni-competent healer of hurts, or as a chief executive officer of a well-run religious corporation, or as the guardian of the pure doctrine whose mere repetition assists, if it does not finally push, its listeners into salvation." Instead of preacher-centered, need-centered, institutionally centered, or content-centered models of preaching, they argued for the image of preacher as storyteller of shared story and of the Story.[58]

More recently, Rice has examined how parable functions as the exemplar of Jesus' own ability to communicate the truth of gospel as story. He claims that speaking in parable is story that is human-centered, realistic speech that can eloquently embody a prophetic point with which listeners can identify. He argues for preaching that offers a parabolic everyday story that says something larger and, like "the classic," speaks to the essential human condition. For Rice, the homily is an expression of both art and liturgy, the fruition of which is best realized when the sermon's story finds its realization in the grace offered in the Eucharist.[59]

Where many who preach in the Sage Voice focus on image, story, and parable, Eugene Lowry has been the theorist most concerned with preaching as a narrative art. He argues for understanding "sermon time" as an ordering of experience rather than ideas, a focusing of events rather than a theme, a following of a plot rather than an outline, with a goal that listeners undergo an experience—where something happens—rather than merely understand what the speaker means.[60] Propositional preaching, he

57. Edmund Steimle, Morris J. Niedenthal, and Charles L. Rice, *Preaching the Story* (Philadelphia: Fortress Press, 1980); see also Richard A. Jensen, *Telling the Story* (Minneapolis: Augsburg, 1980); George M. Bass, *The Song and the Story* (Lima, OH: CSS Publishing, 1984).

58. Steimle et al., *Preaching the Story*, 1–16.

59. Charles L. Rice, *The Embodied Word: Preaching as Art and Liturgy* (Minneapolis: Fortress Press, 1991).

60. Eugene L. Lowry, *Doing Time in the Pulpit: The Relationship between Narrative and Preaching* (Nashville: Abingdon Press, 1985), 27.

maintains, presents reductionist versions of truth, while narrative truth, like a poem, is never reducible to just one thing. Propositional sermons order ideas spatially, while imaging a sermon narratively orders experience temporally: "Ideas seldom have the power to supplant time; a story seldom fails."[61] Narrative preaching may tell a story, but is better understood as a sequencing of sermon material that follows the form of a plot rather than a systematic development of ideas.

Lowry, perhaps more than any other theorist in this voice, treats form as the primary issue at stake, because "[w]hat identifies the usual narrative sermon most readily is its plot form, which always—one way or another—begins with a felt *discrepancy* or conflict, and then makes its way through *complication* (things always get worse), makes a decisively sharp turn or *reversal*, and then moves finally toward *resolution* or closure."[62] Like Rice, he argues that parable is the essential model of story in Scripture and suggests at least four different models of narrative form in preaching the parable.[63] In "running the story" the preacher lets the form and flow of the parable's story control the form and flow of the sermon's design. In "delaying the story" the preacher delays engagement with the biblical story until a context for its insight has been created. In "suspending the story" the preacher acknowledges a hard or troublesome concern raised by the parable that must be examined from some other perspective—whether by flashback, flash-forward, or flash-out—before returning to the rhythm of the parable's story for its resolution. In "alternating the story" the preacher runs the story of the parable, following its form and flow, but alternates this with a second story or exploration of a concern whose rhythm can also follow the form and flow of the parable. This is not an exhaustive list of narrative sermonic design, but much like Craddock's circling model,

61. Ibid., 13.

62. Eugene L. Lowry, *The Sermon: Dancing the Edge of Mystery* (Nashville: Abingdon Press, 1997), 23. See also Lowry, *The Homiletical Plot: The Sermon as Narrative Art Form*, exp. ed. (St. Louis: Westminster/John Knox, 2001).

63. Eugene L. Lowry, *How to Preach a Parable: Designs for Narrative Sermons* (Nashville: Abingdon Press, 1989).

these strategies all share a vision of strategic delay in arriving at homiletic insight, delay that permits listeners to join the preacher on the puzzle that is the sermon journey.

The implicit appeal of such a sermon focuses on the ability of listeners to *undergo* a psychological *gestalt* in which they are suddenly able to see a new reality different from a prior understanding. Rather than nailing down meaning or what is to be appropriated, sermons in the Sage Voice invite listeners on a journey of discovery into the possible meanings of the biblical text. Those who listen to Sage preachers are invited to find themselves in the Scripture text performed in the sermon and to explore how their appropriation, their understanding, their insight of meaning permits them to participate in the continued meaning of the text in their own lives.

Excellence in the Sage Voice

What distinguishes the tenor of the Sage Voice is the way in which it makes its appeal to the individual on a journey of faith. It is the existential emphasis of the phenomenological tradition and its New Hermeneutic and the earlier works of Ricoeur's philosophical hermeneutics that identifies the concerns of this voice. The Sage preacher takes listeners along a carefully chosen pathway to the top of a hill and then points to multiple pathways for them to choose to continue the trip. The Sage brings seekers far enough to see possible futures that further the story, but the choice is the seeker's to make the rest of the journey their own. Lack of excellence in this voice occurs when the preacher fails to invite listeners to take a worthwhile gospel journey. When preaching goes awry in this voice it is often too caught up in a human story that is insufficiently a gospel story, or it may confuse the insight of the humanistic classic with the insight of gospel. Three such cautions are worth noting.

First, Richard Thulin argues for the place of "personal story as a vehicle for Christian proclamation" *if used with care*. For Thulin no sermon can ever be preached authentically unless the preacher has found the connection between her or his own world and the world of the text and/or theological issue. Thulin identifies three areas of potential sermonic abuse of the personal story.

1. *Narcissism*: a proclamation of self rather than Christ;
2. *Privatism*: an idiosyncratic use of self in which no generalized identification with listeners is possible; and
3. *Isolationism*: where there is a complete disconnect between the purpose of the sermon and the purpose of the story.[64]

All are examples of an *egoist* at work. Thulin warns against autobiographical preaching for aesthetic ends. It is not enough for it to be a good story that illustrates the point. When offered, autobiographical stories in sermons need to be vehicles that reveal the shape of the gospel, through which the truth or discovery of the truth of the gospel shines.[65]

Second, though excellent work has been done to describe how preachers can identify the performative dimensions of various biblical literatures (e.g., parables, aphorisms, pronouncement stories, miracles stories, lengthy speeches, historical narratives, parenthetic exhortation, admonition, poetry and hymns, and apocalyptic), the shift to narrative and story-centered preaching has resulted in a significant shift away from preaching Pauline argument.[66] A variety of factors have contributed to this phenomenon. For example, the widespread adoption of the common lectionary in the early 1980s organized around Gospel readings has tended to privilege preaching the Gospel stories rather than the correlated Hebrew Scripture texts, the epistle texts, or the Psalm texts. Other factors, such as shorter sermon length and the increasing biblical illiteracy of listeners, may be factors. Add to this the difficulty for modern

64. Richard Thulin, *The "I" of the Sermon: Autobiography in the Sermon,* Fortress Resources for Preaching (Minneapolis: Fortress Press, 1989), 9.

65. Ibid., 41–42

66. See Mike Graves, *The Sermon as Symphony: Preaching the Literary Forms of the New Testament* (Valley Forge, PA: Judson Press, 1997); Thomas G. Long, *Preaching and the Literary Forms of the Bible* (Philadelphia: Fortress Press, 1989).

listeners to follow epistolary argumentation, and the cumulative effect has been a loss of Paul's message in contemporary preaching. The primacy of Gospel narrative *because* it is narrative has effectively fostered a new canon within a canon that marginalizes texts that make argument rather than tell a story.

The effect, according to James Thompson, has been to relegate twenty-one of the twenty-seven New Testament books to a virtual tertiary status in the canon. Several of Thompson's concerns are relevant to this point:

- "Much of the literature of the new homiletics treats narrative as the primary, if not the only, mode of discourse for preaching, in practice ignoring the revelatory significance of other biblical genres.
- "Narrative preaching is reluctant to speak with authority or to make concrete demands for change in the listeners' lives.
- "Preaching as rational persuasion is not an alien intrusion into a mode of communication that was originally narrative in nature."[67]

Of course homileticians would note that Thompson may have confused story preaching with narrative preaching in this argument. Narrative preaching identifies the performative concern of a text, regardless of its genre, and seeks to preach a concern aligned with this intention. Its purpose is to assist listeners to experience meaning as a process of coming-to-understanding rather than to make points seeking listeners' assent. Thus, good preachers can use narrative approaches to preach the epistles. However, Thompson is probably correct in diagnosing what is happening in actual practice: unfortunately, clergy often find it is simply easier to preach the story of Jesus or one of the patriarchal narratives than to figure out how to narratively perform the concern of epistolary argument.

67. James W. Thompson, *Preaching Like Paul: Homiletical Wisdom for Today* (Louisville: Westminster/John Knox Press, 2001), 9–14.

If a preacher asks, "What is this text doing?" and the answer is, "Making concrete demands for change in the listeners' lives," then this is the performative claim the preacher must help listeners experience. Preaching in the Sage Voice should not avoid the fact that texts may have persuasive claims. Nor should preaching in the Sage Voice treat biblical argument as if it must be preached in a voice of assuredness and is therefore alien to the preacher's preference for ambiguity. The challenge is to reclaim the performative power of the epistolary literature and its argument and invite listeners to explore possible meanings of the text without offering a definitive interpretation of what the listener *should* or *must* do.[68]

Third, in *Sharing the Word: Preaching in the Roundtable Church*, Lucy Rose asks, "Will preachers who seek to perform texts, create new realities, or transform the worshipper be honest that their presentations of texts, new realities, and gospel values, worldviews or ways of being in the world are constructs reflecting their own biases?"[69] Rose challenges that, too often, those who operate with the cultural assumptions of what I call the Sage Voice can become confused, conflating their own convictions as the best convictions without recognizing that they reflect their own biases. When this occurs, preachers are inviting parishioners to join them on a journey of insight that reveals wisdom that is more about a person's sagacity than a participative coming-to-understanding. Rose is wary of the persuasive character and the performative dimension of language because of its ability to mount implicit hierarchies that empower some and disempower others. Behind her concern is a strong rejection of the role of persuasion in preaching not shared by all who, like her, take up the Testifying Voice. On the other hand her concern clarifies a question of excellence in the

68. A helpful guide in this quest is Nancy Lammers Gross's *If You Cannot Preach Like Paul* (Grand Rapids: Eerdmans, 2002). The shift of some homileticians to the Testifying Voice offers promise to redress some of this problem inherent to practice in lectionary preaching. An excellent example of theological inquiry with significant implications for preaching is Douglas Harink, *Paul among the Postliberals: Pauline Theology beyond Christendom and Modernity* (Grand Rapids: Brazos Press, 2003).

69. Lucy Atkinson Rose, *Sharing the Word: Preaching in the Roundtable Church* (Louisville: Westminster/John Knox Press, 1997), 110.

Sage Voice. Sage preachers should never avoid the fact that they are charting the majority of the journey they invite seekers to take. They have defined the parameters of meaningful appropriation even if they have not "nailed it down." Excellence in Sage Voice preaching acknowledges the role of persuasion in structuring the path of a sermon and is always careful to insure that the parameters of its journey are consonant with the gospel and that the sermon does not dominate the listener's final response.

Patterns of preaching that by design lend themselves to the Sage Voice include:

- Sermon as Plot, Whether "From Oops! to Yeah!" or "Sermon by Circled Indirection;"
- Sermons Imaging the Story (as per Troeger and Wilson-Kastner);
- Verse by Verse Exploration of Possibilities;
- Sermon as Personal Narrative; and
- Sermons Primarily Structured by the Performative Movement of the Text.

These strategies of sermon composition do not assume an objectivist orientation to reality and tend to point the way to possible meanings without naming specific implications of meaning listeners should appropriate from the text.

The intention of this kind of preaching is to invite listeners on a journey of self-discovery. Its purpose is to provide listeners with the resources for critical reflection. Sermons in this voice would have listeners respond by saying, "Whoa! What am I going to do with that?" or "What I am going to do about that?" The preacher is the sage who guides them on the pathway, inviting listeners to choose the doorways of their future. The preacher may speak as a prophet within the tradition in question, but it is the listener who must answer the question as to what to do with the understanding achieved as a result of listening to the sermon. A theology or a tradition of teaching may stand behind the preacher's understanding of the text, but this is subordinated to the task of persuasively shaping the sermon in ways that invite individual listeners to consider change that can come through an experience of coming-to-understanding.

A Sample Sermon

As noted above, in *How to Preach a Parable: Designs for Narrative Sermons*, Eugene Lowry suggests that there are four ways narrative preachers tend to approach preaching a sermon: (1) running the story, (2) delaying the story, (3) suspending the story, and (4) alternating the story. The sermon included here as a sample of the Sage Voice is from Barbara Brown Taylor's collection *Home by Another Way* and is an excellent example of what Lowry calls "alternating the story."[70]

Bothering God
Luke 18:1-8
Barbara Brown Taylor

At first reading, Jesus' story about the persistent widow and the unjust judge is one of the funniest in the Christian canon. The humor dissipates, however, with his suggestion that it is a story about prayer. Apparently we too are supposed to make pests of ourselves, in hopes God will respond to us if only to shut us up.

In Luke's Gospel the parable follows right on the heels of Jesus' very scary story about the end of the age. "I tell you," he says to his disciples, "on that night there will be two in one bed; one will be taken and the other left. There will be two women grinding meal together; one will be taken and the other left." Then his disciples ask him, "Where, Lord?" And he says to them, "Where the corpse is, there the vultures will gather."

Then he takes a breath and continues with the parable of the unjust judge, which is our clue that he is not talking about

70. Barbara Brown Taylor, *Home by Another Way* (Cambridge, MA: Cowley Publications, 1999), 197–202.

just any old kind of prayer. He is talking about prayer that asks God to come and come soon—prayer that is more than a little spooked by the idea of being snatched out of bed in the middle of the night—prayer that begs for God's presence, God's justice, God's compassion—not later but right now.

As some of you know, prayer like that can wear your heart right out, if you're not careful—especially when there is no sign on earth that God has heard, much less answered, your prayer. You can knock only so long at a closed door before your hands hurt too much to go on. You can listen to yourself speak into the silence only so long before you start to wonder if anyone was ever there. When that happens—when the pain and the doubt gang up on you to the point that you start feeling dead inside—then it is time to get some help, because you are "losing heart." That is the phrase Jesus uses, and he does not want it happening to anyone he loves. That is why he told his disciples a parable about their need to pray always and not to lose heart.

I have a seven-year-old granddaughter by marriage named Madeline. She is blond, skinny, and tall for her age. When she comes to visit, we cook together. Our most successful dishes to date have been mashed sweet potatoes with lots of butter and crescent dinner rolls made from scratch. From the day Madeline was born, we have been able to look each other straight in the eye with no sentimentality whatsoever. The tartness of our love for one another continues to surprise me. It is easy to forget she is seven years old.

When she came to celebrate her birthday last summer, there were just four of us at the table: Madeline, her mother, her grandfather, and me. She watched the candles on her cake burn down while we sang her the birthday song and then she leaned over to blow them out without making a wish.

"Aren't you going to make a wish?" her mother asked.

"You have to make a wish," her grandfather said. Madeline looked as if someone had just run over her cat.

"I don't know why I keep doing this," she said to no one in particular.

"Doing what?" I asked.

"This wishing thing," she said, looking at the empty chair at the table. "Last year I wished my best friend wouldn't move away but she did. This year I want to wish that my mommy and daddy will get back together. . . ."

"That's not going to happen," her mother said, "so don't waste your wish on that."

"I know it's not going to happen," Madeline said, "so why do I keep doing this?"

Since the issue was wishing, not praying, I left her alone that afternoon, but I know that sooner or later Madeline and I are going to have to talk about prayer. I do not want that child to lose heart. I want her to believe in a God who loves her and listens to her, but in that case I will need some explanation for why it does not always seem that way.

This is the same problem Jesus was having with his loved ones. Things were not going well in the prayer department. The disciples wanted God to make clear to everyone that Jesus was who they thought he was, but instead there were warrants out for his arrest and even he was telling them that his place at the table would soon be empty. By the time Luke wrote it all down twenty years later, things had gotten even worse. Rome was standing over Jerusalem like a vulture over a corpse and there was no sign of the kingdom coming any time soon. Jesus had said he would be right back, only he was not back. People were losing heart, so Luke repeated the story that Jesus had told, about the wronged widow who would not stop pleading her case.

Luke does not say what her complaint is about, but it is not hard to guess. Since she is a widow, her case probably concerns her dead husband's estate. Under Jewish law she cannot inherit it—it goes straight to her sons or her brothers-in-law—but she is allowed to live off of it, unless someone is trying to cheat her out of it. The fact that she is standing alone in the street is a pretty good indicator that none of the men in her family is on her side. If she had any protectors left, they would have kept her home and gone about things in a more civilized manner. No son wants his mother hanging the family laundry in the street. No brother-in-law wants his brother's widow disgracing the family name.

But she has no one holding her back, and as the judge soon finds out, she is quite capable of taking care of herself. This is not a respectable judge, remember. By his own admission, he has no fear of God or respect for anyone. Maybe he thinks that makes him a better judge—more impartial and all that—or maybe he has sat on the bench long enough to know how complicated justice really is. However it happened, he is very well-defended. God does not get to him and people do not get to him, but this widow gets to him, at least partially because she throws a mean right punch.

We cannot hear the humor in the English translation, but in Luke's Greek version, the judge uses a boxing term for the widow. "Though I have no fear of God and no respect for anyone," he says, "yet because this widow keeps bothering me, I will grant her justice, so that she may not wear me out with *continued blows under the eye*." His motivation in responding to her is not equity but conceit. He does not want to walk around town with a black eye and have to make up stories about how he got it. Anyone who has seen the widow nipping at him like a mad dog will know where he got it. Since he cannot stand that idea, he grants her justice to save face.

"Listen to what the unjust judge says," Jesus says to his disciples. This is the part he wants us to pay attention to. *Won't God do the same for you? If you too cry out both day and night, will God delay long in helping you too?*

I am trying to decide whether I really want to tell Madeline this story. What if she concludes that the way to get what she wants is to keep punching God under the eye? Worse yet, what if she gathers that God will answer her not in order to draw her closer but in order to get rid of her?

Actually, I don't think I will say much about God at all. I think I will focus on the woman instead—about how, when she found herself all alone without anyone to help her, she did not lose heart. She knew what she wanted and she knew who could give it to her. Whether he gave it or not was beyond her control, but that did not matter to her. She was willing to say what she wanted—out loud, day and night, over and over—whether she got it or not, because saying it was how she remembered who she was. It was how she remembered the shape of her heart, and while there may have been plenty of people who were embarrassed by her or felt sorry for her for exposing herself like that, there were days when she wanted to say, "Don't knock it until you have tried it."

She would never have believed it herself—how exhilarating it was to stop trying to phrase things the right way, to stop going through proper channels and acting grateful for whatever scraps life dropped on her plate. There were no words for the relief she felt when she finally threw off her shame, her caution, her self-control and went straight to the source to say exactly what she wanted. She did not know she could roar until she heard herself do it.

Give me justice! she yelled at the judge. Do your job! Answer me now or answer me later, but I am coming back every day and every night—forever—until you deal with me.

So he dealt with her, but I am not even sure that is the point. I keep coming back to that sad little question at the end of the parable: "And yet, when the Son of man comes, will he find faith on earth?" It makes you think that Jesus did not know too many persistent widows, or at least not enough of them. He did not know too many people with the faith to stay at anything *forever*. Then as now, most people prayed like they brushed their teeth—once in the morning and once at night, as part of their spiritual hygiene program.

Even the ones who invested more of themselves than that tended to be easily discouraged. They would hang in there for a while, maybe praying as much as an hour a day for weeks on end, but when those prayers seemed to go unanswered they would back off—a little or a lot—either by deciding not to ask so much or by deciding not to ask at all. Superficial prayers turned out to be less painful than prayers from the heart, and no prayers turned out to be the least hurtful of all. Don't ask and you won't be disappointed. Don't seek and you won't miss what you don't find. As for that growing deadness you feel where your heart used to be, well, you will just have to get used to that.

What the persistent widow knows is that the most important time to pray is when your prayers seem meaningless. If you don't go throw a few punches at the judge, what are you going to do? Take to your bed with a box of Kleenex? Forget about justice altogether? No. Day by day by day, you are going to get up, wash your face, and go ask for what you want. You are going to trust the process, regardless of what comes of it, because the process itself gives you life. The process keeps you engaged with what matters most to you, so you do not lose heart.

One day, when Madeline asks me outright whether prayer really works, I am going to say, "Oh, sweetie, of course it does. It keeps our hearts chasing after God's heart. It's how we bother God, and it's how God bothers us back. There's nothing that works any better than that."

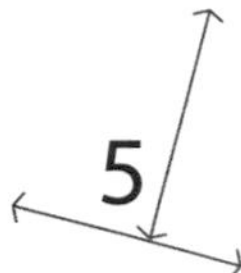

Preaching in the Testifying Voice

I was in my first year of seminary in 1975 when David Tracy published his groundbreaking study, *Blessed Rage for Order: The New Pluralism in Theology*. The book begins by asserting, "That the present situation in theology is one of ever-increasing pluralism is by now a truism. That such a pluralist condition enriches the possibilities for theology would seem equally clear and true. For a theologian to accept the present pluralism as a state of pure enrichment, of gratuitous and unvarnished blessing, is another matter entirely."[1] It was not a required text in any of my coursework, nor were we seminary students ready for the kind of dialogue that Tracy would have had us boldly embrace. In 1975 I approached most encounters with people of other cultures and different religions as evangelistic opportunities. And that is how I responded when Fukashi joined the Sunday school young adult education class I taught.

1. David Tracy, *Blessed Rage for Order: The New Pluralism in Theology* (New York: Seabury Press, 1975; reprint San Francisco: Harper and Row, 1988), 3.

Fukashi was one of three young male Japanese M.B.A. students who joined the ten to fifteen other twenty-something regulars in this class that year. He was invited by a woman who was a member of the congregation I attended. These three men received room and board in her home and accompanied her to church, in part as a courtesy to their host, in part to practice their English-as-a-second-language skills, and in part to satisfy their curiosity about American religious culture. For that year they were among the most faithful in attendance, especially Fukashi.

I recall the day that Fukashi asked if I would stay behind after class to answer a question he had about my lesson. The request came a little more than a month after these visitors had joined our class. The lesson material that particular Sunday had covered the text in Romans 5:12–21. In this biblical text Paul contrasts the gift of grace made possible in Christ with the effect of sin experienced by all people since the first man chose to disobey God. I had carefully explored the analogy between Adam as the first man and Christ as the second Adam. I had contrasted the textual oppositions of sin that brings about condemnation versus the free gift of God's work in Christ that brings about justification. I had shaped the teaching to make the evangelistic message clear: humans are sinners in need of redemption by faith in Jesus Christ. I wondered whether Fukashi's request to meet with me when the others left meant that he was responding to the implied invitation.

When we were alone Fukashi began, "Teacher Reid, please explain to me what this word 'sin' means." I was about to launch into a disquisition on the meaning of sin when I realized that he was asking an English-as-second-language question rather than a theological question. Fukashi was respectfully pointing out that I had spent the hour discussing a concept I assumed as everyone's cultural knowledge.[2] I soon learned what Bible translators have long known—Japanese religious traditions

2. Surprisingly, E. D. Hirsch does not include the word *sin* among the 5,000 essential names phrases, dates, and concepts every American needs to know. In my own experience as an educator in the twenty-first century I would argue that sin is a word that is beginning to have a kind of antiquarian patina for many students; see E. D. Hirsch Jr., Joseph Kett, and James Trefil,

do not have a simple correlate for the Christian concept of sin. It was a bracing immersion into the waters of theological pluralism.

Nine months later I was invited to the going-away party where Fukashi and his fellow students were saying goodbye to their American teachers. Fukashi's English and conversational skills had become more thoroughly Americanized in the intervening months. At one point in the evening he invited me to sit with him again. He said that I had become one of his American teachers much like the M.B.A. faculty members at the party. He began by thanking me for the unexpected education in Christianity he had received in our Sunday school class. Then he said, "I think as my teacher you have hoped I would approve of the teaching of Christianity, but this cannot be. I have read the teachings of Jesus and have come to understand that, if I were to accept these teachings, I would not be able to serve my Japanese employers faithfully. I have raised questions about these teachings in my M.B.A. classes and my American professors have explained that such teachings do not apply to American business, only to American religion. This is still a part of American religion that I do not understand. I will continue to read from the teachings of Jesus when I return home because I want to understand more about them. But I cannot adopt these teachings as my own. I hope you are not offended."

I thought about his words and then responded, "Fukashi, I think perhaps you have understood what I have taught better than all my students this year. I think Jesus would approve of this understanding of his teachings. I believe he would question many practices of both Japanese and American business people today. Doing business is essential to living in community with one another, but doing business honorably without deceit towards others is often very difficult. I am glad you will continue to read Jesus' teachings and I feel honored to be counted among your American teachers." My interaction with Fukashi was my first

---

Cultural Literacy: What Every American Needs to Know, updated and exp. ed. (New York: Vintage Books, 1987).

religious engagement with a person whose value assumptions were so culturally different from my own. It was also my first substantive engagement with issues related to cultural pluralism. It was, however, not the kind of interreligious dialog Tracy envisioned, because I had done all the talking and my goal had been conversion instead of conversation.[3]

In this chapter I explore the implications of the Testifying Voice that takes up the concern of Christian religious identity for post-Christendom pluralists. The diminishment of mainline Christianity's privileged cultural status has led many theologians to consider theologies (and approaches to preaching) that take seriously this new social and religious context.[4] Preaching in this voice still prefers appeals based in ambiguity over assuredness, but this voice turns away from personal appeals that invite radical change and transformation (typical of the Encouraging and the Sage Voices) to make communal appeals grounded in a concern for the significance of tradition and concerns for confessional order as an external locus of authority. The purpose of this approach to preaching is formation of a Christian identity counter to the dominant cultural identity—including the cultural identity that had formerly been at home in Christendom's

3. I am not dismissing the value of cross-cultural evangelism with this story. Rather, I am suggesting that such efforts should emerge out of conversations in which both parties are willing to listen and learn from one another rather than a model of conversion that operates according to a conquering metaphor. Tracy's notion of interreligious dialogue will be described at greater length later in this chapter.

4. Not all would accept pronouncements of Christendom's death, given the political resurgence of the religious right. See editorial, "We're Prime Time, Baby: Evangelicals' New Status Means Deepened Responsibility," *Christianity Today* 49, 7 (July 2005): 23; Pew Research Center Survey Reports, "Religion and Politics: Contention and Consensus," retrieved on June 28, 2005 at http://people-press.org/reports/display.php3?PageID=724. Others see Christendom's effect beyond the vicissitudes of its North American expression; e.g., Phillip Jenkins, *The Next Christendom: The Coming of Global Christianity* (Oxford: Oxford University Press, 2003). For argument on behalf of a North American post-Christendom context see Diogenes Allen, *Christian Belief in a Postmodern World: The Full Wealth of Conviction* (Louisville: Westminster/John Knox Press, 1989); Stanley Hauerwas and William H. Willimon, *Resident Aliens: An Assessment of Culture and Ministry* (Nashville: Abingdon Press, 1989); Stanley Hauerwas and William H. Willimon, *Where Resident Aliens Live: Exercises for Christian Practice* (Nashville: Abingdon Press, 1996); Stanley Hauerwas, *After Christendom: How the Church Is to Behave If Freedom, Justice, and a Christian Nation Are Bad Ideas*, 2d ed. (London: T & T Clark , 1999).

social compact with American civil religion.[5] This approach to preaching aids listeners by providing a dialogical context in which a formative conversation can occur—one in which Christianity is no longer presumed to be the presiding elder at the American religious roundtable. I begin by looking at two different contemporary decentered theologies. One moves out from the need to find culturally commensurate language to express a faithful public witness in a pluralistic environment; it is in contrast to a second theology that moves out from an identity formed by praxis shaped by the text-world of the Bible. I follow this with a brief description of a preaching voice large enough to include both expressions of contemporary theology that indicate what they share in common that differentiate their homiletic expression from the other voices. From this articulation, I then locate efforts to embody this voice in the work of a variety of contemporary homileticians—perhaps the most difficult task in this book, since we are only at the outset of identifying and understanding this movement in homiletics. As with the preceding chapters, I conclude by offering an exemplar of its expression at work.

Twenty-First Century Decentered Theologies

Social observers have little disagreement that there has been a significant retreat from engagement in the public sphere by American citizens. Most contemporary efforts to influence people are directed to a privatized individual who struggles with a culture of consumerism that would have that person work harder to make higher income in order to sustain the amenities making it possible to work harder. The conundrum is not lost on the public, but the alternative is equally elusive for a culture fast becoming,

5. On civil religion as the general religious dimensions of American society distinct from its churches, the degree to which the fabric of a society has been shaped by its religious ethos apart from its specific practices in congregations and synagogues, see Robert N. Bellah, *The Broken Covenant: American Civil Religion in Time of Trial*, 2d ed. (1975; Chicago: University of Chicago Press, 1992).

in Neil Postman's provocative assessment, a technopoly, where technology's usurpation of our previous cultural traditions makes other ways of cultural engagement and living either irrelevant or invisible.[6] This same individual is also in retreat from engagement in the public sphere because of the seeming monolithic immensity of contemporary governmental, organizational, and institutional bureaucracies, the growth of the profit sector of the market economy, and the polarized nature of contemporary public debate.[7]

One result of this phenomenon has been the realization that it is simply easier to direct appeals to listeners with an internal locus rather than an external locus of authority. People are willing to respond to appeals focused on their inner desire to see change or to redirect their life journey or faith journey. Their sense of estrangement from civic responsibility makes it more difficult to motivate based on collective or communal responsibility. There is a reason that Encouraging Voice and Sage Voice appeals strike a chord with North American listeners. Framing appeals that locate truth and meaning in the importance of an external rather than an internal locus of authority is more challenging. Yet this is a task taken on in diverse ways by preachers who seek to speak in a Testifying Voice. Such preachers are always conscious of how they invite listeners to engage in the conversations relevant to their faith and to think about how that conversation relates to the concerns of others.

In a marvelously lucid presentation of our contemporary American theological context, William Placher argues in *Unapologetic Theology* that apologetics—a form of reasoning that assumes an external locus of authority—is once again central in the new post-Christendom reality, in which Christianity is now but one voice in a pluralistic cultural conversation. Placher notes that many contemporary intellectuals who look for language to

6. Neil Postman, *Technopoly: The Surrender of Culture to Technology* (New York: Knopf, 1992).

7. On elements that privilege individual involvement over the collective involvement see Robert Wuthnow, *Producing the Sacred: An Essay on Public Religion* (Urbana: University of Illinois Press, 1994), 14–15.

critique the materialistic values and the skin-deep beliefs of Western culture now look more to Eastern religions for insight—look anywhere but to Christian theology. The problem, of course, is that Western Christianity made its peace with a capitalist, consumer culture as the price of serving as its chaplain. Then the collapse of Christendom came, making way for a new intellectual, social, and religious pluralism that has had considerably less respect for the tired chaplain who still wants to offer North American Christendom answers to post-Christian questions. Given this new cultural reality, Placher suggests, "Perhaps the time has come for a more 'unapologetic' theology."[8]

To get on with this task, Placher argues that an unapologetic theology must be willing to engage issues of pluralism at the intersection of science and religion and at the intersection of an interfaith dialogue with other religions. The two most productive efforts to formulate such a theology in recent years have been David Tracy's project to identify a revisionist theology and George Lindbeck's effort to identify a postliberal theology. Placher summarizes the difference by noting that the primary

> concern of the *revisionist* theology which dominates most academic circles in the United States is to preserve the *public* character of theology, that is, to find ways in which Christians can explain what they believe and argue for its truth in ways that non-Christians can understand. For the recently emerged *postliberal* theology, the theologian's task is more nearly simply to describe the Christian view of things. Postliberal theologians note ad hoc conjunctions and analogies with the questions and beliefs of non-Christians, but their primary concern is to preserve the Christian vision free of distortion, and they mistrust systematic efforts to correlate Christian beliefs with more general claims about human experience, which seem to them always to risk constraining and distorting the Christian "answers" to fit the "questions" posed by some aspect of contemporary culture.[9]

8. William C. Placher, *Unapologetic Theology: A Christian Voice in a Pluralistic Conversation* (Louisville: Westminster/John Knox Press, 1989), 12.

9. Ibid., 154.

Placher argues that it is a distortion to present these theologies as warring camps. I would agree since I believe that in their homiletic expression, both approaches begin with commensurate theological assumptions about the nature of authority appeals and the nature of language appeals. So, with an appreciative nod to Placher, I will try to summarize the strengths and distinctiveness of these two approaches to theology, framing them with reference to their influence on Testifying Voice homiletics.

Revisionist Theology

In 1975 David Tracy canvassed what he termed the pluralist context of contemporary theology and determined that four basic models of theological practice existed: orthodox theology, liberal theology, neo-orthodox theology, and radical theology. Like Paul Ricoeur, Tracy positions theologies in a dialectical conversation in order to find a middle way through. If orthodox and liberal theologies are the outer boundary markers, and neo-orthodox and radical theologies are reactions yet again in opposition, Tracy wishes to describe a post-orthodox, post-neo-orthodox, postliberal, post-radical theology—what he generally calls a revisionist theology. His project is a revision on liberal theology for a post-Christendom, pluralist culture where public discourse must negotiate the dialectic between authentic beliefs, values, and faith in Christian and non-Christian theologies. Christian convictions, he argues, need to be defended according to publicly acceptable criteria for theology's three publics—society, academy, and church.[10] No one of these should control the dialogue. The purpose of a revisionist theology is to challenge both secular and traditional Christian understandings of the role of theology with publicly available criteria of meaning, meaningfulness, and truth.[11] Pluralism is the defining reality that now requires Christian theology to find this different voice necessary to engage in

10. David Tracy, *The Analogical Imagination: Christian Theology and the Culture of Pluralism* (New York: Crossroad Publishing, 1981), 3–46.

11. Tracy, *Blessed Rage*, 34.

a conversation that, in the end, will enrich rather than threaten the meaning of religious truth.[12]

Tracy examines the intersection of three proposals in order to clarify method in revisionist theology. First, he argues that theologians must examine the intersection between biblical texts as examples of classic texts that resist the domestication of reality by illuminating, through their excess of meaning, the truly "common human experience."[13] His second proposal is to privilege dialogue as a form of productive *conversation* that reasons discursively, inquires, and even engages in argument, especially aware of the social and religious tendencies to privilege one's own discourse as hegemonic.[14] His third proposal is to offer a hermeneutic of interpretation that moves between inquiry relevant to these texts and the discursive inquiry of pluralist conversation.[15] In brief, revisionist theology is conducted by way of a theology of common human experience, a rhetoric of dialogic conversation, and a hermeneutic that admits a radical plurality of possible meanings.

Tracy locates his hope in "a Christian faith that revelations from God have occurred and that there are ways to authentic liberation," a belief he negotiates first among Christian theologies in *Blessed Rage for Order* and then as the basis for interreligious dialogue in *The Analogical Imagination*.[16] He argues that it is naïve to assume anything more than family resemblances among

12. The titles of five different works demonstrate how responding to pluralism is central to Tracy's purpose and the progress of his thought concerning public dialogue about the role of faith and religion in a pluralist society: *Blessed Rage for Order: The New Pluralism in Theology* (1975); *The Analogical Imagination: Christian Theology and the Culture of Pluralism* (1981); *Talking about God: Doing Theology in the Context of Modern Pluralism* (1983); *Plurality and Ambiguity: Hermeneutics, Religion, Hope* (1987); and *Dialogue with the Other: The Inter-Religious Dialogue* (1990).

13. David Tracy, *Plurality and Ambiguity: Hermeneutics, Religion, Hope* (Chicago: University of Chicago Press, 1987), 11–18; Tracy, *Blessed Rage*, 43.

14. Tracy, *Plurality and Ambiguity*, 18–27.

15. Ibid., 28–46.

16. Ibid., 113. *Plurality and Ambiguity* is not the projected third volume of Tracy's theological trilogy. He has moved away from trying to find a way to engage in a dialogue amidst the modern "isms" of theological argument to attempt the recovery of language with which to explore the Hidden-Revealed/Comprehensible-Incomprehensible God; see Scott Holland, "This Side of God: A Conversation with David Tracy," *Cosscurrents* 52, 1 (Spring 2002): 54–59.

religions, which is why interreligious conversation will always result in conflicts of interpretation concerning the meaning of common human experience. This is why revisionism is more an attitude of willingness to engage in conversation than an assumption that convergences or universals will be identified. He states,

> whenever any affirmation of pluralism, including my own, past or present, becomes simply a passive response to more and more possibilities, none of which shall ever be practiced, then pluralism demands suspicion. That kind is, as Simone de Beauvoir insisted, the perfect ideology for the modern bourgeois mind. Such a pluralism masks a genial confusion in which one tries to enjoy the pleasures of difference without ever committing oneself to any particular vision of resistance and hope.[17]

This is why theology must be conducted out of its own tradition, engaged in conversation with others, to illumine a way to live in hope amidst pluralism.[18] For Tracy, hope requires that those involved in interpreting our contemporary situation, and those aware of our need to identify locations of solidarity amidst this pluralism, must continue to risk interpreting all the classics of all the traditions. For in that effort to interpret lies both resistance and hope.[19]

Whether the issue is to distinguish meaningful criteria by which Christianity can rejoin the conversation in society and the academy concerning science and religion, or to find points of contact to engage in the necessary work of interfaith conversation between church, synagogue, and mosque, theology must speak in ways that can disclose its truths capable of transforming the

17. Tracy, *Plurality and Ambiguity*, 90.

18. "We find ourselves, therefore, with a plurality of interpretations and methods. We find ourselves with diverse religious classics among many religious traditions. We find ourselves glimpsing the plurality within each tradition while also admitting the ambiguity of every religion: liberating possibilities to be retrieved, errors to be criticized, unconscious distortions to be unmasked. The attempt to understand remains an effort to interpret well. But to interpret as pluralistic, ambiguous, and important a phenomenon as religion is to enter a conflict of interpretations from which there can often seem no exit." (Ibid., 112–13).

19. Ibid., 114.

thought of any intelligent, reasoning, responsible human being: "Any genuine theological proposal that really means what it says about God [should] implicitly address . . . all three publics" of society, academy, and church.[20]

Postliberal Theology

Discussion of postliberal theology must begin with the work of Hans Frei before considering the way George Lindbeck appropriated Frei's project. In the *Eclipse of Biblical Narrative*, published in 1974, Hans Frei concluded that the power of the biblical narrative is lost when an interpreter relocates its meaning in thematized propositions, ideals, and doctrines derived as abstractions from the text.[21] For Frei, these rational abstractions should never replace the way in which biblical narratives interpret experience and theological reflection about it. In Frei's narrative theology the story of Jesus found in the biblical texts invites those who experience it to enter into the world of its story as incomplete, because "Jesus *is* his story." It is an unfinished story because it brooks no division between Christology and eschatology. Frei argues that Gospel stories provide incomplete clues to the rest of Scripture and ambiguous clues to the experience of history that invite an audience, whether readers or listeners, to envision being taken up into, and joining their story with, the story unfolded in the world of the text.[22] It is in this sense that Paul Ricoeur writes, "The whole of contemporary exegesis has made us attentive to the primacy of the *narrative* structure in the biblical writings."[23]

20. David Tracy, "Defending the Public Character of Theology," *Christian Century* 98 (1981): 351.

21. Hans Frei, *The Eclipse of Biblical Narrative: A Study in Eighteenth and Nineteenth Century Hermeneutics* (New Haven: Yale University Press, 1974).

22. Hans Frei, "Remarks in Connection with a Theological Proposal," in *Theology and Narrative: Selected Essays*, George Hunsinger and William Placher, eds. (New York: Oxford University Press, 1993), 43.

23. Paul Ricoeur, "Naming God," in *Figuring the Sacred: Religion, Narrative and Imagination*, Mark Wallace, ed., David Pellauer, trans. (Minneapolis: Fortress Press, 1995), 224.

For Frei it is an issue of one's starting point. If readers begin with the narrative reality of the biblical world and accept its story-world as the defining reality of their meaning and existence, then it constitutes their identity and their citizenship, and it interprets their reality and life by its vision of meaning and identity. This narrative center is important since apologetics too often begins at the point of having thematized the biblical story-world into a comprehensible system of beliefs by which supposedly commensurate argument can be rationally conducted. Frei argues that prior to the eighteenth and nineteenth centuries, literal and figurative interpretation of Scripture served to sustain a unified cumulative narrative of a biblical world story. For example, Christians were able to read Hebrew narratives in light of the New Testament literature and interpretively fuse them into a single narrative story-world. This account functioned as a depiction of the real world in which we live. Then well-intentioned conservatives like Cocceius and Bengel, as well as radicals like Spinoza, interpretively introduced a bifurcated logical interpretive distance between the depicted biblical world and the "real world" by seeking to explain the phenomena of the latter by the frame of the former. This represented a hermeneutical shift in the locus of authority for reading Scripture. Instead of trying to understand the "real world" according to a biblical narrative worldview (the traditional hermeneutic), interpreters increasingly sought to interpret the biblical narrative according to the unfolding events of the real world around them (a critical hermeneutic).

Advances in nineteenth-century liberal theology continued to push this boundary separating literal meaning from its integration with older interpretive approaches (allegorical, typological, and anagogical),[24] leading Frei to conclude that "[i]t is no

24. On the four senses of interpretation for homiletics see Paul Scott Wilson, *God Sense: Reading the Bible for Preaching* (Nashville: Abingdon Press, 2002). The four senses of interpretation were nicely summed up for medieval theology students with the sentence: *Litera gesta docet, quid credas allegoria, Moralis quid agas, quo tendas anagogia* ("The literal sense teaches what actually happened, the allegorical what you are to believe, the moral how you are to behave, and the anagogical where you are going."); Harry Caplan, "A Late Medieval Tractate on Preaching," in *Studies in Rhetoric and Public Speaking in Honor of James Albert Winans*, A. M. Drummond, ed. (New York: Russell & Russell, 1962), 286; see also F. F. Bruce, "The History of New Testament

exaggeration to say that all across the theological spectrum the great reversal had taken place; interpretation was a matter of fitting the biblical story into another world with another story rather than incorporating that world into the biblical story."[25] He argues that many conservative as well as liberal theologians are heirs to this distillation hermeneutic that objectively reduces the biblical story to an estranged set of doctrinal propositions ready-made for apologetic argument. This distillation hermeneutic assumes that stories can be reduced to their point, or at least to some general lesson about human experience and existence. But narratives rarely if ever *mean* one thing, which is why Frei argues on behalf of the narrative center of Christian faith. He rejects other centers of authority, whether American pluralistic culture, Enlightenment critical epistemology, or the apologetic needs of the church. For Frei, any attempt to begin theology with the assumption that a universally accessible system of beliefs can be distilled from the texts—be it a systematic theology or a system of thought used to critique it—leads to a hermeneutic that ignores the narrative character of the biblical text.[26]

In *The Nature of Doctrine*, George Lindbeck takes up Frei's orientation while addressing a set of questions similar to those posed by Tracy. He proposes conceptualizing religion from a cultural-linguistic perspective that approaches the nature of doctrine from a "regulative" or rule-theory approach, rather than an approach that seeks to identify a common human experience as the irreducible basis of conversation.[27] He explores whether a regulative view could be as satisfactory as a propositional theology in allowing for the possibility of doctrinal normative features of religion and permanence. He concludes that it is superior on at least the first point of providing a normative doctrinal grammar of faith.[28]

Study," in *New Testament Interpretation: Essays on Principles and Methods*, I. Howard Marshall, ed. (Grand Rapids: Eerdmans, 1977), 28.

25. Frei, *Eclipse*, 130.

26. Placher, *Unapologetic Theology*, 162.

27. George Lindbeck, *The Nature of Doctrine: Religion and Theology in a Postliberal Age* (Philadelphia: Westminster Press, 1984), 17–19.

28. Ibid., 107.

Like Frei, he wishes to arrive at a normative explication of the meaning of religion from an intratextual rather than an extratextual fashion. Lindbeck accepts that Christianity's narrative center means that the intrinsic Christian identity is a culture into which believers are initiated and trained, that it cannot be reduced to any universal structures of commensurable doctrinal language in order to facilitate intelligible academic conversations across disciplines or meaningful interreligious dialogue. In proposing a cultural-linguistic model of religion, Lindbeck argues for the primacy of the adherent's faith identity as shaped by the cultural socialization process of becoming and being a Christian. This socialization process involves a process of learning a language that is irreducibly shaped by history. It involves the ability to internalize the story of Israel, the story of Jesus, and the story of the early church "well enough to interpret and experience oneself and one's world in its terms."[29] In this sense, Scripture is world-creating, and it is through the formative work of the church that the grammar of this world is learned.

In proposing this cultural-linguistic approach to understanding the nature of doctrine, Lindbeck rejects both propositional and experiential-expressivist theologies. He argues that propositional approaches emphasize the way in which church doctrines function as objective truth claims about reality or as formative systems of propositional belief intended to be readily accepted as cognitively affirmed truths. The experiential-expressivist approach interprets "doctrines as noninformative and nondiscursive symbols of inner feelings, attitudes, or existential orientations."[30] Both approaches locate religious meaning outside the text in either "the objective realities to which it refers or the experiences it symbolizes."[31]

The major contrast between experiential-expressivist and cultural-linguistic approaches to theology—Lindbeck's primary concern in the book—is in how they construe human expres-

29. Ibid., 34.
30. Ibid., 16.
31. Ibid., 114.

sion and human experience. This is a difference he describes as a "reversal of the relationship between the inner and the outer" based on the linguistic turn in Western philosophical hermeneutics. He charges romantic expressivists with assuming that the ability to interpret or understand experience is prelinguistic, as opposed to the assumption that language is a necessary prerequisite for expressing an experience—that one cannot even speak of having an experience if one lacks the capacity to reflect on it linguistically. For Lindbeck, the difference between the cultural-linguistic approach and its alternatives is the degree to which the focus of the former is on intratextual interpretations of praxis rather than on extratextual efforts to identify the nature of truth. He argues that a regulative approach to doctrine with reference to the creedal affirmations of Nicea and Chalcedon "is not how much they can be interpreted in modern categories, but rather how contemporary Christians can do as well or better in maximizing the Jesus Christ of the biblical narratives as the way to the one God of whom the Bible speaks."[32]

Lindbeck argues against the apologetic focus of both the liberal experiential-expressivists and the propositionalists. To argue the credibility of the Christian faith, whether one is a propositionalist or a liberal, requires one to make foundational appeals to universal structures. These efforts may still win popular audiences, he argues, but they have diminishing credibility in the intellectual establishment. Paradoxically, this means "that a postliberal approach, with its commitment to intratextual description, may well have interdisciplinary advantages, while liberal theology, with its apologetic focus on making religion more widely credible, seems increasingly to be a nineteenth-century enclave in a twentieth-century milieu."[33]

Lindbeck recognizes that liberals (including revisionists) would argue that faithfulness in preaching the gospel in currently intelligible forms is scripturally warranted. He disputes simply the utility, not the canonicity, of such claims. "Theology should there-

32. Ibid., 107.
33. Ibid., 130.

fore resist the clamor of the religiously interested public for what is currently fashionable and immediately intelligible. It should instead prepare for a future when continuing dechristianization will make greater Christian authenticity communally possible."[34] Instead of trying to convince a world that no longer believes in a logic capable of proof, Lindbeck argues that the community of faith should absorb the universe into the biblical world rather than seek to export its claims to the world about it.

Contemporary Trajectories of Theology

In *Plurality and Ambiguity*, Tracy demonstrates how a revisionist approach, contrary to the claim of postliberal theology, does assume the linguistic turn's rejection of both positivism and the romantic expressivist understanding of the relationship between language and experience.[35] He argues that positivism fails to understand how its certainties are instrumental constructions of its own rhetoric, while romantic expressivism treats language as a mere instrument to express individualism's notion of the deeper self. What is lost in the interpretations of language-as-instrument by positivism and romantic expressivism is not only the more subtle relationship between language, knowledge, and reality, but also the social and historical character of all understanding through language.[36]

Rachel Sophia Baard writes,

> What Tracy *rejects* is the instrumentalism that believes that language is used to express a deeper self, and that Truth is the possession of the individual. What he *affirms* is the notion of a socially constructed self, the awareness that Ultimate Truth is not the possession of the individual. . . . The decentering of the self in postmodern thought is thus intricately intertwined with the linguistic turn, for the latter implies the social construction of the self, and the impossibility of private access to total truth.[37]

34. Ibid., 134.
35. Tracy, *Plurality and Ambiguity*, 45–65.
36. Ibid., 49.
37. Rachel Sophia Baard, "The Dialectics of Language and Experience in David Tracy's Epistemology: A Response to David Brockman," *Koinonia* XV, 1 (2003): 26.

Baard's assessment could as readily be applied to either revisionist or postliberal theology. Both theologies assume the significance of the linguistic turn, assume that selves are socially constructed, assume the impossibility of private access to total truth, and assume the necessity of developing a decentered theology that responds realistically to the challenge of pluralism. They begin here and then offer different responses that move in distinctly different trajectories.

These theologies have faced challenges, but my purpose here has been to offer a brief description of these emergent theologies. Revisionist theology and postliberal theology are the dominant theologies of the decentered self at the outset of the twenty-first century. They are alternative responses to North American Christianity's post-Christendom context. Other theologies that also address this circumstance include neo-Barthian confessional theology, radical orthodoxy, neo-evangelical emergent theology, political and liberation theologies, radical feminist and Womanist theologies, queer theology, deconstructive theologies, theologies of the Other, etc.[38] This list, which is far from exhaustive, is witness itself to the decentered nature of the contemporary pluralist context. These theologies differ from revisionism and postliberalism only by serving specific constituencies. They all tend to share three things in common. First, they have turned away from appeals to individualism, whether personalist, existentialist, or the transcendentalist invitation to the journey of faith, represented more by the Encouraging and Sage Voices. Second, they tend to have accepted the linguistic turn concerning the nature of language appeals. Third, they take up a concern for what Robert Wuthnow has termed the role of practice-centered faith.[39] As a dimension of the Testifying Voice I take Wuthnow's conception

38. McKim's useful book needs to be updated again to include some of these emerging theologies; Donald K. McKim, *The Bible in Theology and Preaching: How Preachers Use Scripture* (Nashville: Abingdon Press, 1994). For a practical handbook in distinguishing one's own theology in preaching see Burton Z. Cooper and John McClure, *Claiming Theology in the Pulpit* (Louisville: Westminster/John Knox, 2003).

39. Robert Wuthnow, *After Heaven: Spirituality in America Since the 1950s* (Berkeley: University of California Press, 1998), 168–98.

of a practice-centered faith to be that impetus in preaching that values communal conversation and confessional tradition while also being sensitive to how this communal Christian experience may be considered a way of keeping the question of human understanding open in relationship to the mystery of God.

The Testifying Voice in Preaching

The distinctive element of the Testifying Voice is its assumption that the purpose of the sermon is to engage a community of faith's corporately held truths in conversation in a persuasively indeterminate fashion based on the preacher's efforts to wrestle with meaning in conversation with others. The role of preaching is somewhat recast: if the previous voice was the sage on the stage, this voice is more the guide on the side. Here the preacher becomes an activist who seeks to negotiate a place for faith at the table of contemporary options of identity formation. It stakes a claim that a tradition of faith must be a meaningful voice in the pluralist conversation of contemporary meaning. Sermons in this voice operate with interpretivist assumptions about the nature of reality and call forth a corporate identity for listeners. But unlike the Teaching Voice, sermons in this mode refuse to mount a hierarchy that would privilege one cultural reading of the biblical text over another. This voice invites listeners to engage in a formative conversation with their confessional tradition, their contemporaries both within and outside of the church, and the Holy Spirit. The intention is to further engagement with faith. In this voice, any interpretation of preaching's Word is understood as a coming-to-terms that occurs as dialogical engagement within the proclamation community, with the community as an external locus of authority (see Figure 5.1).

The controlling sensibility when preaching in this voice is a desire for listeners to listen to their culture, their convictions, and their confessional tradition as they let this conversation form them as a distinctive people of faith willing to see a world reshaped by concern for "the other." Sermons offered in this voice generally present an interpretation of a text/topic/contemporary thematic that poses a concern raised by culture, conviction, or confessional tradition such that listeners must come to terms with sacred possibilities of being a people of God who speak on behalf of others in response to a call of Christian faithfulness in the face of suffering, oppression, and marginalization. It is preaching shaped in such a fashion that it makes its appeal in a way that invites listeners to respond by saying, "Yes! This conversation matters. Let's keep talking."

Nature of Language Appeals	***Persuasively Indeterminate Appeal***	**The Testifying Voice** Expects: "Yes! This conversation matters. Let's keep talking." ***Formation-Centered***
		Corporate Truth Appeal
		Nature of Authority Appeals

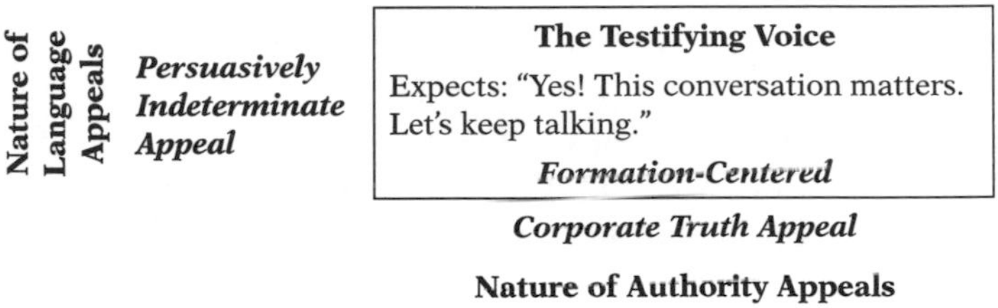

Figure 5.1: The Testifying Voice

The Spectrum of Possibilities

Preachers who take up the Testifying Voice share a common concern to invite listeners to see themselves in relationship with the testimony of Scripture, with their confessional tradition, with those who surround them in congregations, and with others whose voices may have been excluded from its communion table. This exclusion may be an artifact of a dominant culture's privileging of power or the unwillingness of the church to attend to its own exclusionary discourse. Preaching in the Testifying Voice is speech that has turned away from the self to attend to the other, even the otherness of God. Homileticians who address these concerns, whether they are revisionist, postliberal, or proponents of some variation of this type of approach to theology, all distinguish their approaches from the appeal to the individual on a journey of faith in favor of inviting listeners to see themselves as part of a confessional tradition or a community willing to engage the issues of theology in a pluralistic environment.

For example, Mark Ellingsen makes an important distinction between the use of narrative in postliberal preaching and its use by theorists like Craddock, Lowry, and Rice. Narrative-centered homileticians tend to view text and world out of a phenomenological cultural consciousness that understands interpretation as a fusion of horizons occurring in front of the text instead of behind it. These story preachers often relate secular stories, images, or illustrations from the pulpit to illuminate religious points, or they are willing to share their own life story as a means to illuminate the story of Scripture. This represents a critical correlation between the text's story and the interpreter's experience or presuppositions about it. In challenge to this, Ellingsen argues that this kind of sermonic movement changes the conceptual framework of the biblical text, "For if Christianity's claims always must be correlated with contemporary human experience in order that they be God's Word, then the Word of God can never be said to stand unambiguously over against and criticize contemporary experience."[40]

Postliberal preachers, Ellingsen notes, view text and world out of a sociolinguistic cultural consciousness. This means that the postliberal preacher seeks to reverse the flow of traffic on the hermeneutical bridge between Scripture and culture. Instead of explaining Scripture by analogy from the world, world is explained by analogy from Scripture. What ties the church together is not family, job, or self-esteem concerns. The identity listeners shaped by postliberal theology share in common is their baptism, Scripture, and their tradition of belief. Biblical-narrative preaching from the sociolinguistic school of theology begins with this identity-in-Christ and interprets the world by its reality, rather than the other way around.[41] The reader who has followed the argument of this book to this point should be able to hear in this assessment a description of a cultural consciousness that makes its appeal to a believer in community rather than to an individual

40. Mark Ellingsen, *The Integrity of Biblical Narrative: Story in Theology and Proclamation* (Minneapolis: Fortress Press, 1990), 27.

41. Cf. David Fleer and Dave Bland, "Tension in Preaching," in *Preaching From Luke/Acts*, Rochester College Lectures on Preaching, vol. 1, David Fleer and Dave Bland, eds. (Abilene, TX: ACU Press, 2000), 21–37.

in existential isolation. This is preaching that makes its appeal to a practice-oriented spirituality rather than a seeking-oriented spirituality. It makes its appeal to the public rather than private concerns of the listener and has an external locus of authority.

Charles Campbell has been one of the more prolific homileticians exploring the implications of postliberal theology for preaching. In *Preaching Jesus: New Directions for Homiletics in Hans Frei's Postliberal Theology*, he pointedly rejects Craddock's approach to preaching as still subordinating Christ to a liberal theology of human experience and rejects the story and narrative approaches of the New Homiletic as still giving the story of the world priority over the storied identity of Christ in Scripture. This is not surprising since, according to Lindbeck, the hallmark of experiential-expressivist theology is its dominating interest in individual quests for personal meaning, a concern that is indicative, according to my argument, of the Sage Voice.[42] For Campbell, the preacher's interest in narrative is less about emulating its plot and more about ways a preacher can explore how character and incident in the text reveal Jesus' or God's identity. By engaging the congregation in this exploration of Jesus' (or God's) identity, it becomes the listener's task to carry the narrative forward "by becoming a character in the ongoing story of Jesus."[43]

In an eloquent essay that seeks to reclaim preaching from recent concerns to be "relevant," Richard Lischer argues that preachers must reclaim a vision of preaching that has as its purpose the church's ceaseless witness to Jesus Christ. To accomplish this, he argues, preachers need to shift their homiletic metaphor from one of event to one of spiritual formation. Though Lischer makes reference to postliberal theologians like Lindbeck and Hauerwas, his primary interest is to invite preachers to envision preaching as the church's language that prefers *formation* to event, *narrative* to mere illustration, *performance* to translation.[44]

42. Lindbeck, *The Nature of Doctrine*, 22.

43. Charles L. Campbell, *Preaching Jesus: New Directions for Homiletics in Hans Frei's Postliberal Theology* (Grand Rapids: Eerdmans, 1997), 186.

44. Richard Lischer, "Preaching as the Church's Language," in *Listening to the Word: Studies in Honor of Fred Craddock,* Gail R. O'Day and Thomas G. Long, eds. (Nashville: Abingdon Press, 1993), 130.

> Preaching-as-formation is not content with its own eventfulness. It does more than announce a new standing before God or hold up fuzzy correspondences between religion and meaningful experiences. It directs the faithful into the implications of their redemption in Jesus Christ. Instead of demonstrating the likeness of Christian teaching to conventional values, which is the usual method of sermon illustrations, preaching-as-formation explores the differences. In so doing, it becomes the voice of the church as a contrast society.[45]

Preaching must be a performance of the grammar of faith that tells the one great narrative of God's faithfulness to Israel and the church, with a goal to direct the faithful into the formative implications of their redemption in Jesus Christ.

Walter Brueggemann bridges concerns of both postliberal and revisionist theologies. He argues that Christian preaching today should be "analogous to preaching to exiles. More broadly, biblical preaching is addressed to a particular community of believers committed through baptism to the claims of biblical faith addressed to the community of the baptized in order to articulate, sustain, and empower a distinctive identity in the world."[46] In this, Brueggemann argues that the church would do well to realize that *Lamentations* provides a more realistic model for the context of preaching to post-Christendom exiles. For Brueggemann, post-Christendom preaching *demands* an alternative rhetoric of testimony that holds both public and formative concerns in balance. It would be a decentered speech offering *testimony* advocating an odd truth, a truth that is off-centered and in deep tension with the culturally dominant and commonly accepted givens. At the same time, it would be speech offering *testimony* as an advocacy, not a universal claim but a local claim made here and now, and made with reference to the way in which such communities of the baptized can know who

45. Ibid., 126.

46. Walter Brueggemann, *Cadences of Home: Preaching among Exiles* (Louisville: Westminster/John Knox, 1997), 78.

they are in that circumstance.[47] Brueggeman's effort to balance concerns that develop the language of Scripture as a grammar of faith with language that calls listeners to be actively living out that faith as testimony against dominant powers in the culture suggests an effort to negotiate the counterclaims of postliberal and revisionist theologies.

Some revisionist preachers have challenged postliberal homileticians at this point. A proposal for a theology whose primary purpose is to develop a grammar by which adherents can know the Christian view of things is seen as primarily directed inward rather than outward.[48] For example, David Buttrick is at his most acerbic when he labels postliberalism as the "cocooning" of the church. He writes, "The position has swept our churches, perhaps because it seems to offer a theological *raison d'être* for self-preservation while, at the same time, connecting with the biblical theology that has captivated most Protestant clergy during the twentieth century."[49] Of course, Buttrick would argue that his own approach is primarily phenomenological, but unlike Sage Voice preachers, Buttrick wants to shift preaching's focus away from appeals made to the individual in existential isolation and foster appeals to a communal conviction. Like Tracy, he is concerned that gospel be expressed as a liberating challenge to the false idols of dominant culture exploitation. For Buttrick, "Preaching is the Word of God because it functions within God's liberating purpose and *not* necessarily because it is per se biblical."[50]

47. Ibid., 57.

48. Some effort to define a postliberal perspective on evangelism can be found; for example, Rodney Clapp has an early attempt embedded in a larger discussion of postliberalism's implication for Christian practices. However, his orientation depends more on the post-Christendom strategies of communicating gospel of David Bosch and William Abraham than on postliberal theologians; Rodney Clapp, *A Peculiar People: The Church as Culture in a Post-Christian Society* (Downers Grove, IL: InterVarsity Press, 1996), 158–71. For one of the most productive attempts to address this concern see Stanley P. Saunders and Charles L. Campbell, *The Word on the Street: Performing the Scriptures in the Urban Context* (Grand Rapids: Eerdmans, 2000).

49. David Buttrick, *Preaching the New and the Now* (Louisville: Westminster/John Knox, 1998), 41; cf. David Buttrick, *A Captive Voice: The Liberation of Preaching* (Louisville: Westminster/John Knox, 1993), 17.

50. Buttrick, *Captive Voice*, 31.

Buttrick's model for preaching invites preachers to attend to how language forms in human consciousness and how individuals relate what they hear with their own lived experience.[51] Preachers must develop a field of understanding of a text that serves as their convictional understanding of a *text's* contemporary meaning. Then this contemporary field of understanding should be structured in one of three ways of preaching: in the *mode of praxis*, in the *reflective mode*, or in the *mode of immediacy*. Preachers employ an image grid to structure the moves of the sermon. This approach shifts preaching away from the traditional argument mode of making points with a voice of assuredness *without* denying that an argument is being made.

Homileticians who focus on conversation as a model for contemporary preaching, such as Ronald Allen, Lucy Rose, Jeffrey Bullock, and John McClure, all recognize in varying degrees the manner in which revisionist thought has affected their models of preaching. Like Tracy, Ronald Allen draws upon the resources of process theology to help preachers determine how their theology can speak a credible and timely Word both for and to the church.[52] He assumes the pluralistic environment of preaching that is conceived as "a conversation in which preacher and people search together" to interpret a common life from the perspective of the gospel. As one who has made the linguistic turn, he notes that he joins an increasing number of homileticians who believe

51. Ellingsen argues that Buttrick's phenomenological approach groups him with homileticians such as Tom Long, Eugene Lowry, Frederick Beuchner, Edmund Steimle, and other story preachers who have, in Ellingsen's opinion, been too heavily influenced by philosophical *phenomenology.* For Ellingsen, phenomenology as applied to homiletics is heavily influenced by idealism and "purports to concentrate on a description of phenomena without any attempt at metaphysical explanation" (*Integrity*, 55). Ellingsen also classifies Tracy as a theologian guilty of the same problem (55). This is similar to Lindbeck, who wishes to treat all whom he classifies as experiential-expressivists as those who have not made the linguistic turn and are therefore not truly postmodern. However, we have already noted that others have challenged the basis upon which Lindbeck makes his claims. In previous writings I have mistakenly grouped Buttrick's method with other Sage Voice writers. In part this was a chronological artifact of my own effort to understand the emerging New Homiletic and an artifact of my own coming-to-understanding of the difference between the Sage and the Testifying Voices.

52. Clark M. Williamson and Ronald J. Allen, *A Credible and Timely Word: Process Theology and Preaching* (St. Louis: Chalice Press, 1991).

preaching needs to be directed less to individuals and more to that which builds Christian community.[53] He contends for the recovery of preaching as theological reflection.[54] Whether the preacher begins with a text or a topic, Allen believes that preachers should develop a unified theological vision.

Allen's homiletic calls for preaching that assists preachers and congregation together to explore the interrelationship between three theological criteria for preaching: (1) appropriateness to the gospel, (2) intelligibility, and (3) moral plausibility. Different weightings occur among four groups he considers.

> Revisionary thinkers weigh all three about equally. Postliberals place stress on intelligibility, though they too emphasize the importance of being able to understand Christian witness and of the various elements of Christian witness cohering logically. Liberation preachers are especially interested in moral plausibility. Evangelicals, like the revisionary theologians, place great stress on all three criteria, though their understanding of these criteria is modified to fit their worldview.[55]

Allen is particularly interesting for his presentation of the way a sermon embodies openness to the pluralistic conversation it seeks to engender. He is less concerned with identifying problems with other approaches than he is with modeling an irenic spirit of conversation willing to recognize differences among Christian voices.

Allen's model of conversational preaching is quite different from the conversational homiletic offered by the late Lucy Rose. In *Sharing the Word* Rose provides an extensive analysis of various approaches to preaching with a view toward distinguishing these

53. Ronald J. Allen, *Interpreting the Gospel: An Introduction to Preaching*, (St. Louis: Chalice Press, 1998), xii; Ronald Allen, "Individual and Community in Postmodernity," in *Theology for Preaching: Authority, Truth, and Knowledge of God in a Postmodern Ethos*; essays by Ronald J. Allen, Barbara Shires Blaisdell, and Scott Black Johnston (Nashville: Abingdon Press, 1997), 137–60.

54. Ronald J. Allen, *Preaching Is Believing: The Sermon as Theological Reflection* (Louisville: Westminster/John Knox Press, 2002).

55. Allen, *Interpreting the Gospel*, 88.

approaches from her own proposal. She offers a model of preaching that envisions the sermon as an opportunity to express the solidarity already present between preacher and worshipers while not privileging the voice of the preacher. Rose's approach is significantly shaped by feminist challenges to hierarchical ways of knowing and concern for the marginalization of voices. At the same time it is also shaped by the possibilities of autobiographical truth shared in a communal context that helps facilitate connectedness and solidarity. She is concerned that preachers must take seriously preaching's contemporary decentered language context.

Rose's approach would more accurately be described as a confessional homiletic interested in recovering the possibilities of transcendence in preaching that can occur if truth is conceived of as an intertextual intelligibility rather than truth presented as a universal, a kerygmatic, or a performative representation of reality. She challenges Traditional Voice preaching as being overly committed to persuasion, presenting "as normative and universal that which is particular and individual."[56] Similarly, she argues that preaching that invites commitment by treating sermonic language as if it can be consubstantial with salvation too readily confuses the representational nature of language of its "gospel" with the saving work of God. She also challenges approaches to preaching that share many of the elements I have termed as preaching in the Sage Voice. Here, she argues that preaching that seeks to perform a text, or attends to what the text does rather than what it says, must not ignore the degree to which performing intentions is still a mental construct of the preacher reflecting her or his biases. Rose expresses concern with the ethics of indirection and narrativity that acts as if it is not persuading, while it lets the form rather than the content carry the burden of this task.

Her model emphasizes the power of sermonic language that is both confessional and evocative in a way that spotlights Chris-

56. Lucy Atkinson Rose, *Sharing the Word: Preaching in the Roundtable Church* (Louisville: Westminster/John Knox Press, 1997), 110.

tian formation as a discursive understanding of truth expressed in the community's ongoing, interpretive conversation.[57] Of course, one of the speakers from the three other voices she has problematized might ask her whether transcendence is actually recovered in her model of preaching if truth becomes an intertextual intelligibility established through the interpretive understanding of a decentered language. Or more simply, "Will preachers permit gospel to become so pluralized that it stakes no interpretive claim concerning meaning apart from *dialogue with* confessional tradition and no transcendence beyond the community's own interpretive context?"[58] Though she distances her model of preaching from Tracy's revisionist concept of conversation, this is the same challenge that postliberals would make against Tracy's theology.[59]

Rose is particularly uncomfortable with preaching's historic relationship to persuasion, because "[p]ersuasive preaching and leadership styles have been abusive to many in the church whose experiences and convictions have been consistently ignored or dismissed."[60] She argues that continued discussion of the relationship in homiletic theory is potentially dangerous because it gives presence to a relationship that can be understood to still sanction previous definitions and practices. Though her model shares some communal concerns with postliberal preaching, her commitment to exploring the personal quest for meaning by way of personal-journey narratives suggests that her approach still shares some elements in common with what I have described as Sage Voice preaching. I will return to her concern with the role of persuasion in preaching at the outset of the next chapter.

Jeffrey Bullock critiques Rose's rejection of ontological truth in favor of eschatological, nonhierarchical truth implied in the "play" of preaching that never persuades and never arrives. He suggests that she implicitly draws on Derrida's notion of "play,"

57. Ibid., 110.

58. See Robert Reid, "Faithful Preaching: Preaching Epistemes, Faith Stages, and Rhetorical Practice," *Journal of Communication and Religion* 21, 2 (1998): 173.

59. On Rose's reference to Tracy see Rose, *Sharing the Word*, 9–10.

60. Ibid., 133n 1.

a posture that resists the hegemonic limit always at work in quests to nail meaning down. Yet Bullock notes that Rose wants preaching as conversation that never finally articulates any position. His homiletic assumes that the preacher brings intention to the conversation that leaves open space for listening to others and acknowledgement that meaning can be arrived at in the "space" that occurs in true dialogic listening. He argues for an approach to preaching that adopts a phenomenological, Gadamerian conception of "conversational play," which is willing to arrive at an articulated "position," but one that is "always on the way to becoming, always already on the way to being worked out in community life."[61]

Bullock has no interest in nailing down a center or providing a final word, but he recognizes that congregations desire that sermons need to *arrive* somewhere that *points* to something that surpasses the understanding of both preacher and congregation. Bullock's preacher is a herald who views the sermon more as *process* than *product*. Rather than viewing the sermon as an act of retrieval and exposition of the text as object, preachers who engage in conversational *homileo*-ing would explore meaning as a collaborative dialogue between preacher, text, and community.

John McClure also employs the metaphor of conversation to frame his understanding of the context of preaching. His *Other-Wise Preaching: A Postmodern Ethic for Homiletics* is a decentered homiletic that invites preachers to exit the cultural consciousnesses that assume a representational epistemology and/or a propositional deductive hermeneutic. Like the other proposals for a conversational homiletic, McClure urges preachers to offer testimony rather than answers. He is particularly concerned that gospel testimony speak witness in its concern for "the other," a

61. Jeffrey Francis Bullock, *Preaching with a Cupped Ear: Hans-Georg Gadamer's Philosophical Hermeneutics As Postmodern Wor(L)D*, Berkeley Insights in Linguistics and Semiotics (New York: Peter Lang Publishing, 1999), 102. Bullock contends that one of the problems of trying to employ Derrida's critical practice for homiletics is that Derrida is a critic "who performs his criticism, and his performance takes place through a style of writing that resists the 'theological presence of a center.'"

concern he finds to be *central* to a gospel orientation. His model lays challenge to the phenomenological homiletics of Buttrick and Bullock, the process-relational *logos* of Allen, as well as post-liberal, critical, and other testimonial homiletics.[62] At the same time, McClure points to the work of various homileticians like Phillip Wogoman, Christine Smith, and Walter Burghardt, who have identified elements of a constitutive rhetoric of *other-wise* preaching.[63]

McClure's study *The Roundtable Pulpit* offers a modest attempt to describe the practice that supports this ethic of preaching. He encourages preachers to form listening groups whose reflections on text and the preacher's preparatory exegesis can be shared in the sermon, bringing voices other than that of the preacher to the conversational table. Rather than preaching biblical *insights* or biblical *mandates*, this is a model of preaching as a "coming to terms" that occurs first in conversations of the community focused on discerning the Word of God and then finds expression in the proclamation of the community. Preaching the collaborative work of a community's coming to terms focuses on the relational work of that community's effort to enact faith. "It implies that members of the community of the Word decide on ways to stand *with* and stand *for* one another by claiming tentative *directions* of thought and action as God's Word."[64] His model represents a collaborative, dialogic homiletic in which the biblical text is treated as Word of God emerging from a conversation in which the meaning and purpose of the gospel is at stake.

There are obviously other models for preaching that could serve as theory for the Testifying Voice, but the present list is suggestive of the spectrum available as witness that names God and names grace in this voice.

62. John S. McClure, *Other-Wise Preaching: A Postmodern Ethic for Homiletics* (St. Louis: Chalice Press, 2001).

63. Others whom McClure identifies as *other-wise* preachers include Justo Gonzáles and Catherine Gonzáles, Kathy Black, James H. Harris, William Sloane Coffin, Lenora Tubbs Tisdale, and Charles Campbell and Stanley Saunders (Ibid., 133–38).

64. John S. McClure, *The Roundtable Pulpit: Where Leadership and Preaching Meet* (Nashville: Abingdon Press, 1995), 23–24.

Excellence in the Testifying Voice

The biblical-narrative, sociolinguistic model is but one of several ways in which the Testifying Voice is expressed, and not all would accept its critique of story preaching. For example, David Buttrick and others accept the argument that preaching story needs to make its appeal in ways that invite listeners to constitute themselves as part of a community of practice without accepting the argument that all "story" must cross the bridge from only one direction; e.g., Jesus' parables began in this world to create new images for identification with the kingdom come.

What is common here is that Testifying Voice strategies of sermon composition seek to emulate or open up a dialogue in which Christian formation and/or awareness of an enlarged worldview or understanding of Christian responsibility is in view. Sermons in this voice often represent an effort to enact the storied identity of biblical characters or writers as counter-image or counter-speech, subverting contemporary assumptions of culture. These sermons explore how the language of Scripture and tradition provide the means to resist the influence of the dominant culture that would otherwise define the identities of listeners. They suggest ways to embrace the unfinished nature of the language of Scripture's story to go on in our own Christian formation.

John McClure argues that preaching must attend to four different tensions or concerns:

1. Theo-symbolically coming to terms with a Christian *worldview*;
2. Semantically coming to terms with a Christian understanding of *truth*;
3. Culturally coming to terms with the *experience* of the hearers; and
4. Scripturally coming to terms with the sermon text's possibilities of *meaning*.

His roundtable model of preaching suggests that a sermon attending to these concerns would be plotted in four sequenced moves:

first name a tension, offer a partial resolution, then bring more critical reflection to bear, and finally propose a more constructive understanding reflecting possible meanings.[65]

This approach is similar, at least in its conceptual moves, to Ronald Allen's framework of a Second *Naïveté* approach to preaching.[66] I have adapted Allen's threefold movement to a fourfold division to suggest the relationship with McClure's model for sermon movement:

1. A First *Naïveté* move is made in which the preacher and congregation name a tension in a text, doctrine, practice, or topic in a precritical way.
2. Partial resolutions are named.
3. A critical-reflection move is then made that indicates the inadequacy of such resolutions of the text, doctrine, practice, topic, or text.
4. A Second *Naïveté* move is made where the pastor and congregation return to the original matter informed by the critical reflection, viewing the text/story in a more constructive fashion and appropriating a new set of meanings to be associated with the world of the text/story/practice.

This pattern of preaching reduces Walter Wink's fivefold synthesis of Ricoeur's model of the act of interpretation into homiletic moves. These still incorporate Ricoeur's model of "coming to understanding," which moves though an initial fusion, then a negation of fusion through suspicion of the object, followed by the creation of distance, leading to a negation of the negation through suspicion of the subject and finally resolving into interpretive communion.[67]

65. John McClure, *The Four Codes of Preaching: Rhetorical Strategies* (Minneapolis: Fortress Press, 1991).

66. Ronald J. Allen, *Patterns of Preaching* (St. Louis: Chalice Press, 1998), 98–100.

67. Walter Wink, *The Bible in Human Translation* (Philadelphia: Fortress Press, 1973), see chapter three. Ron Allen wisely observes that when it comes to preaching, "In the unending cycles of interpretation, one generation's second *naïveté* may become the equivalent of a first *naïveté* for a subsequent generation" (Allen, *Interpreting the Gospel*, 197). Allen cites an essay

Homiletician Carol Miles is particularly attracted to this model as a pattern of thinking one's way through the movement of a sermon. For Miles the challenge of interpreting biblical texts is to take words spoken for people in a different time and a different place and find their relevance today. When it comes to preaching she says, "We have to learn to model that in the pulpit—distancing the text from us by looking at it critically so that we might bring it near again in that 'second *naïveté*': 'This text still has something to say to me!'" Regarding her own practice she notes, "That's what I try to model when I do interpretative work with these texts for my students. I think lay people need to see those kinds of moves being made in the pulpit so they become more sophisticated readers of the Bible themselves."[68] In this approach the preacher frames ideas with phrases that admit:

- "This is tough,"
- "This bothers me about this text,"
- "I don't know how you felt when you heard this text read but I know the first thing that leaps out at me is this hard word."

When Miles hears questions like these in a sermon she finds that "[i]t makes me feel regarded. I also feel there's an honesty there and an integrity. I don't feel like what is being said to me on Sunday morning is part of some ideology."[69]

Excellence in preaching in the Testifying Voice does not coerce listeners toward the predetermined right answer. Preaching in the Testifying Voice admits the ambiguity of our efforts to

by Ted Peters as formative in his own development of this approach to preaching: Ted Peters, "Hermeneutics and Homiletics," *Dialog* 21 (1982): 121–29.

68. Carol Miles: "Hearing the Gospel in a Different Voice: An Interview," *Insights: The Faculty Journal of Austin Seminary* 119, 2 (Spring 2004): 16. Available at http://www.austinseminary.edu/news/insights_spring_04.pdf.

69. Ibid., 16. In context Miles is using the popular notion of ideology that blurs the distinction between ideology and an ideologue, an often blindly partisan advocate or adherent of a particular ideology. All preaching presumes some ideology, but it need not presume it blindly or in an ardently partisan manner.

understand ourselves and our identity in relationship to others, acknowledges the work necessary to better understanding, and points the way to possible resolutions that name God and name grace as ways of discovering meaning that matters for a Christian *worldview*, for Christian understanding of *truth*, for coming to terms with our *own experience* and the *experience of others* and with the sermon text's possibilities of *meaning*.

Strategies that can help a preacher let the Testifying Voice control the purpose of the sermon, that invite preachers to take up this voice, include: (1) Sermons *Imaged* as Phenomenological Play (e.g., Buttrick; Bullock), (2) Sermon as Developmental Improvisation (e.g., Campbell; Lischer), (3) Quadrilateral Sermons (e.g., Allen), (4) Roundtable Conversation Sermons (e.g., Rose; McClure), and (5) Second *Naïveté* sermons (e.g., Allen; Miles). Sermons designed in these fashions invite listeners to find themselves in conversation with those whom they are seated next to, with fellow participants in their culture, and with the theological tradition engaged. The congregation's theology or its tradition of interpretation plays a central role in shaping the sermon, but rather than seeking affirmation of some explanation offered, the intention is to invite listeners to continue on in the conversation, to respond by saying, "Yes! This conversation matters. Let's keep talking." Sermons in a Testifying Voice tend to be controlled by the persuasive intention of helping listeners be formed and reformed by an engagement with their corporate community's tradition of faith released to do a work of spiritual formation in their lives together. Sermons in this voice use language to re-form memory and set congregational consciousness free from a kind of culturally imposed amnesia.[70]

A Sample Sermon

The essential elements of the Testifying Voice are readily apparent in the following sermon by Ronald J. Allen. As with all

70. Charles Campbell, *The Word before the Powers: An Ethics of Preaching* (Louisville: Westminster/John Knox, 2002), 110–11.

the voices, there are moments where the Teaching Voice, the Encouraging Voice, and the Sage Voice occur, but the Testifying Voice is clearly in control of the desired outcome to invite listeners to participate in a conversation that can direct faith's practice.

Professor Allen makes use of a "From First to Second *Naïveté*" sermon design that invites listeners to be part of a conversation engaged in a critical reflection on the implications of the text for contemporary Christian practice. The sermon begins with a typical precritical response to the text. From here Allen proceeds to offer an initial critical reading of the biblical text, but one that does not resolve all of the tensions of the biblical story. A second, more-nuanced question is posed, and the sermon concludes with a proposal for understanding a more-nuanced contemporary appropriation of meaning that makes possible a more textured (a second *naïveté*) response to the story.

Praying for Justice with Your Feet
Luke 18:1-8
Ronald J. Allen

Not long ago I was leading a Bible study in a damp church basement. After we read the parable of the widow and the unjust judge, one of the people thumped her Bible and said, "That judge is the sorriest picture of God I ever heard." "What do you mean?" "Well, that judge is obviously God. That judge had no feeling for that widow. She had to keep coming, and the only reason the judge paid her any mind was to get rid of her."

God looking upon people in situations of injustice as annoyances? They keep coming to God, and coming, and coming. They become such pests that God *must* notice them. But then only to get rid of them. That would be a sorry God.

But if you take a step back you can hear that this parable is not a case of one thing being another. The name for that is "allegory." The Gospel of Luke does have a parable with an allegorical interpretation—the parable of the sower, the seed, and the four soils. The seed *is* the Word and each kind of soil *is* a different hearer (Luke 8:4–15). However, to the everlasting theological relief of everyone who has thought, "Such a sorry God," the parable of the widow and the unjust judge is not an allegory.

But if not an allegory, then what? Take another step back and listen to what Luke adds to the parable. "And [Jesus] said, 'Listen to what the unjust judge says. And will not God grant justice to [the] chosen ones who cry to [God] day and night? Will God delay helping them?'" (Luke 18:7). The parable is not an allegory, but a comparison. This text is a first-century rabbinic way of making an argument from the lesser to the greater. To paraphrase an earlier passage, "If I as a parent know how to give good gifts to my children, how much more does God give to the human family!" (Luke 11:13).

The situation of the woman before the judge is a comparison of the situation of the community to whom Luke wrote and God. Since the lesser circumstance is true (the unjust judge giving in to the persistence of the woman), how much more true is the greater circumstance (God responding to the pleas of the needy for justice).

So what is the greater—the situation Luke has in mind? "Jesus told them a parable about their need to pray always and not to lose heart." The context is teaching on prayer. So we need to remember that in the Gospel of Luke and the Book of Acts, prayer has a special meaning. Prayer is the intentional opening of self and community to the present and coming realm of God.[71] Many Jewish people expected this realm to be a time and place when God's purposes would be completely fulfilled. Everyone would experience love in every moment and have every material resource needed for a full life. No poverty, no racism, no arbitrary barriers to abundance and community.

Luke believes that realm is already making a beginning through Jesus, and that it will come in fullness when Jesus comes back. This theme echoes in the question that ends today's reading. "When [Jesus] returns, will [Jesus] find faith on earth?" Luke

71. For example, Ronald J. Allen, *Preaching Luke-Acts*, Preaching Classic Texts (St. Louis: Chalice Press, 2000), 46–47; Ronald J. Allen, "The Story of the Church according to 'Luke,'" in *Chalice Introduction to the New Testament*, Dennis E. Smith, ed. (St. Louis: Chalice Press, 2004), 215.

raises this issue not as a general musing but as a question to the listening community. "When Jesus returns, will he find that *you* have prayed as desperately for the realm as this widow sought justice from the judge, or will you give up?"

To pray in Luke and Acts is to ask God to bring the realm, and then to live as if the realm is on its way. The prayer that Jesus teaches the disciples is a prayer for the realm, "Hallowed be your name. Your [realm] come" (Luke 11:2). The early community in Acts models the realm by sharing all things in common, thereby providing for all (Acts 2:42–47; 4:32–37). Stephen, stones bruising his dying body, prays for God to forgive the persecutors (Acts 7:59). When Peter and Cornelius pray, the reunion of Jewish and Gentile peoples begins (Acts 10:3–33). The apostles pray in jail, and God opens the doors. On a sinking ship, Paul prays and is saved to carry the news of the realm to Rome (Acts 27:29).

On the one hand, I am drawn to part of Luke's perspective. To pray is not to ask for a new bicycle, a passing grade on the final exam, or a nice promotion. To pray, for Luke, is to seek for God's realm to become all in all. It is to seek a world in which everything happens according to God's purposes—in every heart, every home, every congregation, neighborhood, state, nation, and planet. If a corrupt judge will respond to a solitary widow, how much more will the loving God bring the realm?

How could God not be moved by the cry of the innocent civilian in Iraq holding the bloody stump where her arm was before the car bomb exploded seconds ago? When you see such things, what else can you do but pray for the realm to come *now*?

On the other hand, I admit I am skeptical about other aspects of Luke's perspective. Will God "*delay* long in helping [the needy who cry day and night]? I tell you [God] will *quickly* grant justice to them." Oh? What does "quickly" mean? For 2,000 years suffering widows have cried for justice, yet God has been anything but "quick" in bringing the realm. Two thousand years gives new meaning to the term *delay*.

Of course, as human beings we must admit that our limited minds cannot fully fathom God's purposes. But 2,000 years of hunger, poverty, violence, and death raise the question of what purpose God could possibly have in delaying the coming of the realm. If God has the power singularly to create a new world and does not do so, then God is complicit with evil.

Faced with such issues, some Christians pointedly raise the question of whether we can think that God is simultaneously all loving, altogether just, and completely powerful. I think it makes sense to think with a small group of Christians and Jewish people who revise their view of God that God is all loving and altogether just, but not completely powerful.[72] God has limited God's own self. No, God is by nature limited.

To be sure, God is more powerful than any other entity. But from this point of view God cannot simply dictate things to happen. People who believe this way—and perhaps you can tell I am among them—believe that God works in the world not through brute power but by luring individuals and communities to cooperate with God's purposes of love and justice for all. God works in cooperation with others—people and nature—to help the world take on qualities of the realm.

In every moment God offers us choices that can lead the world to become more like the divine realm. By refusing God's alternatives, we keep the realm at arm's length.

Each way of thinking has its benefits and its losses. With Luke's way of thinking, you have the security of an all-powerful God who will intervene and eventually make things right. But you live with the bitter issue of more and more widows and others experiencing injustice. And I have to say, you wonder what difference your prayers make if God is not going to intervene in history until God is good and ready. With the revised way of thinking, you get more intellectual credibility in that you resolve the nagging question of why God does not act quickly to grant justice. And you recognize that what you do to cooperate with God's purposes—or not to cooperate—makes a real difference not only to God but to helping qualities of the realm become manifest in our world.

72. An elegant and persuasive statement of this perspective is found in Clark M. Williamson, *Way of Blessing, Way of Life: An Introduction to Theology* (St. Louis: Chalice Press, 2002).

To be painfully straightforward, some situations have little likelihood of change. Cancer sometimes reaches the stage where it is almost impossible to turn back. Even then, however, God is constantly present. The awareness that we are never alone often helps us make our way through such circumstances.

So where does the revised way of thinking leave us with respect to the parable of the widow and the unjust judge?

- Aspects of our world are often like the circumstance of the widow: in need.
- However, God seeks love and justice in every situation. God wants every human being and every community to live in a world that is more like the realm than the way things are now.
- Prayer is the opening of self and community to God and to how our lives and world can take on more qualities of the realm. Like the widow, we do need to pray "day and night" to be available to God's lures.
- Through prayer and study we discern actions we can take to participate with God in moving toward circumstances of love and justice in our personal lives, homes, congregations, wider communities, and the world.

The widow went on her feet day after day to the judge. In a sense, we, too, pray for justice with our feet. We open ourselves to God through prayer, and then do what we can do to join with God. We "keep coming . . . day and night." We keep doing what we can do, not to bother God but to respond to the fact that God is constantly present, ever offering new opportunities for love and justice.

When things cannot change, we embrace the divine presence that is always with us—holding us so that we are never alone.

In 1943, the Nazis in Berlin began to round up about 2,000 Jewish husbands who were married to Aryan women. These husbands were taken to a building on Rosenstrasse, Rose Street, that had been a welfare center for the Jewish community but in a bitter irony was now converted into a prison. The husbands were to be held there until they were shipped to the concentration camps.

Before the husbands could be loaded on the trains, their wives and other women came and stood outside the prison. Day after day, they demanded the release of their husbands. In the words of a reviewer of the film *Rosenstrasse*, "Unarmed, unorganized, and leaderless, they faced down the most brutal forces at the disposal of the Third Reich."[73] A haunting scene from the film portrays the women, bundled against the cold, framed by a gray sky, crying with increasing intensity, "Give us back our husbands."[74]

They prayed with their feet. The guards unlocked the doors.

I know things don't always work out that way. But suppose those women had never gone to the prison?

When we pray, we increase God's opportunities to bring love and justice into our world. Where can you pray with your feet today?

73. From a review by Richard S. Levy of Nathan Stolfuss's book *Resistance of the Heart: Intermarriage and the Rosenstrasse Protest in Nazi Germany*. Copyright © 1997 by H-Net. Retrieved on June 20, 2005 at http://fcit.coedu.usf.edu/holocaust/timeline/rosenstr.htm.

74. Margarethe von Trotta, director, *Rosenstrasse* (IDP Distribution, 2003).

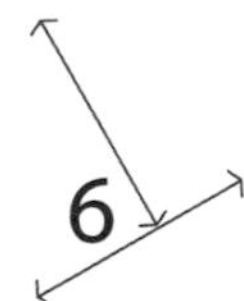

Developing Authenticity of Voice

Branch Rickey, the famous former owner of the Brooklyn Dodgers, quipped, "Luck is the residue of design." Apply this to preaching and we could say, "Response is the residue of design." Good preaching is not a matter of luck. It is the result of the match between testimony that authentically names God and names grace, and the preacher's control of the persuasive appeals implicit to the structural design of the sermon. Few things in a sermon are more signature than the preacher's assumptions about the role of persuasion. It is a primary indicator of the potential response from listeners, whether the preacher believes sermons must offer an argument or tries to minimize persuasive effect based on the belief that conviction should be the work of the Holy Spirit. Whatever passion the sermon expresses is part of this persuasive fabric. Whatever reasons it offers are hopefully crafted with an eye to their anticipated influence. Whatever authenticity it personifies arises from the preacher's ability to speak in ways that connect her or his own faith experience and understanding with that of the listeners. In all of this, persuasion matters especially as it relates to the ability to develop an authenticity of voice in preaching.

As indicated in the last chapter, some homileticians have become convinced that any effort to persuade undermines the purpose of preaching. Lucy Rose has even argued that continued use of the word in preaching is "potentially dangerous in sanctioning previous definitions and practices."[1] Unfortunately this debate confuses issues of argument and the possibility of its manipulation with the very processes of communication itself.[2] Persuasion has unquestionably been abused in preaching, but most communication theorists would be either amused or amazed if preachers tried to argue that they were unwilling to be persuasive in preaching. As Herbert Simons observes, for persuasion to occur there need only be an act of communication in which one person has an intent to influence another person who has the ability to form a judgment or make a choice in response. He defines persuasion as "human communication designed to influence the autonomous judgments and actions of others."[3] Screaming at the dark is not a persuasive act of communication. Knocking on someone's front door is. Confusion arises because of the common assumption that there is a difference between informative and persuasive speaking. Though a useful artifice for coursework in public speaking, it does not hold up under scrutiny. When is a formal occasion of speech, let alone a sermon, less than a knock at the door?

The problem confuses speech that provides information with speech in which some element of controversy focuses the ar-

1. Lucy Atkinson Rose, *Sharing the Word: Preaching in the Roundtable Church* (Louisville: Westminster/John Knox Press, 1997), 133.

2. For the basic disciplinary debate see Lucy Hogan, "Rethinking Persuasion: Developing an Incarnation Theology of Preaching," *Homiletic* 24, 2 (1999): 1–12, and the response by Richard Lischer, "Why I Am Not Persuasive," *Homiletic* 24, 2 (1999): 13–16. Homileticians expressing doubts about the role of persuasion include Rose, *Sharing the Word*; Richard Lischer, "Preaching as the Church's Language," in *Listening to the Word: Studies in Honor of Fred Craddock,* Gail R. O'Day and Thomas G. Long, eds. (Nashville: Abingdon Press, 1993), 113–30. For a more positively disposed assessment of the role of persuasion see Thomas Long, "And How Shall They Hear? The Listener in Contemporary Preaching," in *Listening to the Word*, 167–88; David Buttrick, "Who Is Listening?" in *Listening to the Word*, 189–206; Fred Craddock, "Is There Still Room for Rhetoric?" in *Preaching on the Brink: The Future of Homiletics*, Martha J. Simmons, ed. (Nashville: Abingdon Press, 1996), 66–74; Robin R. Meyers, *With Ears to Hear: Preaching as Self-Persuasion* (Cleveland: Pilgrim Press, 1993). For the more Barthian negotiations of this tension see James F. Kay, "Reorientation: Homiletics as Theologically Authorized Rhetoric," *Princeton Seminary Bulletin* XXIV, 1 (2003): 16–35.

3. Herbert W. Simons, *Persuasion in Society* (Thousand Oaks, CA: Sage Publications, 2001), 7.

gument.[4] For example, there is no question but that the basic airline safety speech is intended to influence the autonomous judgment of people who need to prepare for their flight. Yet those of us who have been on flights rarely experience the talk as persuasive because it lacks the element of controversy. We think of it as informative even if the airline industry has a deep desire to influence our behavior. Imagine what would happen in the aisles if a United Airlines flight attendant began by sternly warning passengers not to follow the Northwest Airlines safety procedures because they are dangerous. Magazine pages would remain unturned. Cell-phone users would hurry their goodbyes. Controversy transforms this too-familiar speech into a dispute. Whenever someone speaks to others, the effort is naturally guided by an intention that seeks a response. That intention, for better or worse, implies a process of persuasion.

Throughout this study I have been guided by a rhetorical perspective of communication that assumes humans use language to *affect* purposes with others, with a goal to be *effective* in those purposes.[5] Without such an assumption it would have been impossible to argue on behalf of excellence in preaching. Without such an assumption it would have been difficult to sustain the argument that each of the four voices embodies an implicit set of appeals that invite listeners to construct faith as a response. Perhaps the better question to ask is how preachers can respond with a sense of authenticity that is ethically responsible within a voice.

4. Homileticians concerned about the effect of persuasion would do better to explain the persuasive nature of human communication that seeks to influence autonomous human judgment, in order to help preachers to develop language capable of using the influential nature of language responsibly. George Campbell's distinction between speech that instructs versus speech that proves arguments, raised in Chapter Two, addresses differences between motives for speaking, not the presence or absence of a desire to influence autonomous judgment; George Campbell, *The Philosophy of Rhetoric*, rev. and exp. ed., with critical introduction by Lloyd Bitzer, ed. (Carbondale: Southern Illinois University Press, 1988), 2.

5. See Harold Barrett, "Maintaining the Self in Communication," in *Bridges Not Walls: A Book about Interpersonal Communication,* John Stewart, ed. (Boston: McGraw Hill, 2002), 96. Source: Barrett, *Maintaining the Self in Communication: Concept and Guidebook* (Incline Village, NV: Alpha and Omega, 1998). On the gray areas of persuasion where there may be no overt intention to persuade see Simons, *Persuasion*, 7–10.

This chapter raises this issue of responsible preaching as it relates to the expression of voice. Where the previous chapters have primarily been descriptive, in this chapter I shift to language that is more explicitly prescriptive and practical, exploring the implications of voice for one's preaching identity, what is involved in deciding to shift a preaching identity to a different voice, and the enduring influence of a ministry in one clear and coherent voice for those who hear sermons. For reasons that will become clear, I will refer to these hearers in this chapter by the potential of what developing clarity of voice can help them become—listener-learners.

Discovering a Preaching Identity

Understanding the relationship between a preaching voice and the expectation of its response is the first step toward accepting one's own cultural consciousness as an identity in preaching. There are obviously other aspects of a preaching identity. For example, Burton Cooper and John McClure have provided an invaluable guide to assist preachers in the effort to identify the basic theological framework that informs their preaching. They provide a grid that distinguishes such content concerns as basic theological orientations, dissimilarity in sources of authority, various theistic worldviews, different orientations to relationships between church and world and between Christianity and other religions, as well as alternatives in assumptions about theodicy, the atonement, and what happens in the eschaton/eternity. Their study provides a brief, accessible road map to help preachers (and parishioners) understand the distinctions in relation to others regarding the content of a preacher's theological identity.[6]

In a sense, Cooper and McClure's inventory is akin to the Myers-Briggs personality indicator that measures the responses of test-takers across four tensional sets that can be categorized into sixteen different personality frames. People may be more or

6. Burton Z. Cooper and John S. McClure, *Claiming Theology in the Pulpit* (Louisville: Westminster/John Knox Press, 2003).

less one of the types of identity as opposed to the other, but the test is fairly reliable as a means of categorizing what matters in the respondent's worldview and how respondents differ in the way that they relate to one another. Cooper and McClure's set of distinctions are sufficiently clear that they can be reduced to a two-page check-off list at the end of the book. The proposal of the Four Voices of Preaching as four distinct preaching identities is less overt, since it describes a person's taken-for-granted cultural convictions rather than their deeply held personal convictions. Where Cooper and McClure help preachers locate their distinctive theological identity, *The Four Voices of Preaching* has as its purpose to assist preachers (and those who listen to preachers) to discover the cultural assumptions implicit in their *rhetorical* identity.

In this book I have treated identity more as a function of what happens rhetorically in talk rather than as either an exploration of a personal interior state or an artifact of one's social psychology.[7] In addition, I have assumed that preaching intentions are designs, whether implicitly or explicitly understood by the preacher, that *affect* purposes with listener-learners with a goal to be *effective* in those purposes. Preachers desire that there would be some influence and some response to having heard a sermon. If excellence is admitted as a quality that preachers should aspire to in their efforts to communicate, then learning how to shape sermons in light of the homiletic question, "What do I want to have happen as a result of having heard this sermon?" would be one way to begin to realize one's preaching identity. Since all voices can occur within any sermon, it is the

7. Perhaps another way to say this is to return to one of the definitions introduced in chapter one. There I noted that in 1877 Phillips Brooks proposed that "[p]reaching is the bringing of truth through personality," which is to say that it is communication that is simultaneously an expression of the divine and the human. Rather than treat the "personality" dimension of this definition as a psychological construct, I have viewed it more as a social construct of cultural orientation. See Phillips Brooks, *Lectures on Preaching* (New York: E. P. Dutton, 1877), 5. Willimon notes that when coediting *The Concise Encyclopedia of Preaching*, he realized that this was the definition most cited by the various contributors. He writes that it is not surprising, because the "definition strikes experienced preachers as essentially right" (William Willimon, *Pastor: The Theology and Practice of Ordained Ministry* [Nashville: Abingdon Press, 2002], 157–58).

sermon's expected response that reveals the primary preaching intention of a specific sermon. The arrangement theories listed at the close of each of the preceding chapters provide a suggestive list of patterns to help in permitting a particular voice to take the wheel that directs a sermon toward a specific preaching intention.

While some homiletic textbooks treat sermon arrangement designs as if they are a toolkit that can add variety to a preaching ministry, I have argued that sermon forms often support very different preaching intentions—intentions that reveal radically different cultural consciousnesses at work. Some forms are argument-centered, some are advocacy-centered, some are journey-centered, and some are formation-centered. *Sermon form does not create a voice. Rather, it is an individual's cultural assumptions about the nature of language and the nature of authority that provide the center of gravity that places one or another voice behind the wheel that brings a sermon to a successful destination.* The preacher's task is to make a match between the cultural assumptions that serve as his or her rhetorical resources and the sermonic intent of an arrangement theory that assists listener-learners in realizing a sermonic intention.

Let me be clear. One does not take up a different voice in preaching by deciding to use a different arrangement theory in preaching. Discovering a preaching voice is not a proposal for a cookbook of personas one can don for different homiletic occasions. Such a view subverts authenticity. Basic assumptions about the differing natures of language and authority mark the choices of a Rubicon many preachers would not choose to cross. And those who would should wonder why others see such a disparity in the choice.

For example, in *Deep Memory, Exuberant Hope: Contested Truth in a Post-Christian World*, Walter Brueggemann states,

> My thesis is that preaching is *sub-version*. You will recognize the play I intend. Preaching is never dominant version; never has been. It is always a sub-version, always a version, a rendering of reality that lives under the dominant version, or an alternative

> strategy of showing our "under-version" to be in deep tension with the dominant version.[8]

It is unlikely that the author of such a statement could find the voice to preach with objectivist assumptions about the nature of reality. Nor would he be interested in making individualistic persuasive appeals. *He would likely find these other voices to be inauthentic testimony coming from his mouth.*

Voices, when they are true, represent the marriage of form, content, and cultural consciousness to achieve an excellence of intention. A preaching voice reveals the deep cultural commitments of the "terministic screen" that frames the way a preacher sees life and world. It reveals what counts as truth (whether the preacher prefers ambiguity or assuredness; prefers the question or the answer) and what counts as the "social mooring" of preaching's appeal (whether she or he is more concerned with affirming social solidarity or inviting individual transformation). These tensions have been explored in the preceding chapters as a preacher's negotiation of the sermon's bases of appeal in the nature of authority and the nature of language.

Your preaching voice (or your pastor's preaching voice) matters because there is a direct relationship between developing coherent intentions in preaching and the experience by listener-learners of preaching's authenticity of *voice*. Authenticity—that sense that the preacher has found his or her voice—is directly correlated to the ability to negotiate the bases of a sermon's appeal and communicate that intention in a manner that helps listener-learners realize its aspiration. When a preacher's voice is inconsistent or incongruent, listener-learners will experience the sermon as lacking a sure footing. My argument throughout has been: *authenticity of voice is more likely to be experienced by parishioners if preachers learn to turn an intuitive understanding of voice into an explicitly understood rhetorical resource.* Preachers must work to discover the boundaries of rhetorical congruence for control of their voice.

8. Walter Brueggemann, *Deep Memory, Exuberant Hope: Contested Truth in a Post-Christian World* (Minneapolis: Augsburg Fortress, 2000), 5.

Implications for Preachers and for Listener-Learners

In trying to identify their preferred cultural consciousness as a preaching identity, preachers may ask, "So, does finding my voice mean that my preaching options are limited? Do I only get to preach out of one voice for the rest of my ministry?" In a word, "No." Few preachers operate out of one and only one cultural consciousness. Occasions will arise when preachers intuitively elect to draw upon the resources of a different voice. Usually, when this happens, the preacher in question tends to choose one "footing" on which to rest the weight of his or her convictions while trading out the other "footing," either one to the left or one to the right. In practice this means that a preacher who generally speaks out of a Sage Voice (personal truth—persuasively *in*determinate) may decide that a special circumstance or occasion calls for a different preaching intention. So our preacher may choose to trade out the assumption of ambiguity in favor of a tentative voice of assuredness and speak out of an Encouraging Voice (personal truth—persuasively determinate). Or our preacher may hold on to ambiguity but trade in appeals to personal transformation in favor of the Testifying Voice (corporate truth—persuasively *in*determinate) with its ability to make appeals to social solidarity and confessional order. However, it would be inadvisable for our preacher to adopt the Teaching Voice (corporate truth—persuasively determinate), because it would require an ability to surrender both legs of the cultural assumptions of his or her preaching identity.

For Preachers

There may be moments in the sermon when the preacher might elect to speak with a Teaching Voice, since all four voices regularly occur in any sermon. However, it is unlikely that our preacher would want to preach out of a voice that did not represent any aspect of his or her personal sense of cultural gravity. If there is a preacher facile enough to shift the grounds of his cultural identity in this manner, it is unlikely that a congregation would readily experience the same leap as an "authentic witness." Voices are not flavors of ice cream to be tried out for variety's sake. A preacher who would shift voices over and over would likely find a congregation in revolt.

Of course, occasions arise that tempt preachers to try out a new voice. The choice should be made with conscious care. For example, a preacher accustomed to speaking in the Encouraging Voice may be asked to speak before the annual conference meeting of her denomination. It is easy to imagine reasons why she may seize on the invitation as an opportunity to change her typical preaching intention. Keep in mind, however, that this would be a temptation to move the boundaries of the cultural consciousness that gives power to her current ability to name God and name grace for her listener-learners. Is this the best time to try out a new voice? Would it likely be experienced as an authentic expression of her witness of God? Is it the best time to change the basis of appeal that has made her preaching effective with her home congregation? On the other hand, if she is aware that the voice that rings true within her own congregation might seem to be experienced as inauthentic with this other audience, she may decide that shifting the "footing" of her voice would be wise.

Other occasions tempt for good cause. This same preacher may come to a point in her pastoral ministry where she determines that her cultural consciousness assumptions and those of the congregation have become so congruent that little real challenge is occurring in her preaching—congruence has become too comfortable, resulting in predictable rather than challenging messages. Through prayer she may find her own faith moving in a different direction and feel the need to gently begin to call the congregation to hear the gospel in a new voice.

Similarly, a minister newly appointed to a congregation may come to realize that the cultural assumptions that form his voice are far from the assumptions that form the faith of his parishioners. Where he may tend to preach out of the assumptions of the Sage Voice, he may discover that over the years the faith of the congregation has primarily been formed by someone who spoke out of the assumptions of the Teaching Voice. One solution might be to consciously choose to shape sermons out of the preaching intentions of the Encouraging Voice. Here, both preacher explicitly and listener-learners implicitly can choose to share at least one leg in common. These choices have significant ethical implications, but these are better faced by the preacher who can make a conscious choice and seek change with integrity rather than intuitively blundering into the divide without knowing why something does or does not work.

Recently, I met with a pastor who was struggling to identify why the strategies for change that had emerged out of much work by the congregational leadership had produced so little measurable growth. This evangelical congregation had adopted a new mission statement that put personal transformation near the top of its core values and sought to prioritize ministries that would be more inviting to "spiritual-seekers" rather than continue to seek growth from the already converted who were moving into the community. They had shifted their worship commitments to express this new emphasis and restructured power away from an institutional model to a more missional model that sought to treat the congregation as an embodiment of a faith movement rather than a faith institution.[9] The pastor understood that none of this could guarantee "growth," but he was surprised at how little response occurred as a result of these changes. So we looked at the talk of the church (especially his sermons) and the degree to which they embodied the ideals of the new mission commitments.

Since the congregation had adopted many of the strategies that make for ministry in a transformational model—a model whose cultural consciousness shares many of the assumptions of the Encouraging Voice in preaching—I looked to see if the pastor's preaching voice tended to make its appeal out of the voice of assuredness that invited people on a journey of personal transformation. It was readily apparent that the pastor's sermons were structured by the assumptions of the Teaching Voice—a voice that

9. For these and similar ideas of congregational transformation see Bill Easum, *Unfreezing Moves: Following Jesus into the Mission Field* (Nashville: Abingdon Press, 2001).

had historically served the church when its mission was to be a congregation that appealed to people looking for a congregation with a specific theology that served a general denominational identity. This pastor's sermons were arranged either as verse-by-verse expository explanation of the meaning of the text or as sermons-that-make-points. In both types of preaching his sermons authoritatively interpreted the meaning of the text and proposed specific applications. The sermon appeals were "persuasively determinate" in ways that invited "corporate assent" to the truth of the interpretation. We discovered that the espoused values of the church were written and organized in ways that would assume the cultural consciousness of the Encouraging Voice, but the basic assumptions of the taken-for-granted beliefs and perceptions of the pastor were still being voiced in the Teaching Voice.

I turned to Edgar Schein's highly influential book *Organizational Culture and Leadership* to help the pastor see the "disconnect." Schein contends that if we look at any organization we can see lots of activity and cultural artifacts. For Schein these include such manifestations as work product, physical plant architecture and work environment arrangements, the technologies, artistic creations, manner of dress, address, myths, stories, published materials, et cetera, of the organization—all of its "stuff." These artifacts are to be differentiated from its espoused values. The latter are often "assumptions supported by articulated sets of beliefs, norms, and operational rules of behavior."[10] They represent the idealized ideology of the organization meant to serve as a guide to deal with uncertainty and direct the intention of innovation. A third level of corporate culture is an organization's "basic assumptions." Basic assumptions are "the implicit assumptions that actually guide behavior, that tell group members how to perceive, think about, and feel about things."[11] Figure 6.1 arrays these three levels of organizational culture.

10. Edgar H. Schein, *Organizational Culture and Leadership*, 2d ed. (San Francisco: Jossey-Bass, 1992), 20. For a briefer and more accessible summary of this approach to organizational culture see Edgar H. Schein, *The Corporate Culture Survival Guide: Sense and Nonsense about Culture Change* (San Francisco: Jossey-Bass, 1999).

11. Schein, *Organizational Culture*, 22.

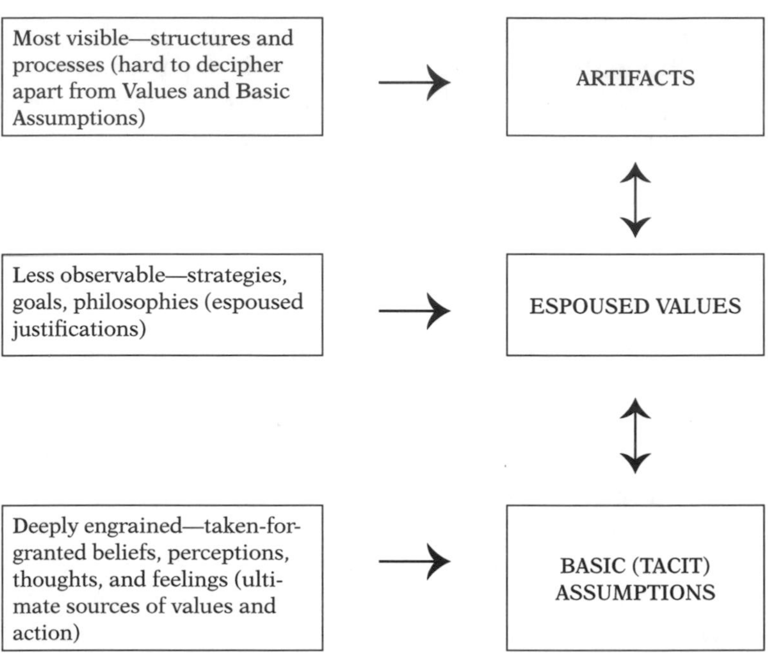

Figure 6.1: Schein's Layers of Organizational Culture

Most organizations neither confront nor debate their basic (tacit) assumptions, which is why these are the hardest elements of organizational life to change. Schein writes,

> To learn something new in this realm requires us to resurrect, reexamine, and possibly change some of the more stable portions of our cognitive structure, a process that . . . others have called double loop learning or frame breaking. . . . Such learning is intrinsically difficult because the reexamination of basic assumptions temporarily destabilizes our cognitive and interpersonal world, releasing large quantities of basic anxiety.[12]

He finds that when there is a basic congruence between the tacit assumptions and the espoused values, then the articulation of the values can serve as a source of identity that can help the

12. Ibid.

organization realize its mission. But when there are significant "disconnects" between the tacit assumptions and the espoused values, it represents a contradiction between the organization's aspirations for the future (espoused values) and the ultimate, taken-for-granted sources of its values and action. The latter will invariably trump the former in day-to-day decisions. The tacit assumptions represent the essential cognitive structures that frame what counts as reality and the real identity of the organization.

In talking with the pastor we were able to see how Schein's conception of the layers of organizational culture could be used to identify the disconnects between the aspirations for missional change that had been articulated by the leadership (what the church was saying it wanted to be) and how this was "out of line" with the missional culture his preaching voice was actually affirming. Schein concludes, "It is important to recognize that artifacts are easy to observe but difficult to decipher and that [espoused] values may only reflect rationalizations or aspirations. To understand a group's culture, one must attempt to get at its shared basic assumptions. . . . As we shall see, culture change, in the sense of changing basic assumptions, is, therefore, difficult, time consuming, and highly anxiety provoking."[13]

So, the pastor and I began to explore how he might shift the question of what he wanted to have happen as a result of people listening to his sermons to imagine how his preaching could become more culturally congruent with the Encouraging Voice aspirations rather than the tacit assumptions of his Teaching Voice. The task of reframing his own cultural consciousness would not be easy, but it was necessary if he wanted to live into and model the way of the new missional aspirations he and the leaders had developed for the congregation. As Schein's work clarifies, changing the cognitive structures of one's cultural consciousness is difficult work. Taking others with you in the change is even more challenging.

13. Ibid., 26–27.

For Listener-Learners

I suspect that those who listen to sermons may also find several implications of this study. I will take up two here and address a more significant one in the next section of the chapter. First, I can envision opportunities that lay members may have as participants in a pastor's sermon group or in one-on-one relationships with a preacher. The basic question, "What do you hope will happen as a result of our listening to that sermon you plan to preach?" is a powerful place to start useful conversations about voice in preaching. The one who asks needs to help his or her pastor to stay fixed on the question rather than settling for an answer about the big idea of the sermon or some other aspect of its thematic content. Sensitive lay people can serve as able listener-learners who can assist preachers in determining whether they have found their voice or have been too apt to let more than one preaching intention behind the wheel of the sermonic purpose.

A second area in which sermon listener-learners may exercise influence in matters of voice is during congregational transition. In many Protestant congregations a search committee or other delegated individuals often have a significant role in determining who the interim will be, and in proposing the candidate to be voted on as the new pastor or a new associate. Several years ago I worked closely with a congregation in which a long-term pastor had left. During the transition this church, a "flagship" congregation for its denomination, brought in a senior-level interim pastor to supervise the large staff and to preach in the four services of worship held every weekend. With the able leadership of the previous pastor this congregation had witnessed steady growth over the past two decades. The previous pastor had consistently preached in the Encouraging Voice.

The first task of the search committee was to help the congregation find a qualified interim senior pastor. They found an individual with broad and capable experience who had committed his ministry to assisting congregations during this kind of transition. It seemed to be the right match, but it turned out to be disastrous. Privately, the interim pastor told me that he self-identified as someone trained in the "liberal" tradition but was proud that he had been able to adapt to the cultural needs of other "evangelical" churches in which he had served productive interims. His secret was that he avoided sermons and subjects that could polarize these congregations and avoided taking positions on controversial issues, since this is not the "job" of an interim pastor.

He was accustomed to preaching sermons that made points and had found that this approach had served him well in these other more-conservative congregations. As stated earlier, the Teaching Voice serves old liberal as readily as fundamentalist and doctrinal preaching. He was shocked and chagrined as groups formed in opposition to his preaching. He would examine his sermons to look for the content that was disturbing and found none. He asked listeners to tell him what they found objectionable. They had difficulty naming it. Instead, the disgruntlement was summarized with statements like, "He never calls us to anything!" "Where's the hope?" "Where's the connection to my concerns?" "What ever happened to grace?" "Why is he always talking about theology?" "He tells us what things mean and never tells us why any of it matters!" Unfortunately, he had no idea that it was his preference for the Teaching Voice in preaching that proved to be his greatest challenge in providing leadership for this community.

It is difficult for anyone to follow a long-term, popular pastor—and no less for the person who must immediately fill these shoes. Unfortunately, for this interim and for the congregation, which began losing people who went looking elsewhere for inspiration, the problem was really an inability to describe the dilemma as a problem of a mismatch between the congregation's communal faith consciousness and the preacher's voice. Had the search committee understood the significance of voice in preaching, they would have looked for an interim who would have been able to sustain the same cultural consciousness—the same basis of appeals—in her or his preaching. Eventually, this congregation turned to the associate pastors to "fill the pulpit," most of whom had been originally chosen because they talked and preached out of the same cultural assumptions and looked at life and faith through the same "terministic screen" (out of the same cultural consciousness) as the original pastor. When a new pastor was presented to the congregation, though very different in personal style and interests than the previous pastor, it should be no surprise that his preaching was clearly conducted in the same voice as the previous senior pastor. The interim minister had helped the congregation to identify rather clearly the kind of voice with which a successful pastor would have to speak.

Congregations in transition can experience less turmoil if they develop a clear notion of their own communal faith identity—the general cultural consciousness of its way of "doing" faith. In this sense, a cultural consciousness is something we can view as an expression of a "faith consciousness." This leads to a third practical implication for listener-learners, but one that will be taken up as the substance of the next section.

Preaching and Listener-Learner Faith Consciousness

In *Claiming Theology in the Pulpit* Cooper and McClure note in passing that contemporary sociological research presents findings that seem to support the argument of the relative unimportance of preaching today. They suggest that such findings may simply indicate a lay reaction to contemporary preaching that, in its effort to be relevant, too often seems to lack theological substance. But is there really more of a problem with preaching today, or do we only think so because sociologists can now formulate quantifiable questions in an effort to determine whether preaching matters?[14] In gathering a collection of contemporary essays on the subject, Mike Graves reminds readers of Harry Emerson Fosdick's timeless essay "What's the Matter with Preaching Today?" In

14. For example, a report from the Barna Research Group found no significant difference between Christians and non-Christians in moral social practices or provision of assistance to the poor and hungry—matters regularly raised in preaching. See George Barna, *Report to the Promise Keepers Organization* (Colorado Springs: The Barna Group, 1999), as cited in Lori Carrell, *The Great American Sermon Survey* (Wheaton: Mainstay Church Resources, 2000), 30.

1928 Fosdick offered an answer, and many of the modern contributors to Graves's book add their own response in a series of fresh essays. Yet in his introduction Graves also reminds us that the pundits in every era have complained about the quality and value of preaching. Perhaps the modern listener-learner would do better to ask, "What do I expect of sermons? How should they matter for my practice of faith?"

Homileticians have only recently tried to determine how listeners experience a ministry of preaching as part of their own faith formation.[15] Joseph Jeter Jr. and Ronald Allen have identified a variety of typologies that would help preachers categorize different listener worldviews. They begin with a generational typology as a frame through which one can also view Fowler's faith stage development typology, the Myers-Briggs typology of personality types, the neurolinguistic typology of mental processing styles, various gendered typologies, et cetera. Each can provide preachers with new ways of understanding how to be responsive to the different kinds of listener-learners present in congregations and how one might frame both sermonic materials and appeals relevant to them.[16] As Jeter and Allen note, in passing, I had already raised interest in the way that Fowler's project is particularly relevant to providing a link between the cultural consciousness of the preacher and the adult stage of faith of those who listen to sermons.[17]

For my purpose here I am particularly interested in Fowler's project concerning adult faith development, because he recently reframed his project's language away from stage theory to suggest that he had actually gathered data on what amounts to different "cultural consciousnesses" of adult faith. This language is commensurate with my inquiry into the cultural conscious-

15. See John S. McClure, Ronald Allen, Dale P. Andrews, L. Susan Bond, Dan P. Moseley, and G. Lee Ramsey Jr., *Listening to Listeners: Homiletical Case Studies* (St. Louis: Chalice Press, 2004); Ronald J. Allen, *Hearing the Sermon: Relationship, Content, Feeling* (St. Louis: Chalice Press, 2004); and Carrell, *The Great American Sermon Survey*.

16. Joseph R. Jeter Jr. and Ronald J. Allen, *One Gospel, Many Ears: Preaching for Different Listeners in the Congregation* (St. Louis: Chalice Press, 2002).

17. Ibid., 186n 6.

nesses of those who preach, making a comparison between the four cultural consciousnesses of preaching voices and the four cultural consciousnesses of faith pertinent. The degree to which they appear to map the same phenomenon would prove helpful in providing language to describe the shape and structure of the faith called forth from listener-learners by the different voices of preaching.

Some background to Fowler's project may help demonstrate its value at this point.[18] James Fowler began his work in the 1970s by describing developmental differences in faith in the language of stage theory typical of developmental theory from this period.[19] He and his students identified seven distinct "stages of faith" based on how individuals interpret and respond to factors of contingency, finitude, and ultimacy in their lives. His four stages of adult faith are *Synthetic-Conventional, Individuative-Reflective, Conjunctive*, and *Universalizing.*[20] He summarizes his research project in the following way:

18. An earlier version of this argument can be found in Robert Stephen Reid, "Faithful Preaching: Faith Stages, Preaching Strategies, and Rhetorical Practice," *Journal of Communication and Religion* 21, 2 (1998): 164–99. Language from that essay is adapted here. Jeter and Allen note my effort to apply Fowler's categories in *One Gospel, Many Ears,* 186n 6. Unfortunately, they read my four divisions through the grid of Lucy Rose's efforts to define historically distinctive approaches to preaching in *Sharing the Word* rather than as a proposal of four different cultural consciousnesses.

19. Fowler envisioned his project as an effort to clarify what research in faith development can add to the overall assessment of the normative visions of human wholeness supplied by adult developmental theories. He reworked the structuralism of Piaget, the psychology of Erickson and Levinson, the moral development theories of Kohlberg and Gilligan, and integrated these with the theologies of Niebuhr and Tillich in an effort to clarify an understanding of faith as a way of knowing and valuing.

20. Fowler defines faith as "[t]he process of constitutive knowing underlying a person's composition of a comprehensive frame (or frames) of meaning generated from the person's attachments or commitments to centers of supraordinate value which have the power to unify his or her experience of the world, thereby endowing the relationships, contexts, and patterns of everyday life, past and future, with significance" (James Fowler, *Stages of Faith: The Psychology of Human Development and the Quest for Meaning* [San Francisco: Harper and Row, 1981], 25–26). Craig Dykstra surveys the variety of ways Fowler has tried to answer the question, "What is faith?" and concludes that Fowler may well succeed in juggling the tension between social science and theology because, aside from all his careful social-scientific attempts to qualify what he is saying, people of faith still recognize themselves and something of their own journey of faith in his descriptions of the stages of faith; see "What Is Faith? An Experiment in the Hypothetical

> Over the past ten years, in a variety of settings, we have conducted in-depth, semi-clinical interviews with approximately 500 persons. Among other interests we have sought to test whether certain developmental patterns that seem to hold in the domains of cognitive, psychosocial, and moral growth have developmental parallels in this area of faith. Our underlying questions have been these: How do persons awaken to and begin to form (and be formed) in the life stances of trust and loyalty, of belief and commitment that carry them into the force fields of their lives? Are there predictable stages or revolutions in the life of meaning-making? Must we, in order to become fully adult and to be fully human, have a deep-going and abiding trust in and loyalty to some cause or causes, greater in value and importance than ourselves? [21]

Fowler and his associates have conducted many more interviews since this first statement with people of a variety of ages, sexes, and orientations to metaphysical matters.

He summarizes the basic distinctions between his four adult stages of faith by correlating them to life stages. Like other developmental theorists, he argues against the assumption that any one stage should be viewed as superior to another. He summarizes their distinctiveness in this way:

> *Synthetic-Conventional faith* (adolescence and beyond): New cognitive abilities make mutual perspective-taking possible and require one to integrate diverse self-images into a coherent identity. A personal and largely unreflected synthesis of belief and values evolves to support identity and to unite one in emotional solidarity with others.
>
> *Individuative Reflective faith* (young adulthood and beyond): Critical reflection upon one's beliefs and values, utilizing

Mode," in *Faith Development and Fowler*, Craig Dykstra and Sharon Parks, eds. (Birmingham: Religious Education Press, 1986), 46.

21. James Fowler, *Becoming Adult, Becoming Christian: Adult Development and Christian Faith* (San Francisco: Harper and Row, 1984), 51–52. No prior assumption of the "validity" of faith was made other than a belief that humans are "language-related, symbol-borne and story telling creatures . . . [who] do not live long or well without meaning" (50).

third-person perspective-taking; understanding of the self and others as part of a social system; the internalization of authority and the assumption of responsibility for making explicit choices of ideology and lifestyle open the way for critically self-aware commitments in relationships and vocation.

Conjunctive faith (early midlife and beyond): The embrace of polarities in one's life, an alertness to paradox, and the need for multiple interpretations of reality mark this stage. Symbol and story, metaphor and myth (from one's own tradition and others') are newly appreciated (second, or willed, *naïveté*) as vehicles for expressing truth.

Universalizing faith (midlife and beyond): Beyond paradox and polarities, persons in this stage are grounded in the oneness with the power of being. Their vision and commitments free them for a passionate yet detached spending of self in love, devoted to overcoming division, oppression, and violence, and an effective anticipatory response to an in-breaking commonwealth.[22]

As noted above, Fowler recently correlated the first three of these stages among educated American adults with what he now describes as "tempers of cultural consciousness." It is important to note that he views these more as cultural frames of reference than as faith viewed from a theological perspective.[23] He views Synthetic-

22. James Fowler, *Weaving the New Creation: Stages of Faith and the Public Church* (San Francisco: HarperCollins, 1991), 18.

23. James Fowler, *Faithful Change: The Personal and Public Challenges of Postmodern Life* (Nashville: Abingdon Press, 1996), 161. James Loder has argued that "Fowler wants to concentrate on the human aspect of faith, but the decisive question is how Fowler's constructs relate to biblical understandings of faith." Of course the question is, "Decisive for whom?" Fowler's project maps faith from a human perspective for both developmental theorists and people of faith. Loder offers a profound exploration of faith development from a theological perspective. The same challenge will undoubtedly be leveled at this study, since I have classified approaches to faith from a perspective of human cultural consciousness rather than theological perspective. That is why it is an anthropology of preaching rather than a theology of preaching. Within the limits of what it seeks to accomplish, Loder finds Fowler's work to be an important contribution to the study of faith development. See James E. Loder, *The Logic of the Spirit: Human Development in Theological Perspective* (San Francisco: Jossey-Bass, 1998), 256–57.

Conventional faith as a temper rooted in a pre-Enlightenment worldview of orthodoxy; Individuative-Reflective faith as a temper rooted in Enlightenment rationalism with its appeal to individualism; and Conjunctive faith as a temper located in the post-Enlightenment, postmodern worldview. One is left to assume that no cultural consciousness is depicted as commensurate with Universalizing faith, because he argues that it does not occur with sufficient frequency yet in his surveys to warrant conclusions about its cultural assumptions.

For my purposes Fowler's Universalizing faith can be readily correlated (at least in theory) with the Testifying Voice. He argues that the defining characteristic of Universalizing faith include its selfless call to a communal consciousness, its incarnational activism, and its thorough embrace of the social imperatives of doing justice and expressing love for the other. Compare this to Charles Campbell's argument calling for preaching committed to a peculiar speech that redescribes contemporary life in such a way as to construct a passionate yet detached spending of *self* in love expressed as a faith "in community" with others who are devoted to overcoming division, oppression, and violence.[24] Or consider Walter Brueggemann's argument about preaching's purpose expressed earlier in this chapter. Fowler's description of a decentered concern for the other as the central characteristic of the orientation to faith would be as acceptable to a revisionist as it would to a postliberal.

The other voices can readily be related to Fowler's faith consciousnesses. The Teaching Voice, with its commitment to make appeals that are persuasively determinate in order to reinforce social solidarity, can readily be associated with Synthetic-Conventional faith's acceptance of the beliefs and values supported by an external authority that "evolves to support identity and to unite one in emotional solidarity with others." The Encouraging Voice, with its commitment to make persuasively determinate appeals in order to invite listeners on a journey of individual transfor-

24. Charles L. Campbell, *Preaching Jesus: New Directions for Homiletics in Hans Frei's Postliberal Theology* (Grand Rapids: Eerdmans, 1997), 237.

mation, can readily be associated with Individuative-Reflective faith's critical reflection upon one's own beliefs, its internalization of authority, and its assumption of responsibility for making explicit ideological and lifestyle choices. The Sage Voice, with its commitment to make appeals that are persuasively indeterminate while inviting listeners on a journey of individual transformation, can readily be associated with Conjunctive faith's embrace of polarities, its alertness to paradox, and its need for multiple interpretations of reality that take account of the power of symbol and story, metaphor, and myth. As indicated in Figure 6.2, the Voices can readily be compared to Fowler's four adult cultural consciousnesses of faith.[25]

	The Teaching Voice Calls Forth	**The Encouraging Voice Calls Forth**	**The Sage Voice Calls Forth**	**The Testifying Voice Calls Forth**
Adult Cultural Consciousnesses of Faith	Synthetic-Conventional Faith Consciousness	Individuative-Reflective Faith Consciousness	Conjunctive Faith Consciousness	Unversalizing Faith Consciousness
Fowler's Foci of These Faith Consciousnesses	Tacit; interpersonal; noncritical; external locus of authority	Explicit; autonomous; critical-reflective; internal locus of authority	Multiple perspectives and systems accepted; second naiveté appreciated	Beyond multiple perspectives—a decentration of self realized in favor of the communal needs; commitment to an embraced pluralism

Figure 6.2: The Four Voices and Fowler's Cultural Consciousnesses of Faith

25. Adapted from Reid, "Faithful Preaching," 164–99. Since Fowler does not provide tempers of cultural consciousness for Universalizing faith, I have projected them here.

Applied to preaching, Fowler's model of faith consciousness can be viewed as a model of the degree of complexity and ambiguity listener-learners find reasonable in faith and in faith presentations. Fowler argues that it is important to note that no one cultural consciousness of faith should be treated as superior to another. Similarly, I have argued that one must beware of assuming that one voice is superior to another for preaching. What matters, whether one is examining the faith of individuals or how that faith is expressed by a preacher, is the authenticity of its expression.

The correlation between Fowler's project and my proposal of four culturally distinct voices of preaching has ethical implications. It is up to preachers to determine whether they desire to match their voice to the expectations of a congregation's normative expression (Fowler refers to this as the congregation's modal development level) of faith consciousness or to preach in a voice that calls for a different faith consciousness from listener-learners.[26] Preachers can make that choice only if they understand the assumptions that distinguish different voices in preaching. Preachers need to determine whether they are trying to shift the communal faith-consciousness of a congregation as a matter of convenience or out of a sense of gospel faithfulness. The latter is complicated by the temptation to assume that one's own faith consciousness is the consciousness most faithful to the claims of the gospel.

Theological training and ordination do not bestow the right to declare one's own faith consciousness as the truth and demand

26. Though intended to describe that which was measured (individual expressions of faith), Fowler uses his descriptive categories to talk broadly about the "modal developmental level" of communities as the average expectable level of development for adults in a given community.

In faith terms, it refers to the conscious or unconscious image of adult faith toward which the educational practices, religious celebrations, and patterns of governance in a community all aim. The modal level operates as a kind of magnet in religious communities. Patterns of nurture prepare children and youth to grow up *to* the modal level—but not beyond it. Persons from outside the community are attracted to the community because of its modal development level. The operation of the modal development level in a community sets an effective limit on the ongoing process of growth in faith (*Stages of Faith*, 294).

Fowler's generalization of his use of the phrase *modal development level* is akin to the notion of a cultural consciousness reflective of the communal faith of a particular congregation.

that everyone else use it as the measuring stick. At the same time it is difficult to imagine how one can speak an authentic word to a congregation with whom no footings are shared. It might be "prophetic Word," but it will be Word that is less likely to be heard. In a very real sense, unpacking the assumptions that function as the pre-understanding of one's own voice leads to challenging questions about the responsibility of voice to bring about change in faith or to challenge a communal faith that may have become too culturally content with its existing assumptions.[27] The issues are thorny and difficult to weigh, because it is difficult to separate personal motives from gospel claims. The task is challenging. It should be.

In presenting this typology of Four Voices of Preaching in the contemporary North American context, I have begun the task of identifying the cultural assumptions relevant to an anthropology of preaching.[28] Rather than a univocal anthropology, I have attempted to describe four distinctly different cultural consciousnesses that would lead to four distinctly different orientations to an ethic of preaching. Just as there can be no univocal anthropology of preaching, there can be no univocal ethics of preaching.[29] Ethical explorations of voice will need to be equivocal explorations of what would make for a coherent conception of responsible preaching within each voice.[30]

For the present purpose I will simply note that Wayne Booth states that all encounters between the one who speaks and the listener-learner are ethical because they are rooted in the character

27. On "pre-understanding" see Paul Ricoeur, "The Task of Hermeneutics," in *Hermeneutics and the Human Sciences*, John B. Thompson, ed. and trans. (Cambridge: Cambridge University Press, 1981), 56–57.

28. An anthropology of any kind of religious discourse would approach its subject from human perspective, in my case a cultural and rhetorical approach that generally assumes a phenomenological and hermeneutical perspective.

29. For an example of a univocal ethics of preaching, see Raymond W. McLaughlin, *The Ethics of Persuasive Preaching* (Grand Rapids: Baker, 1979). Though McLaughlin tries to address what he terms the emerging notion of "ethical relativism" in the 1970s, his argument begins with the assumptions that preachers should speak with the voice of assuredness and make appeal based on an external locus of authority.

30. This ethic of variously voiced identities in preaching would be the next step in developing an equivocal anthropology of preaching, but one that is beyond the scope of this study.

(*ethos*) of the participants. Listener-learners "keep company" with the speaker (or in our case the preacher) and in the process are changed by the experience, which interprets life, tells us about our life, and introduces us to other possible lives.[31] In the homiletic dance where spoken word becomes Word of God, the human and the divine voice come together in the preaching moment. It is here that a preacher's own rhetorical anthropology must join with a practice of a theology in development of an ethic of preaching that can help in realizing a faithful witness of naming God and naming grace.

A Concluding Analogy

Design's Residue: Learners

A final prescriptive assessment is offered here, one that takes up the challenge to attend to the relationship between voice and designs that help provide rhetorical coherence to preaching intentions. To the average preacher this concern for theory and the way it enacts a specific cultural consciousness may seem heady stuff, with little relationship to the real practice of communicating the gospel. That would be a significant misreading. The revolution happening in higher education offers an important parallel. In the last two decades schools and universities have begun to tackle the question of what makes for educational excellence. Two radical reorientations have emerged as the way forward—the learner-centered paradigm shift and the focus on the relationship between curricular design and expected outcomes.[32]

31. Wayne Booth, *The Company We Keep: An Ethics of Fiction* (Berkeley: University of California Press, 1988), 3–20. My first effort to identify the "next step" in developing a full anthropology of preaching was a proposal for an ethics of preaching presented before the Academy of Homiletics in 2002 entitled "Irresponsible Preaching."

32. These are radical in that they challenge ways we have institutionalized learning over much of the twentieth century. They are a "reorientation" of these ways that are actually a recovery of ancient understandings that communication is best when it is dialogical (Plato's concern) and is clear about its desired outcome with listeners (Aristotle's concern).

First, educators are learning how to shift away from a teacher-centered paradigm of education to a learner-centered paradigm.[33] In the former it was assumed that knowledge was passively transmitted from professor to student with the teacher as the primary information provider. In the latter educators are coming to understand that students learn best when they actively construct knowledge by integrating new information through inquiry, discussion, critical thinking, and problem solving. Professors have had to give up the cherished lecture and shift away from thinking of education as an information delivery system. Education is not about "the more you know." Education is about the "the more you do." To shift from knowing to doing, educators have had to learn how to move away from a competitive, individualistic mode of teaching and learn how to create classroom contexts that facilitate cooperative and collaborative forms of learning. Of course professors still provide lectures, but instead of serving as an end, they are being redesigned as the fuel for the means of this cooperative and collaborative learning.[34] Ask any student who has had a course built around effective use of case study discussion, rather than tests, which form of learning they prefer.

The best homiletic methodologies in each of the voices canvassed in this study have already shifted away from a preacher-centered, content-centered paradigm to a listener-centered paradigm. What is needed now is a learner-centered paradigm in preaching. Preachers would do well to realize that in the Great Commission Jesus invited his followers to go and "make learners" (*mathêteusate*) rather than "make listeners" of all nations. In the twenty-first century parishioners will increasingly come to expect preachers to discover how to make sermonic learning a more collaborative venture.

The rhetorical task of the twenty-first-century pulpit will be to shift preaching away from knowledge lectures, where the burden has been to discover the insight as yet unseen by listeners, to rediscover how sermons can become formative Word of

33. Mary E. Huba and Jann E. Freed, *Learner-Centered Assessment on College Campuses: Shifting the Focus from Teaching to Learning* (Boston: Allyn and Bacon, 2000), 5.

34. Donald A. Bligh, *What's the Use of Lectures?* 6th ed. (San Francisco: Jossey-Bass, 2000).

God that invites listener-learners to live into faith. The sermon clearly matters, but a learner-centered homiletic must provide the formative materials for the conversations and actions that create and sustain faith. Clearly this was the model of much black preaching in the midst of the civil rights movement, where sermons urged parishioners to do the gospel in their boycotts, at the courthouses, and in the streets, where sermons emerged out of the immediate materials of what had happened for everyone that week. The shift to a listener-centered approach to preaching in the latter quarter of the twentieth century was the first step in reaching for homiletic excellence of engagement, but this reorientation must go further and shift the focus from sermons shaped for listeners to sermons that make learners.

Second, the focus on the relationship between curricular design and expected outcomes has been the other half of the revolution that is making for excellence in education. Anyone who has been in a university classroom in the last decade knows that the syllabus is no longer a single piece of paper with the prof's office hours, the textbooks, and the course catalog description. The syllabus is now the deliverable on a contractual promise between the university and the student. It spells out what the student can expect to gain as a result of taking the course. Assessment is no longer the standard three tests and a final paper for every course. That is a teacher-centered, content-centered orientation to learning.

Universities are challenging their educators to rethink the role of assessment and its relationship to desired outcomes by asking the more difficult question, "What do I want to have happen as a result of students participating in this class?" Division chairs are learning to ask, "What do we want to have happen as a result of students' having taken our course of curricular study?" Regional accrediting agencies increasingly require that all universities and seminaries have a clear sense of institutional mission, with the specific mission of each educational division tied to the educational institution's larger mission and each course specifically tied to achieving the divisional objectives. Gone are the days that a course is taught on the whim of Professor Does-his-own-thing or Professor Needs-to-teach-an-extra-course-and-this-might-be-of-interest. Students rightly want to know that there is coherence to the educational curriculum they are offered as professional preparation. Professors still committed to the teacher-centered paradigm often complain that they are losing their freedom in this outcomes-education system. Yet in too many instances, that freedom was at the expense of overall program coherence and what we now know makes for educational excellence in a learner-centered paradigm of education.[35] Accrediting agencies would be quick to assure professors and universities that the focus is not on assessment per se, but rather on the relationship between teaching intentions and learner outcomes. The task has become how to find ways to make excellence more measurable.

Thank God the church does not get to hold final exams to determine the outcomes of preaching. Most of us still believe this is God's work, not ours. But gone need to be the days when Reverend Hopes-for-the-best still confuses the sermon's focus statement with its preaching intention. The focus statement is oriented to the sermon content. The preaching intention is oriented to the response. If "response is the residue of design," then preachers need to be rigorous in asking, "What do I want to have happen as a result of learners' having heard this sermon?" That is a learner-centered question rather than a preacher-centered, a content-centered, or even a listener-centered question. It is a question that is the stepping stone to developing an authenticity of voice that can make for excellence in the rhetorical dimensions of preaching. Grasping the relationship between clarity of

35. Many places of employment now ask professionals to design performance evaluation objectives in line with the missional objectives of the division and the company. This orientation is beginning to pervade all sectors of professional practice. There is still some debate as to just how far outcomes-based education should let mission drive curricular design, but no educator who has crossed the divide believes that education should return to the lecture as data dump in a teacher-centered paradigm of education. See Standford Erickson, *The Essence of Good Teaching: Helping Students Learn and Remember What They Learn* (San Francisco: Jossey-Bass, 1984); T. Dary Erwin, *Assessing Student Learning and Development: A Guide to the Principles, Goals, and Methods of Determining College Outcomes* (San Francisco: Jossey-Bass, 1991); Education Commission of the States, *Making Quality Count in the Undergraduate Education* (Denver: Education Commission of the States, 1995).

preaching intention and clarity of voice is the first step toward moving from muddling through to excellence in preaching—the measurable in a design-centered, learner-centered approach to preaching.

■

Of course design can be only the carrier of that which calls for response. It must be joined to witness that names God and names grace if it is to become a faithful testimony embodying Word of God for listener-learners. Preachers need to learn how to use preaching designs that help listener-learners realize a sermon's preaching intention. Combined with the ability to make the theology of a text or a perspective apparent for listener-learners, control of the cultural assumptions of a voice helps preachers realize a preaching identity that structures what Phillips Brooks once called "personality" as the bearer of gospel truth. A preacher who finds his or her own preaching identity in the coherence of one of the Four Voices of Preaching may discover, through a ministry of preaching that strives for excellence in a faithful expression of that voice, that the residue of design is not just response. It is actually learners—people discovering faithfulness as they live into a clear and coherent witness that becomes Word of God in their lives.

Subject Index

Author Index